Warman's®

WORLD WAR II
COLLECTIBLES

3RD EDITION

IDENTIFICATION & PRICE GUIDE

John Adams-Graf

Published by

Krause Publications, a division of F+W Media, Inc.
700 East State Street • Iola, WI 54990-0001
715-445-2214 • 888-457-2873
www.krausebooks.com

To order books or other products call toll-free 1-800-258-0929
or visit us online at www.krausebooks.com

Cover photography by Library of Congress (General Dwight D. Eisenhower); collectibles, front cover: German 2nd Model paratrooper's helmet, $5,500 (£3,410), Hermann-Historica.de; German MP40 submachine gun, $19,305 (£11,969), PoulinAntiques.com; USMC Fleet Marine Force PFC's tunic, $95-$125 (£59-£78), AdvanceGuardMilitaria.com; U.S. Army lightweight service gas mask, $65-$85 (£40-£53), AdvanceGuard-Militaria.com; Japanese good luck flag, 72cm x 82cm, $195-$215 (£121-£133), AdvanceGuardMilitaria.com; and Soviet Union Order of Lenin, Type V medal, $1,000-$1,500 (£620-£930), Hermann-Historica.de

ISBN-13: 978-1-4402-4070-6
ISBN-10: 1-4402-4070-1

Cover Design by Kevin Ulrich
Designed by Kevin Ulrich
Edited by Mary Sieber

Printed in China

AUTHOR DEDICATION
To my sister, Celine Lauermann.
May you always experience peace and contentment.

Contents

Robert F. Sargent, CPhoM, USCG

Acknowledgments

A work of this nature does not evolve over a short period of time. Rather, it has taken 45 years to develop the familiarity with the military material culture of World War II to even feel comfortable considering such a project.

I will never fully appreciate my parent's tolerance. As a young boy, I never stopped asking my father, a World War II veteran, or my mother, a college student during the war, about their experiences and memories. They never stifled my enthusiasm. My dad let me sit with his war buddies when they got together at our family-owned grocery store to reminisce, and my mom kept me supplied with books and toys and explained photographs to me.

Perhaps the moment that cemented my fascination with World War II was the day my father let his six-year-old son march alongside him and his fellow American Legion members in our city's Memorial Day parade. Clad in camouflage pajamas, plastic camouflaged helmet, and wearing my dad's M1936 musette bag on my back (packed with my blanket and teddy bear), I marched with the pride of knowing that these guys had been to war. They were the true "relics." The stories they told me, the souvenirs they showed to me, and the pride they demonstrated in their participation in the liberation of Europe and the Pacific has stuck with me to this day. I am indebted to all the veterans of World War II for the sacrifices they made. Without them, I would not enjoy the freedom to pursue my own dreams and passions.

More recently, I wish to extend my gratitude to Jefferson Shrader and Anna McCoy of Advance Guard Militaria. They opened the records of their businesses to me in order to determine realistic values of military relics based on their actual sales history. Without this data, this price guide would not have been possible. The collecting hobby will benefit from this generosity for years to come. Similarly, Ernst-Ludwig Wagner of Hermann Historica OHG, Craig Gottlieb of HistoryHunter.com, Patrick F. Hogan of Rock Island Auction Company, James D. Julia of James D. Julia, Inc., Heritage Auctions, and Nick Poulin of Poulin Antiques and Auction Company graciously took time from their busy auction schedules to retrieve photos and sales data for me to use in compiling the final data and illustrations for this work.

Chris William responded to my request to photograph his collection simply by saying, "How soon can we do it?" His depth of collection was a veritable one-stop-shop for photography.

Peter Suciu took time from his own busy writing career to photograph his helmet collection. His generosity has provided images of many unusual and rare examples that won't be seen in any other work (unless, of course, he sits down and writes a comprehensive guide to helmet collecting…he is the one person I hope would consider such a project).

Several fine dealers and collectors of World War II memorabilia came forward and contributed past catalogs, auction and sale results, photographs, and their specialized knowledge. This group of individuals includes: Doug Bekke, Kevin Born, Fred Borch, Fred Borgmann, Collin R. Bruce II, George Cuhaj, Bill Combs, John Conway, Joseph S. Covais, Vera Crist, Chris Depere, Rick Fleury, Brennan Gauthier, Nathan Hannah, Gary Harvey, Robert Jaques, Thomas R. Kailbourn, Clement V. Kelly, Reto and Kanae Kleinpeter, Jim McCloskey, Trisha Majestic, Dennis Matheney, Larry Menestrina, Mike Morris, Kelly Nelson, Freja Andersen Ó Coileáin, Lisa Oakes, Charles D. Pautler, Harold Ratzburg, Bruce R. Tuttle, Sandra Schleif, Mary Schmidt, Andrew Turner, Thomas Wittmann, and Judy Voss.

I owe a debt of gratitude to my dear friend and fellow-author David Doyle. David understands the pitfalls of authoring a book of this scope and never wavered in his encouragement to me when I felt myself falter. A friend such as David, who possesses a strong professional and moral ethic, is a rare thing…more valuable than any double-decal SS helmet or identified paratrooper's jacket. I am grateful for the information, vintage photographs, professional empathy and friendship he has shared with me.

And finally, the depth of thanks I owe to Diane Adams-Graf of the Minnesota Historical Society cannot be measured. She is the consummate museum professional and the finest partner I could ever imagine. I look forward to a long, caring life together so that I can attempt to repay her patience for the nights and weekends that I selfishly spent writing this book.

If I have left anyone off this list, it is the result of a messy filing system! Thank you all for making this book available to the thousands of World War II collectors and enthusiasts.

John Adams-Graf

Introduction

During the nearly seven decades since the end of World War II, veterans, collectors, and nostalgia-seekers have eagerly bought, sold, and traded the "spoils of war." Actually, souvenir collecting began as soon as troops set foot on foreign soil. Whether Tommies from Great Britain, Doughboys from the United States, or Fritzies from Germany, soldiers eagerly looked for trinkets and remembrances that would guarantee their place in the historic events that unfolded before them. Helmets, medals, Lugers, field gear, daggers, and other pieces of war material filled parcels and duffel bags on the way back home.

As soon as hostilities ended in 1945, the populations of defeated Germany and Japan quickly realized they could make money selling souvenirs to the occupation forces. The flow of war material increased. Values became well established…a Luger was worth several packs of cigarettes, a helmet, just one. A Japanese sword was worth two boxes of K-rations, an Arisaka bayonet was worth a Hershey's chocolate bar.

Over the years, these values have remained proportionally consistent. Today, that "two-pack" Luger might be worth $5,000 and that one-pack helmet, $1,500. The Japanese sword might fetch $1,200 and the Arisaka bayonet $95. Though values have increased dramatically, demand has not dropped off a bit. In fact, World War II collecting is the largest segment of the miltaria hobby.

Surprisingly, the values of items have been a closely guarded secret. Unfortunately, the hobby has relied on paying veterans and their families far less than a military relic is worth with the hope of selling later for a substantial profit. This attitude has given the hobby a bad reputation.

The advent of the Internet, though, significantly leveled the playing field for sellers and buyers. No longer does a person have to blindly offer a relic for sale to a collector or dealer. Simply logging onto one of several Internet auctions will give the uninitiated an idea of value.

But a little information can be dangerous. The value of military items resides in variation. Whether it is a difference in manufacturing technique, material or markings, the nuances of an item will determine the true value. Don't expect 20 minutes on the net—or even glancing through this book—to teach you these nuances. Collectors are a devoted bunch. They have spent years and hundreds, if not thousands, of dollars to establish the knowledge base that enables them to navigate through the hobby. Use the basic information that you will gain from this book to begin the foundation of your negotiations.

Who Needs This Book?

This book was not written for the "hardened" or "veteran" collector or World War II memorabilia. Because of their years of handling objects and study, they can pick up a piece of militaria and generally recognize its value. They will not benefit from this book. In fact, they may actually dislike this book! Why? Because *Warman's World War II Collectibles* is for the person who is *not* an ardent collector of military objects.

Using *Warman's World War II Collectibles*, the non-collector will be able to evaluate military objects that he or she may find in attics, closets, flea markets, garage sales, or thrift stores. This book is also for the families who encounter a box or trunk in an attic filled with the souvenirs and remembrances of a relative's service to his or her country. Often, they just want to know what "Dad's old army stuff" is worth. This book will answer those questions.

This book does not attempt to be an identification guide. The more than 1,800 images of artifacts don't begin to scratch the surface of the vast mounds of relics that are available. The World War II collectibles field is vast; there are thousands of titles dedicated to a variety of subsets ranging from bayonets and hand grenades to machine guns and Nazi Party membership badges. *World War II Collectibles* will provide a basis of pricing information for thousands of items, but apart from the images included in this book, the reader will have to dig further for identification purposes.

This book will make the non-collector or the novice collector a smarter consumer. It will provide the information that will protect you from making a financial mistake in buying or selling a World War II object.

What is Covered?

Warman's World War II Collectibles does not attempt to be comprehensive in listing all of the uniforms, weapons, insignia, and accoutrements worn by the millions of men and women in service between 1939 and 1945. Rather, it does list the items most commonly encountered in the 21st century, whether in an antiques shop, at a flea market, in a long-forgotten trunk, or in an online auction.

In each of the eight chapters, items from a variety of nations will be presented. The majority of the items originated in the military formations of the United States, Great Britain, Germany, and Japan, though the reader will find items from other nations as well.

Is Hitler's China Listed?

While it is true that the occasional soldier grabbed valuable artwork or pieces of some notable's silverware to take home, they were, by far, the exception. Of the hundreds of thousands of soldiers and sailors who returned to their homes at the end of World War II, most wore their uniform and carried a duffel bag of personal belongings and, perhaps, some mementoes for families and friends. They weren't art critics, looters, or investment speculators. In fact, most never considered the monetary worth of the objects they carried as souvenirs. The objects they brought home were simply reminders of—and perhaps some sort of compensation for—the extreme sacrifice they had made to their country. For some veterans, the objects represented a deep, personal meaning that could never be quantified in a dollar amount.

In the following pages, the reader will find a catalog of a wide range of World War II militaria that is typically found in veterans' estates. This book does not attempt to identify all of the great rarities or one-of-a-kind items that tend to cause a seasoned collector's jaw to drop. Rather, the items described in these pages range from a soldier's own uniform and personal items to the trophies he or she may have carried home at the conclusion of their service.

How to Use This Book

The person who will benefit the most from this book is one who probably isn't a militaria collector. A lot of the listings may appear to be gibberish. For example, how is the uninitiated to know the difference between

a "Shirt, OD, flannel, enlisted man" and a "Shirt, forest green, wool, USMC, enlisted man?"

Warman's World War II Collectibles does not attempt to be an identification guide. The scope of the uniforms, weapons, and equipment of nations involved in World War II is beyond what one book can cover. A variety of excellent references exist (and are listed in the bibliography of this book) that will help a person identify a particular object. Once an identity has been established, this book will help assign a value.

The nomenclature used in this book tends to emulate what a particular government or army called an item. Collector-determined names will often appear in parentheses however. For example, most collectors use the name "Model 41 jacket" or "Parsons jacket" (a reference to the officer who popularized this garment) to refer to the khaki-colored poplin field jackets that U.S. Army soldiers commonly wore in combat in both the European and Pacific theaters. The Army's name for these garments, though, was "Jacket, field, OD (second pattern)." The listing in this book will combine both the official nomenclature as well as popular collector terminology. In the case of the field jacket, the listing will appear as "Jacket, field, OD, cotton poplin (second pattern, often referred to as an M1941 jacket)."

Even though both "official" and "collector" terminology are presented, the reader may not have a clue as to what a particular item might be. For example, how is a non-collector to know the difference between a "jacket, field, OD, cotton poplin" and a "jacket, field, lined, ETO?" Though it is hoped that this book will be used in conjunction with other valuable photo references, more than 1,800 illustrations are included here to assist the novice with object identification.

This book deals only with items made before the autumn of 1945 when the last of the Axis surrendered to the Allied powers. The items listed are typical of what a soldier would have carried or encountered on a daily basis. It does not address items primarily used by civilians from this period (such as glassware, toys, or other decorative arts or home-front items) or produced after the cessation of hostilities.

Availability, Price and Reproduction Alert

At the start of each chapter, there is a rating chart. Three ratings are represented: Availability, Price, and Reproduction Alert. An attempt has been to make a general rating for each category. Each rating is represented by one to five stars with the meaning as follows:

Availability:

✪✪✪✪✪ You should be able to find these items at a general antiques show.

✪✪✪✪ Commonly found through online auctions or through most dealers.

✪✪✪ Encountered with frequency at military relic shows.

✪✪ May find the items through private sales lists.

✪ Very rare, available through advanced dealers.

Price:

✪✪✪✪✪ $5,001 and up

✪✪✪✪ $1,001-$5,000

✪✪✪ $251-$1,000

✪✪ $51-$250

✪ Less than $50

Reproduction Alert:

✪✪✪✪✪ Extreme care needed. It is safe to assume that the item you have encountered is a reproduction. Get proof that it isn't before making a purchase.

✪✪✪✪ Be extremely careful. Reproductions are misrepresented as original on a regular basis.

✪✪✪ Be careful. Reproductions are known to exist and are misrepresented.

✪✪ Reproductions might exist, but most often, misidentification is of more concern.

✪ Items in this category are rarely, if ever, reproduced.

Several pros and cons for collecting the items represented in a particular chapter are also listed. These are not provided as a definitive list of reasons to collect or not collect that group of objects, but rather, to advise the reader to consider liability, storage, and fraudulent representation before making a purchase.

Pricing

Values are presented first for items as issued, followed by listings of soldier-used items. For example, in the uniform chapter, the reader will first see listings for uniforms without any insignia. One can think of these listings as "base models." These listings are followed by soldier-used or worn items with all of the insignia, markings, or accessories showing unique ownership, and therefore, affect current values. These latter items and prices are from sales of actual objects as reported by various dealers and auction houses, thereby providing the reader with a window into "real world" values.

The reader will notice that pricing is given in U.S. dollars and English pounds. Prior to the Internet dominating the hobby, there was often a huge discrepancy in prices paid for similar objects in the United States and abroad. However, in the last few years, prices have stabilized throughout the world.

Demand varies from nation to nation. U.S. and German material is in high demand in England, Europe, and Japan. However, Canadian gear is in higher demand in Canada than it is in the United States or Germany. The laws of supply and demand apply in this hobby as well. Highest prices will be realized in the nation of origin or that of a direct wartime opponent.

Where to Do Business?

Whether you are hoping to buy or sell, chances are there is a military collector living near you. Check your local classifieds. Advanced collectors often run "Military Items Wanted" ads in local papers and classified ad websites. Even if you are hoping to buy items, a call may open a conversation that will lead to subsequent deals.

Militaria shows take place throughout the United States, Europe, England, and Japan. Ranging from a dozen dealers to more than 2,000, these shows are the best source of fresh material for collectors. *Military Trader*, a monthly magazine published in the United States, contains a worldwide listing of military shows. Check the calendar of events, called the "Battle Plan," online at www.militarytrader.com.

Before you buy or sell any object, remember you are the person who needs to be happy with the final transaction. You can only sell an object once, so be sure you are ready to sell and are happy with the price. Be realistic. A dealer buys items to sell to other collectors. He needs to make a profit, generally about twice what he will pay. Be aware of the basic values of your items before you visit a dealer. Don't ask him to price your item—that will be uncomfortable for both of you. Likewise, don't waste his time by shopping an item around. He doesn't want to make an offer on an item only for you to take that offer somewhere else to leverage a few more dollars from another dealer.

Finally, keep in mind that these relics represent the sacrifices of millions of men and women who fought for what they believed was a better way of life. As this generation passes on, these relics will be the only tangible links to the horror, pain, honor, and glory that engulfed our world from 1939-1945.

Chapter 1

Uniforms & Footwear

Little evokes the sense of a soldier's personal commitment and sacrifice quite the way an original GI's field jacket or an SS officer's tunic does. After the conclusion of World War II, many discharged soldiers (of all nationalities) were allowed to keep their dress uniforms, if not all of their issued clothing. For years following the war, surplus and used clothing stores purchased mountains of uniforms. Customers eagerly purchased the durable goods for outdoor activities, as work clothes, or simply as cheap collectibles.

Uniforms, however, were not a common "trophy" piece for combat troops. Perhaps the items were simply too personal—it is easy to imagine the individual who wore a jacket, pair of trousers, or some other garment. Most likely, though, it was a matter of economy—something that collectors have to deal with today as well. Combat clothing tends to be bulky. A soldier on the campaign could carry a rucksack full of medals, documents, or other small trophies compared to one tunic that would fill the same space. Collectors are faced with the same dilemma: A lot of small items can be stored in the same space as one full uniform.

Uniforms are very desirable, nonetheless. Collectors eagerly seek entire uniforms or the various components to complete an outfit worn by a particular type of soldier. For example, a collector might begin with a German M36 combat tunic and focus on assembling the full uniform and equipment of a Wehrmacht soldier as he appeared during the 1940 campaign. Often, collectors like to display full uniforms on mannequins, thereby gaining a sense of a soldier's full load on campaign or appearance in garrison.

Uniforms: Dress or Fatigue?

Uniforms, regardless of the nationality, can be broken into two groups: Dress and fatigue. The former tends to be much more elaborate and includes the insignia and awards that a soldier had earned up to a certain time. The latter is more representative of the jobs for which soldiers were trained. Fatigue uniforms can range from a mechanic's coveralls to a combat infantryman's wool trousers.

Dress uniforms are still quite plentiful. This is because discharged soldiers often wore their uniforms home. After changing into their civilian woredrobes, the former soldiers carefully stored their uniforms as remembrances of their service. Many of these dress uniforms haven't seen the light of day since 1945. As estates are settled and dispersed, these uniforms are emerging from trunks, attics, and closets, to the delight of collectors.

The value of a dress uniform tends to come from the insignia that adorns it. Whether one is evaluating a U.S. Army Air Corps lieutenant's Class A jacket, a British Service Dress uniform, or a German Waffenrock, it is the insignia and accessories that determine whether the garment is worth a few dollars or hundreds of dollars. The nuances of the insignia, however, requires a great deal of study to know what patches, insignia, and medals add the most value.

Conversely, the value of fatigue or "combat" uniforms is determined by function. A sailor's rain jacket doesn't evoke the strong mental images of survival in combat as does an SS soldier's camoflauge smock. Even though a U.S. first pattern winter parka might be more "scarce" than a U.S. Pattern of 1941 field jacket because fewer were made of the former, the latter is the more desirable (and therefore, more valuable) item. The field jacket represents the common GI in the field. Virtually every American foot soldier who saw combat wore one of these. A general rule to follow is, if an item was worn by a soldier in combat, it will have a greater value than a non-combatant item.

Don't Tear Off the Tag

Collectors, especially those who focus on U.S. uniforms, pay a premium for uniforms that have complete and legible tags. These tags generally detail the contract under which the garment was made, the date of the contract and pattern, the official nomenclature for the garment, and the size.

Privately purchased tags imprinted with the original owner's name can often be found sewn into garments. These help a collector to establish a provenance for the garment.

And finally, many soldiers simply used pens to write their name, serial number or other information in their garments. These markings also can add to the intrigue—if not to the value—of a uniform. No attempt should be made to obliterate or remove such markings.

Shoes and Boots

Footwear follows the same general value structure of uniforms. That is, dress shoes and boots are less valuable than their combat-intended counterparts. One of the most recognizable icons are hobnailed German "jack boots." Because of their popularity with combat troops, these have become the quintessential footwear to display with German uniforms (even though ankle-high shoes were just as commonly issued to soldiers in the field). American "rough-out" service shoes, though issued in numbers equivalent to chrome-tanned "smooth" service shoes, conjure images of soldiers slogging it out in North Africa or Italy. That image has led to the lesser quality, rough-out shoes commanding a higher price today.

Size *Does* Matter

It is important to remember who is buying uniforms today. Basically, there are two types of consumers: collectors and reenactors. Collectors approach the hobby with the reverence of museum curators. The artifacts are handled with care. Originality and provenance command the premium prices from this group.

The other group, reenactors, don't care as much about the provenance of a uniform or even the originality or the totality of insignia that is present. In fact, the less insignia, the better for this group. Original insignia simply drives up the price of the garment. This group of buyers plans to wear the uniforms in the pursuit of their hobby. Essentially, reenactors are looking for used clothing rather than uniforms "with a story." For this group, size is what commands the premium prices. The larger the garment, the higher the price. Scores of reenactors will pass by a mint condition size 34 paratrooper's jacket (for which a collector would gladly pay $600-$800 / £410-£496) but will scramble to purchase a size 46 Class A jacket with no insignia (which would be worth about $25-$35 / £16-£22 to a collector).

Are Uniforms For You?

Uniform collecting is an extremely rewarding aspect of the militaria hobby. A person can assemble a meaningful display with a reasonable amount of investment. Items are available and can even still be found in antique shops, estate sales, and family attics.

Remember, though, uniforms require plenty of room for storage. If you specialize in uniforms, bear in mind that it will be the acquisition of yet another tunic, coat or other garment that will satisfy your collecting urges. It doesn't take too many uniforms to fill a closet!

Displaying uniforms can be difficult. Many feel that display on mannequins or clothing forms is the best way to enjoy a collection. If you thought a few

uniforms filled a collecting space quickly, wait until you buy a couple of mannequins! The alternative is to "flat-display" uniforms by hanging them on walls. Again, it doesn't take many jackets to cover all available vertical space in a room. Sooner or later, all uniform collectors surrender to storing the bulk of their collections out of sight in closets, attics, trunks, or boxes.

If you decide that uniform collecting is for you, exercise caution. As with any aspect of the hobby, fakes exist. Although most fakes tend to be of expensive uniforms like those of paratroopers, SS soldiers, or Panzer troops, a lot of uniforms can consist of all-original period components that had been assembled after the war. It does not take long to replace a less desireable shoulder patch or collar tab with an example from an elite unit.

Also keep in mind that people have been reenacting in an organized fashion for more than 40 years. Some early reenacting clothing, if worn hard on the campaign and put away dirty, will have some convincing-looking patina. Learn to recognize appropriate period construction techniques, fabrics, and styles before making your first purchase.

A Jacket's Value is in the Detail

If one looks at the various listings in this book and then compares them to listings found on dealers' lists or Internet sales and auction sites, one might be confused. Why do the dealer and auction prices seem so high?

The answer is found in the details, and specifically, the insignia. Most uniform component production ran into the hundreds of thousands, so generally speaking, the actual uniform piece is not the price determinant. Rather, the real value comes from the insignia on a particular uniform. For example, a simple U.S. Army Ike jacket with no insignia is worth about $35. However, an identical paratrooper's jacket with original insignia, including the divisional patch, campaign and citation ribbons, paratrooper wings, special unit awards, rank chevrons, and service stripes is worth $385 or more, depending on whether the name of the paratrooper is known (thereby establishing provenance).

When trying to determine the value of your uniform jacket or tunic, first determine the price of the basic garment without any insignia. Then look at the collar, shoulders, and sleeves to determine the value any insignia adds to the jacket or tunic. Finally, make note of any markings or oral tradition that can establish the soldier who originally wore the garment. Remember, the more combat a soldier saw, the higher the value of the uniform!

Collecting Hints

Pros:

- Uniforms are extremely personal and convey a direct sense of a soldier's commitment and service.
- Plentiful supply and variety available with prices in all collecting strata.
- Easy to find items with a known provenance.

Cons:

- Bulky! It takes plenty of space to assemble, display and store uniforms.
- Uniforms require special handling and care to preserve.
- It is difficult to recognize if the insignia is original to a particular garment or if it has been applied after 1945 to artificially inflate the value.
- Reproductions of combat clothing abound.

Availability: ✪ ✪ ✪ ✪
Price: ✪ ✪ ✪
Reproduction Alert: ✪ ✪ ✪

AUSTRALIA

Outerwear, Male

Australian RAAF summer flying overalls.
$175-$195 (£109-£121)
AdvanceGuardMilitaria.com

Coats, Jackets, Male

Australian RAAF officer's uniform, flight lieutenant observer.
$95-$135 (£59-£84)
AdvanceGuardMilitaria.com

Australian RAAF officer's summer uniform, squadron leader air gunner.
$195-$235 (£121-£146)
AdvanceGuardMilitaria.com

Australian RAAF pilot's summer dress tunic, flight lieutenant. **$185-$235 (£115-£146)**
AdvanceGuardMilitaria.com

Australian RAAF officer's summer dress tunic, flight lieutenant observer. **$160-$185 (£99-£115)**
AdvanceGuardMilitaria.com

Australian RAAF flight officer's tunic, sank U-470. **$710 (£440)**
AdvanceGuardMilitaria.com

Australian RAAF officer's uniform, flying officer air gunner. **$140-$165 (£87-£102)**
AdvanceGuardMilitaria.com

Australian RAAF officer's summer dress tunic, flying officer bombardier. **$125-$165 (£78-£102)**
AdvanceGuardMilitaria.com

Australian issue service dress trousers, 1943. **$35-$65 (£22-£40)**
AdvanceGuardMilitaria.com

Australian RAAF officer's uniform, identified flight lieutenant air gunner. **$140 (£87)**
AdvanceGuardMilitaria.com

CANADA

Outerwear, Male

Canadian khaki work coveralls. **$95-$135(£59-£84)**
AdvanceGuardMilitaria.com

Coats, Jackets, Male

Canadian Pattern 1940 6th Division battle dress jacket, Canadian Fusiliers. **$295-$345 (£183-£214)**
AdvanceGuardMilitaria.com

Canadian RCAF pilot flight sergeant's tunic, Pathfinder. **$225-$295 (£140-£183)**
AdvanceGuardMilitaria.com

Canadian RCAF flying officer pilot's Type D serge blouse.
$175-$265 (£109-£164)

AdvanceGuardMilitaria.com

Canadian RCAF flying officer summer tunic, air gunner.
$65-$115 (£40-£71)

AdvanceGuardMilitaria.com

Canadian RCAF summer dress squadron leader pilot's tunic.
$95-$145 (£59-£90)

AdvanceGuardMilitaria.com

Canadian RCAF flying officer pilot's tunic.
$285-$345 (£177-£214)

AdvanceGuardMilitaria.com

Canadian RCAF aerial gunner corporal's summer dress tunic. **$135-$165 (£84-£102)**

AdvanceGuardMilitaria.com

Canadian RCAF air gunner pilot officer's tunic. **$125-$175 (£78-£109)**

AdvanceGuardMilitaria.com

Canadian RCAF flying officer pilot's tunic, American volunteer. **$220-$300 (£136-£186)**

AdvanceGuardMilitaria.com

Trousers, Male

Canadian RCAF flying trousers. **$95-$135 (£59-£84)**

AdvanceGuardMilitaria.com

Coats, Jackets, Female

Canadian Women's Army Corps tunic. **$115-$135 (£71-£84)**

AdvanceGuardMilitaria.com

Values at a Glance

Commonly encountered uniform pieces:

• U.S. Army Class A Jacket, no insignia	$25
• U.S. Army "Ike" Jacket, no insignia	$20
• U.S. Army M43 Jacket, no insignia	$95
• U.S. Army Overcoat, no insignia	$35
• U.S. Navy Jumper, no insignia	$15
• U.S. Army "Double Buckle" boots	$95
• USMC Dress Blue Jacket	$65
• U.S. Army Air Corps A-3 Shearling Trousers	$85
• German Felt "Eastern Front" Boots	$75

CZECHOSLOVAKIA

Coats, Jackets, Male

Czechoslovakian Tank Corps officer's tunic.
$295-$365 (£183-£226)
AdvanceGuardMilitaria.com

ENGLAND

Outerwear, Male

RAF Irvin flight jacket. **$650-$850 (£403-£527)**
Manion's International

British Royal Field Artillery lt. colonel's tunic and breeches. **$145-$195 (£90-£121)**
AdvanceGuardMilitaria.com

"On base we wore khaki shirts and slacks. Goggles were no longer worn once we had flown solo."

—Flight Lt. Reg Everson, Royal Air Force

British National Fire Service greatcoat. **$15-$45 (£9-£28)**
AdvanceGuardMilitaria.com

RAF flight lieutenant's greatcoat. **$85-$100 (£53-£62)**
AdvanceGuardMilitaria.com

British RAF 1941 Pattern flying suit. **$295-$365 (£183-£226)**
AdvanceGuardMilitaria.com

British leather jerkin. **$80-$100 (£50-£62)**
AdvanceGuardMilitaria.com

Coats, Jackets, Male

British RAF pilot flight lieutenant's tunic,
Canadian volunteer. **$115-$150 (£71-£93)**
AdvanceGuardMilitaria.com

British World War II Royal Field Artillery lieutenant
colonel's tunic and breeches. **$145-$195 (£90-£121)**
AdvanceGuardMilitaria.com

British RAF pilot group captain's summer
dress tunic. **$115-$135 (£71-£84)**
AdvanceGuardMilitaria.com

British RAF signaller flight sergeant's tunic.
$145-$165 (£90-£102)
AdvanceGuardMilitaria.com

British Royal Tank Regiment lieutenant colonel's battledress jacket. **$200-$385 (£124-£239)**

AdvanceGuardMilitaria.com

British Air Raid Protection battle dress blouse. **$65-$85 (£40-£53)**

AdvanceGuardMilitaria.com

British Seaforth Highlanders Scottish service dress jacket and tartan trousers. **$165-$200 (£102-£124)**

AdvanceGuardMilitaria.com

British RAF khaki drill NCO pilot's tunic. **$115-$135 (£71-£84)**

AdvanceGuardMilitaria.com

British RAF No 8 Group Pathfinder Force flying officer uniform, air gunner. **$425-$495 (£264-£307)**

AdvanceGuardMilitaria.com

RAF identified flying officer signaller's tunic, Indian-made. **$235 (£146)**

AdvanceGuardMilitaria.com

RAF NCO pilot's tunic, North Africa service. **$215-$265 (£133-£164)**

AdvanceGuardMilitaria.com

British flight sergeant's battledress jacket, American volunteer. **$195 (£121)**

AdvanceGuardMilitaria.com

British RAF warrant officer navigator's battle dress uniform and medals. **$565-$625 (£350-£388)**

AdvanceGuardMilitaria.com

Shirts, Male

British RAF khaki drill bush shirt and shorts.
$85-$95 (£53-£59)
AdvanceGuardMilitaria.com

British RAF airman's issue shirt.
$75-$95 (£47-£59)
AdvanceGuardMilitaria.com

Trousers, Male

British issue
service dress
trousers. **$25-$45
(£16-£28)**
AdvanceGuardMilitaria.com

Footwear, Male

British rest/athletic shoes.
$100-$125 (£62-£78)
AdvanceGuardMilitaria.com

British RAF 1941
Pattern flying
boots. **$285-$345
(£177-£214)**
AdvanceGuardMilitaria.com

RAF flying boots, Australian-made, 1936 Pattern. **$445-$525 (£276-£326)**
AdvanceGuardMilitaria.com

British WAAF utility pattern working suit. **$385-$435 (£239-£270)**
AdvanceGuardMilitaria.com

Outerwear, Female

British Women's Land Army overalls coat. **$35-$55 (£22-£34)**
AdvanceGuardMilitaria.com

Coats, Jackets, Female

British WAAF Airwoman's service dress jacket and cap. **$315-$350 (£195-£217)**
AdvanceGuardMilitaria.com

Footwear, Female

British WAAF service shoes. **$125-$145 (£78-£90)**
AdvanceGuardMilitaria.com

FRANCE

Outerwear, Male

French greatcoat group. **$335-$450 (£208-£279)**
Hermann-Historica.de

1920 Pattern greatcoat for French Colonial forces. **$400-$450 (£248-£279)**
Hermann-Historica.de

Coats, Jackets, Male

French uniform of the National Police, 1940-1944. **$300-$500 (£186-£310)**
Hermann-Historica.de

Summer uniform belonging to Gen. Charles Noguès. **$2,680 (£1,662)**
Hermann-Historica.de

French 1935 Pattern greatcoat and 1938 Pattern tunic. **$400-$550 (£248-£341)**
Hermann-Historica.de

French 1st Hussar NCO tunic and trousers. **$150-$200 (£93-£124)**
AdvanceGuardMilitaria.com

French First Army officer's tunic. **$155-$165 (£96-£102)**
AdvanceGuardMilitaria.com

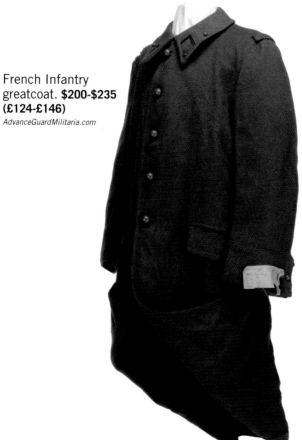

French Infantry greatcoat. **$200-$235 (£124-£146)**
AdvanceGuardMilitaria.com

Footwear, Male

French shearling flying boots. **$165-$200 (£102-£124)**
AdvanceGuardMilitaria.com

Favorite Find: Uncle Don's Coveralls

by Kevin Born • Originally published in Military Trader

What's my favorite World War II relic? When I saw the question in the *Military Trader*, I didn't hesitate; I knew exactly what it was.

As a young child growing up in the Midwest in the late 1960s, I frequently visited my grandmother with my family. Dad was the next-to-youngest of nine brothers. All but one had served in the military, either during World War II or the Korean War.

I looked forward to going to Grandma's house because, carefully tucked away in a closet in the basement, were all the duffle bags brought home by her eight sons. I'd spend delightful hours digging through old wool uniforms, navy jumpers, starched fatigues, pistol belts, canteens, and other military treasures. I'd put on the jackets and feel the chevrons and ratings on the sleeves and the ribbon bars on my chest. I tried to imagine what military service was like.

There was always one uniform to which I was drawn—a jump suit, or rather, a one-piece camouflage uniform that had belonged to my Uncle Don. He had served in World War II. I had no clue what it was or what Uncle Don had done in the war, but it was cool!

Whenever I went to Grandma's house, it was the first uniform I pulled out of the duffle bag. Eventually, after being asked many times, Grandma let me take home this treasured camo uniform.

For several years, through the late 1960s and early 1970s, I played soldier in this uniform behind my house and in neighborhood kids' yards, vanquishing Nazis or fighting behind Japanese-held enemy lines with plastic rifles or pointed sticks.

The uniform was packed away and forgotten at my parent's house when I went off to college. While there, my father died. When I was serving at my first Army duty station on the West Coast, my mother moved and had to get rid of my accumulated World War II uniforms. I thought the camo uniform I'd grown to love was now just a memory.

Many years later, when I was visiting my mother's new house, she said she had something special for me. To my surprise, she pulled a box from a closet, and in it was the long-lost camo uniform! She knew how much it meant to me and had saved it all of those years.

Much later I learned the uniform was a set of highly sought-after herringbone twill camouflage coveralls worn by both the Army and Marines in World War II. While they were in mint condition when I received them, they sustained years of hard play. Regardless, they are still in good condition, albeit missing the maker's tags and sporting a small hole near the bottom of the zipper.

I later learned that "Uncle Don" had been Technical Sergeant Donald Born, who had served in Horham, England, flying combat missions as a top turret gunner on a B-17 named "Little Joe." Assigned to the 335th Bomb Squadron, 95th Bomb Group of the 8th Air Force in December 1944, Don successfully flew 35 missions over Germany. He earned six Air Medals for this dangerous work.

I asked him about the camo coveralls a few years ago, but he had no idea where he had found them. All he could remember was that he had received them in a trade for something.

Until he died in 2008, Uncle Don kept the fuse safety pin tags from bombs his plane had dropped, carefully marked with the dates and locations of each of his bombing missions. These he had hanging in his basement, a reminder of all those dangerous missions over Germany.

The camo coveralls remain one of my prize possessions. They are a connection to my Uncle Don and the first piece of militaria that I had ever "collected." Those joyous moments nearly 45 years ago in my grandmother's basement with Uncle Don's camo coveralls eventually led me down the path to a lifelong passion for military collecting and a career as an Army officer.

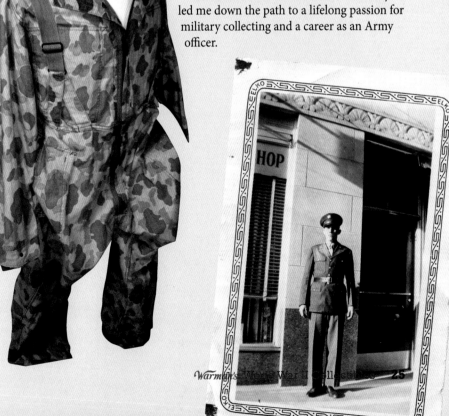

GERMANY

Outerwear, Male

Heer Infantry Captain's Infantry greatcoat. **$385-$435 (£239-£270)**
AdvanceGuardMilitaria.com

Overcoat for a field chaplain. **$2,850-$3,500 (£1,767-£2,170)**
Hermann-Historica.de

Reversible winter jacket in autumn camouflage. **$2,000-$3,000 (£1,240-£1,860)**
Hermann-Historica.de

Heer splinter camouflage reversible winter parka. **$520-$695 (£322-£431)**
AdvanceGuardMilitaria.com

Winter camouflage uniform in splinter pattern. **$1,000-$1,600 (£620-£992)**
Hermann-Historica.de

Coats, Jackets, Male

Heer Model 1941 field jacket, infantry private. **$1,285-$1,395 (£797-£865)**

AdvanceGuardMilitaria.com

Heer Model 1943 field jacket, infantry gefreiter. **$1,395-$1,450 (£865-£899)**

AdvanceGuardMilitaria.com

Tunic for eastern volunteer to German Army. **$2,275-$2,500 (£1,411-£1,550)**

Hermann-Historica.de

Special issue Panzer clothing for an Oberleutnant. **$4,288 (£2,659)**

Hermann-Historica.de

Waffenrock for a captain of the Panzer Grenadiers. **$2,500-$3,000 (£1,550-£1,860)**
Hermann-Historica.de

Wraparound jacket for an officer candidate sergeant of the Assault Artillery. **$3,000-$3,500 (£1,860-£2,170)**
Hermann-Historica.de

Field tunic for tropical or southern front, unissued condition. **$1,950-$2,300 (£1,209-£1,426)**
Hermann-Historica.de

Field tunic for a captain of a propaganda company. **$1,850-$2,000 (£1,147-£1,240)**
Hermann-Historica.de

Wraparound jacket for a sergeant of Assault Gun Unit of "Großdeutschland" Division. **$6,500-$8,000 (£4,030-£4,960)**

Hermann-Historica.de

White jacket for SS orderlies. **$5,000-$6,000 (£3,100-£3,720)**

Hermann-Historica.de

SS Judicial Service Sturmführer black tunic. **$10,000-$12,000 (£6,200-£7,440)**

HistoryHunter.com

Service tunic (private purchase) for a Standartenführer of the Standarte "Germania." **$11,390 (£7,062)**

Hermann-Historica.de

Waffen SS NCO "Deutschland" M43 combat tunic and awards. **$8,500-$9,000 (£5,270-£5,580)**
Manion's International

SS field tunic. **$12,000-$14,000 (£744-£8,680)**
HistoryHunter.com

Reversible lace-up camouflage smock.
$11,000-$13,000 (£6,830-£8,060)
Hermann-Historica.de

Model 43 Waffen SS camouflage suit in Erbsttarn pattern. **$4,000-$5,000 (£ 2,480-£3,100)**
Hermann-Historica.de

Paratrooper's jump smock ("Knochensack"), 3rd Model in Splinter Pattern camouflage. **$10,000-$13,000 (£6,200-£8,060)**
Hermann-Historica.de

Waffen SS Panzer wraparound officer's tunic. **$10,000-$12,500 (£6,200-£7,750)**
HistoryHunter.com

Evening uniform for a Luftwaffe flight Oberleutnant. **$1,000-$1,250 (£620-£775)**
Hermann-Historica.de

M44 camouflage blouse in dot pattern for the Waffen-SS. **$2,800-$3,500 (£1,736-£2,170)**
Hermann-Historica.de

Walking out dress for a Luftwaffe lieutenant of flight or paratroop personnel. **$2,500-$3,000 (£1,550-£1,860)**
Hermann-Historica.de

Luftwaffe Field Division camouflage jacket.
$1,500-$3,000 (£930-£1,860)
Hermann-Historica.de

Luftwaffe lieutenant's (flying personnel)
tropical tunic. **$1,100-$1,400 (£682-£868)**
HistoryHunter.com

Leather jacket for Luftwaffe pilot,
Oberleutnant. **$1,850-$2,250 (£1,147-£1,395)**
Hermann-Historica.de

Luftwaffe service tunic of an
Oberleutnant of a Flak unit.
$750-$975 (£465-£605)
Hermann-Historica.de

Jacket of a Wehrmacht
official of admiral's rank.
$2,800-$3,350 (£1,736-£2,077)
Hermann-Historica.de

Field tunic for a Zugführer
of the Technical Emergency
Service. **$2,500-$3,500
(£1,550-£2,170)**
Hermann-Historica.de

Service tunic for a Luftschutz-
Truppmann. **$1,200-$1,475
(£744-£9,145)**
Hermann-Historica.de

Kriegsmarine of U-boat
flotilla machinist uniform
group. **$2,825 (£1,752)**
Hermann-Historica.de

Walking-out uniform for
enlisted men of the National
Socialist Flying Corps.
$1,500-$2,000 (£930-£1,240)
Hermann-Historica.de

Shirts, Male

Wehrmacht pullover sweater.
$195-$245 (£121-£152)
AdvanceGuardMilitaria.com

Sport shirt for SS member.
600-$700 (£372-£434)
Hermann-Historica.de

Heer M1933 pullover shirt.
$245-$275 (£152-£171)
AdvanceGuardMilitaria.com

Heer M1934 pullover shirt.
$265-$295 (£164-£183)
AdvanceGuardMilitaria.com

M1933 Wehrmacht pullover
shirt. **$125-$145 (£78-£90)**
AdvanceGuardMilitaria.com

Trousers, Male

Kriegsmarine tropical shorts.
$375-$395 (£233-£245)
AdvanceGuardMilitaria.com

Heer mounted breeches made from
Italian materials. **$325-$395 (£202-£245)**
AdvanceGuardMilitaria.com

Model 1933 Austrian-made stone gray
issue trousers. **$650-$750 (£403-£465)**
AdvanceGuardMilitaria.com

Model 1933 Austrian-made stone gray
issue breeches. **$585-$685 (£363-£425)**
AdvanceGuardMilitaria.com

Full-length trouser for tropical uniform. **$950-$1,275 (£589-£791)**
Hermann-Historica.de

Stiefelhose für Hitler Youth Leader. **$350-$400 (£217-£248)**
Hermann-Historica.de

Trousers for the M 43, 1st Model camouflage suit. **$3,300-$4,300 (£2,046-£2,666)**
Hermann-Historica.de

M44 enlisted trousers, depot piece. **$1,500-$1,900 (£930-£1,178)**
Hermann-Historica.de

Trousers for flying personnel.
$275-$350 (£171-£217)
Hermann-Historica.de

$325-$400 (£202-£248)
AdvanceGuardMilitaria.com

Luftwaffe leather trousers for fighter pilots.
$3,500-$5,000 (£2,170-£3,100)
Hermann-Historica.de

Footwear, Male

Heer 1937 Pattern hobnailed ankle boots.
$145-$195 (£90-£121)

AdvanceGuardMilitaria.com

First Pattern shoes for tropical uniform.
$950-$1,350 (£589-£837)

Hermann-Historica.de

Tropical issue boots.
$1,000-$1,500 (£620-£930)

Hermann-Historica.de

Eastern Front winter boots.
$195-$215 (£121-£133)

AdvanceGuardMilitaria.com

Third Reich officer's boots.
$195-$225 (£121-£140)

AdvanceGuardMilitaria.com

Third Reich NCO field boots.
$225-$295 (£140-£183)

AdvanceGuardMilitaria.com

Heated, fur-lined Luftwaffe flight boots.
$375-$475 (£233-£295)

Hermann-Historica.de

Luftwaffe flight boots. **$265-$350 (£164-£217)**

Hermann-Historica.de

Luftwaffe or Field Police brown leather
marching boots. **$245-$285 (£152-£177)**

AdvanceGuardMilitaria.com

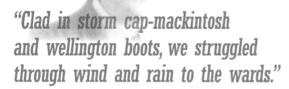

"Clad in storm cap-mackintosh and wellington boots, we struggled through wind and rain to the wards."

—Britsh Army nurse in field hospital at Gebeit

Coats, Jackets, Female

Female RAD uniform jacket.
$1,000-$1,200 (£620-£744)
Hermann-Historica.de

Uniform for a female Luftwaffer helper, Luftnachrichten-Führerin.
$3,000-$3,500 (£1,860-£2,170)
Hermann-Historica.de

HUNGARY

Shirts, Male

Hungarian issue shirt. **$185-$225 (£115-£140)**
AdvanceGuardMilitaria.com

Outerwear, Male

Hungarian Infantry overcoat. **$350-$450 (£217-£279)**
AdvanceGuardMilitaria.com

Coats, Jackets, Male

Hungarian Infantry 1922 Pattern tunic. **$695-$895 (£431-£555)**
AdvanceGuardMilitaria.com

Trousers, Male

Hungarian Infantry wool trousers. **$295-$385 (£183-£239)**
AdvanceGuardMilitaria.com

ITALY

Outwear, Male

Italian Alpini Mountain parka and gaitered trousers. **$395-$465 (£245-£288)**
AdvanceGuardMilitaria.com

Italian Infantry officer's greatcoat.
$315-$350 (£195-£217)
AdvanceGuardMilitaria.com

Coats, Jackets, Male

Uniform jacket of a general.
$350-$650 (£217-£403)
Hermann-Historica.de

Italian lieutenant general's tunic.
$315-$395 (£195-£245)
AdvanceGuardMilitaria.com

Italian Infantry lieutenant's tunic.
$275-$295 (£171-£183)

AdvanceGuardMilitaria.com

Italian Infantry captain's tunic and breeches.
$325-$385 (£202-£239)

AdvanceGuardMilitaria.com

Italian Alpini officer's service
dress tunic. **$285-$365 (£177-£226)**

AdvanceGuardMilitaria.com

Italian Nizza Cavalry Regiment
officer's tunic. **$395-$465 (£245-£288)**
AdvanceGuardMilitaria.com

Italian fatigue jacket.
$95-$125 (£59-£78)
AdvanceGuardMilitaria.com

Italian North African Campaign tropical
uniform. **$565-$585 (£350-£363)**
AdvanceGuardMilitaria.com

Italian Carabinieri officer's black service tunic.
$235-$265 (£146-£164)
AdvanceGuardMilitaria.com

M1937 field tunic of an engineer NCO. **$500-$650 (£310-£403)**

Hermann-Historica.de

Italian Tropical Sahariana tunic. **$340-$385 (£211-£239)**

AdvanceGuardMilitaria.com

JAPAN

Outwear, Male

Japanese Army pilot's privately purchased jacket and trousers. **$255-$285 (£158-£177)**

AdvanceGuardMilitaria.com

Japanese Army tanker's jacket. **$375-$425 (£233-£264)**

AdvanceGuardMilitaria.com

Japanese Army officer's rain cape. **$85-$115 (£53-£71)**

AdvanceGuardMilitaria.com

Japanese Army Type 3 overcoat. **$85-$115 (£53-£71)**

AdvanceGuardMilitaria.com

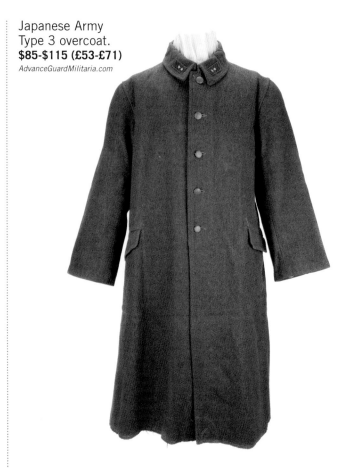

Japanese Army Type 98 raincoat with hood. **$175-$195 (£109-£121)**

AdvanceGuardMilitaria.com

Japanese Army Type 3 Army raincoat. **$100-$125 (£62-£78)**

AdvanceGuardMilitaria.com

Coats, Jackets, Male

Japanese Naval Landing Force tropical tunic, captain. **$295-$325 (£183-£202)**

AdvanceGuardMilitaria.com

Japanese Army tropical combat shirt and shorts. **$385-$425 (£239-£264)**

AdvanceGuardMilitaria.com

Japanese Preparatory Flight School summer tunic.
$165-$185 (£102-£115)

AdvanceGuardMilitaria.com

Japanese Army cotton tunic.
$165-$185 (£102-£115)

AdvanceGuardMilitaria.com

Trousers, Male

Japanese Army Type 98 wool tunic.
$135-$165 (£84-£102)
AdvanceGuardMilitaria.com

Japanese Army Type 3 wool enlisted issue trousers. **$100-$135 (£62-£84)**
AdvanceGuardMilitaria.com

Japanese Army 3rd Type tropical tunic.
$135-$165 (£84-£102)
AdvanceGuardMilitaria.com

Japanese Army winter work trousers.
$135-$165 (£84-£102)
AdvanceGuardMilitaria.com

Japanese Army late war Type 98 trousers of simplified construction.
$95-$115 (£59-£71)
AdvanceGuardMilitaria.com

Footwear, Male

Japanese Army Class B boots.
$145-$185 (£90-£115)
AdvanceGuardMilitaria.com

Japanese Army Tabi shoes.
$95-$125 (£59- £78)
AdvanceGuardMilitaria.com

Japanese officer's shoes.
$135-$165 (£84-£102)
AdvanceGuardMilitaria.com

Japanese Army wood-sole slippers.
$35-$45 (£22-£28)
AdvanceGuardMilitaria.com

NEW ZEALAND

Outerwear, Male

New Zealand RNZAF flight lieutenant's greatcoat. **$60-$95 (£40-£59)**
AdvanceGuardMilitaria.com

Footwear, Male

New Zealand ankle boots. **$85-$125 (£53-£78)**
AdvanceGuardMilitaria.com

POLAND

Coats, Jackets, Male

Polish enlisted Wz. 36 summer service tunic. **$535-$665 (£332-£412)**
AdvanceGuardMilitaria.com

Trousers, Male

Polish enlisted summer service trousers. **$225-$300 (£140-£186)**
AdvanceGuardMilitaria.com

Footwear, Male

Polish Model 1939 issue ankle boots. **$395-$465 (£245-£288)**
AdvanceGuardMilitaria.com

SOVIET UNION

Outwear, Male

Soviet amoeba-pattern camouflaged sniper suit. **$800-$1,200 (£496-£744)**
AdvanceGuardMilitaria.com

Coats, Jackets, Male

Soviet World War II M.35 enlisted infantry gymnastiorka. **$325-$365 (£202-£226)**
AdvanceGuardMilitaria.com

Soviet Infantry officer's M43 gymnastiorka. **$165-$195 (£102-£121)**
AdvanceGuardMilitaria.com

Trousers, Male

Soviet M43 field tailored gymnastiorka.
$150-$175 (£93-£109)

AdvanceGuardMilitaria.com

Soviet Cavalry officer's field service
breeches. **$200-$235 (£124-£146)**

AdvanceGuardMilitaria.com

Model 1943 Infantry enlisted
gymnastiorka. **$185-$235 (£115-£146)**

AdvanceGuardMilitaria.com

Soviet Union Army enlisted man's breeches.
$125-$165 (£78-£102)

AdvanceGuardMilitaria.com

Footwear, Male

Soviet Infantry boots. **$165-$225 (£102-£133)**

AdvanceGuardMilitaria.com

Soviet Union enlisted boots.
$165-$200 (£102-£124)

AdvanceGuardMilitaria.com

UNITED STATES

Outerwear, Male

AAF 5th Air Force officer's
elaborately embroidered M41 field
jacket. **$1,400-$1,600 (£868-£992)**

AdvanceGuardMilitaria.com

3rd Armored Division "Tanker" jacket.
$395-$450 (£245-£279)

AdvanceGuardMilitaria.com

U.S. Army mackinaw coat, 1938 Pattern.
$95-$135 (£59-£84)

AdvanceGuardMilitaria.com

AAF B-15 flight jacket. **$325-$335 (£202-£208)**

AdvanceGuardMilitaria.com

U.S. Army enlisted ETO jacket, First Pattern.
$235-$300 (£146-£186)

AdvanceGuardMilitaria.com

AAF 19th Fighter Squadron A-2 flight jacket.
$1,295-$1,500 (£803-£930)

AdvanceGuardMilitaria.com

AAF 13th Air Force 5th Bomb Group aerial gunner's painted A2 flight jacket. **$2,650 (£1,643)**
AdvanceGuardMilitaria.com

AAF 10th Air Force A-2 flight jacket. **$975-$1,250 (£605-£775)**
AdvanceGuardMilitaria.com

AAF A-2 flight jacket. **$725 (£450)**
AdvanceGuardMilitaria.com

AAF A-2 flight jacket with 374th Fighter Squadron insignia. **$435 (£270)**
AdvanceGuardMilitaria.com

AAF B-7 "Alaskan Suit" shearling flying parka. **$335-$435 (£208-£270)**
AdvanceGuardMilitaria.com

USN naval aviator's M-445A fleece flying jacket. **$255-$285 (£158-£177)**
AdvanceGuardMilitaria.com

AAF 9th Air Force B-14 flight jacket. **$165-$195 (£102-£121)**
AdvanceGuardMilitaria.com

AAF B-13 officer's flight jacket. **$185-$195 (£115-£121)**
AdvanceGuardMilitaria.com

AAF B-3 flight jacket.
$495-$585 (£307-£363)
AdvanceGuardMilitaria.com

USMC P1942
reversible
camouflage
combat trousers.
**$365-$450
(£226-£279)**
AdvanceGuardMilitaria.com

**AAF 370th Bomb Squadron B-15A
flight jacket. $185-$225 (£115-£140)**
AdvanceGuardMilitaria.com

**USN M456 goatskin heated flying suit.
$325-$385 (£202-£239)**
AdvanceGuardMilitaria.com

82nd Airborne soldier's jump jacket and trousers, including paratrooper M2 knife. **$3,200-$3,865 (£1,984-£2,296)**

AdvanceGuardMilitaria.com

Coats, Jackets, Male

USMC 4th Division Ordnance Company unit-marked P41 HBT utility coat. **$185-$235 (£115-£146)**

AdvanceGuardMilitaria.com1

USMC P1941 HBT jacket and trousers. **$225-$265 (£140-£164)**

AdvanceGuardMilitaria.com

USMC P1941 HBT jacket, unissued. **$225-$250 (£140-£155)**

AdvanceGuardMilitaria.com

AAF 8th Air Force aerial gunner
enlisted ETO jacket, First Pattern.
$255-$325 (£158-£202)

AdvanceGuardMilitaria.com

AAF CBI senior pilot's bush jacket.
$180-$225 (£112-£140)

AdvanceGuardMilitaria.com

CBI service pilot's bush jacket.
$165-$225 (£102-£140)

AdvanceGuardMilitaria.com

AAF British-made ETO jacket,
Technician 4th Grade. **$182 (£113)**

AdvanceGuardMilitaria.com

82nd Airborne sergeant's uniform.
$345-$400 (£214-£248)
AdvanceGuardMilitaria.com

Four-Pocket "Class A" Coats

AAF 15th Air Force 301st Bomb Group master sergeant's service coat. **$235-$265 (£146-£164)**
AdvanceGuardMilitaria.com

USMC baseball uniform. **$300-$365 (£186-£226)**
AdvanceGuardMilitaria.com

Colonel's dress white uniform and visor cap.
$265-$295 (£164-£183)
AdvanceGuardMilitaria.com

AAF 20th Air Force CBI pilot's uniform.
$120-$135 (£74-£135)

AdvanceGuardMilitaria.com

AAF CBI staff sergeant air crew member's
jacket, bullion insignia. **$265-$335 (£164-£208)**

AdvanceGuardMilitaria.com

AAF CBI aerial gunner technical sergeant's
tunic, bullion insignia. **$145-$185 (£90-£115)**

AdvanceGuardMilitaria.com

AAF 8th Air Force pilot lieutenant's jacket,
combat crew. **$165-$185 (£102-£115)**

AdvanceGuardMilitaria.com

U.S. Forces in Austria quartermaster major's complete uniform. **$265-$295 (£164-£183)**
AdvanceGuardMilitaria.com

AAF Airborne troop carrier officer's uniform. **$115-$165 (£71-£102)**
AdvanceGuardMilitaria.com

AAF 12th Air Force sergeant's uniform. **$110-$125 (£68-£78)**
AdvanceGuardMilitaria.com

U.S. Air Transport Command jacket. **$80-$95 (£50-£59)**
AdvanceGuardMilitaria.com

Field "Eisenhower" or "Ike" Jackets

1st Cavalry Division
soldier's uniform.
$55-75 (£34-£47)
AdvanceGuardMilitaria.com

AAF 3rd and 12th AAF
photographer's Ike jacket
and shirt, bullion insignia.
$195-$235 (£121-£146)
AdvanceGuardMilitaria.com

69th Division / XIX Corps
Field Signal NCO's Ike jacket.
$75-$95 (£47-£59)
AdvanceGuardMilitaria.com

Desert Air Force major
pilot's tan Ike jacket, flew
with Canadians. **$195 (£121)**
AdvanceGuardMilitaria.com

World War II AAF 12th Air Force pilot's jacket, bullion insignia. **$145-$165 (£90-£102)**
AdvanceGuardMilitaria.com

USMC Coats and Jackets

USMC 2nd Marine regiment colonel's jacket. **$345-$395 (£214-£245)**
AdvanceGuardMilitaria.com

USMC 6th Marine Division NCO's uniform. **$65-85 (£40-£53)**
AdvanceGuardMilitaria.com

USMC 1st Marine Division staff sergeant's dress blue uniform. **$145-$175 (£90-£109)**
AdvanceGuardMilitaria.com

10th Mountain Division engineer's uniform. **$125-$175 (£78-£109)**
AdvanceGuardMilitaria.com

USN Line ensign pilot's khaki tunic.
$85-$115 (£53-£71)
AdvanceGuardMilitaria.com

U.S. Navy Uniforms

USN Minecraft Crewman uniform group.
$85-$145 (£53-£90)
AdvanceGuardMilitaria.com

USN Lieutenant of the Line white service dress jacket. **$55-$75 (£34-£47)**
AdvanceGuardMilitaria.com

USN Seabee petty
officer's uniform.
$45-$75 (£28-£47)
AdvanceGuardMilitaria.com

Stars and Stripes reporter's shirt.
$95-$125 (£59-£78)
Author's Collection

Shirts, Male

Army tank destroyer corporal's shirt.
$35-$55 (£22-£34)
AdvanceGuardMilitaria.com

NCO's wool shirt. **$25-$34 (£16-£21)**
Author's Collection

Trousers, Male

USMC P1944 HBT trousers, unissued.
$165-$185 (£102-£115)
AdvanceGuardMilitaria.com

World War II navy blue denim "dungarees"
trousers. **$245-$325 (£152-£202)**
AdvanceGuardMilitaria.com

Army Mountain Troops issue poplin ski
trousers. **$285-$325 (£177-£202)**
AdvanceGuardMilitaria.com

A-3 shearling trousers. **$95-$145 (£59-£80)**
AdvanceGuardMilitaria.com

Footwear, Male

U.S. Army M1943 service shoes. **$165-$225 (£102-£140)**

AdvanceGuardMilitaria.com

Marine issue combat shoes. **$125-$165 (£78- £102)**

AdvanceGuardMilitaria.com

U.S. early war Army cap-toe service shoes. **$165-$225 (£102-£140)**

AdvanceGuardMilitaria.com

AAF A-6 winter flying boots. **$175-$225 (£109-£140)**

AdvanceGuardMilitaria.com

Unissued double-buckle combat boots. **$200-$250 (£124-£155)**

AdvanceGuardMilitaria.com

A-6A winter flying boots and socks. **$245-$285 (£152-£177)**

AdvanceGuardMilitaria.com

Army service shoes, February 1943 Pattern.
$225-$265 (£140-£164)

AdvanceGuardMilitaria.com

U.S. Army cap-toe service shoes.
$175-$225 (£109-£140)

Author's Collection

Outerwear, Female

WAC enlisted utility overcoat. **$95-$135 (£59-£84)**

AdvanceGuardMilitaria.com

WAVES raincoat and havelock. **85-$125 (£53-£78)**

AdvanceGuardMilitaria.com

Army Nurses Corps cape. **$135-$165 (£84-£103)**

AdvanceGuardMilitaria.com

USMC Women's Reserve overcoat. **$95-$125 (£59-£78)**

AdvanceGuardMilitaria.com

Enlisted WAC wool overcoat. **$100-$135 (£62-£84)**

AdvanceGuardMilitaria.com

Army nurse overcoat. **$125-$145 (£78-£90)**

AdvanceGuardMilitaria.com

Jackets, Female

Army Nurses Corps M1940 blue uniform jacket. **$195-$245 (£121-£152)**

AdvanceGuardMilitaria.com

7th Service Command WAC uniform. **$185-$235 (£115-£146)**

AdvanceGuardMilitaria.com

Early Army
Nurses Corps
blue tunic.
**$145-$175
(£90-£109)**
AdvanceGuardMilitaria.com

Army Nurses
Corps field
hospital
seersucker
duty uniform.
**$145-$175
(£90-£109)**
AdvanceGuardMilitaria.com

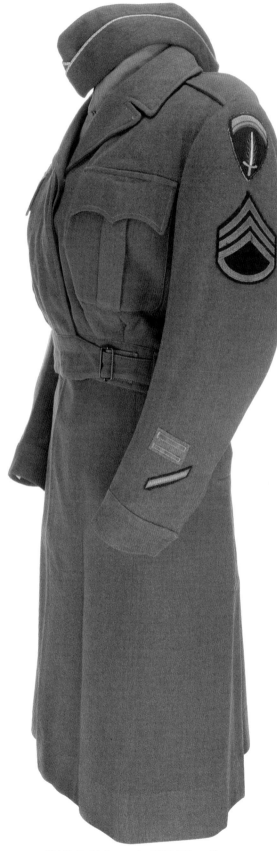

WAC British-made SHAEF uniform.
$495-$550 (£307-£341)
AdvanceGuardMilitaria.com

WAAC enlisted winter tunic, unissued with cutter tags. **$80-$100 (£50-£62)**
AdvanceGuardMilitaria.com

ANC lieutenant's khaki summer service uniform. **$165-$195 (£102-£121)**
AdvanceGuardMilitaria.com

AAF Army Flight Nurse flying uniform, identified. **$585 (£363)**
AdvanceGuardMilitaria.com

SPARS enlisted uniform.
$225-$250 (£140-£155)

AdvanceGuardMilitaria.com

Female Civil Defense worker's
uniform. **$175-$195 (£109-£121)**

AdvanceGuardMilitaria.com

Army nurse blue off-duty dress. **$325-$365 (£202-£226)**

AdvanceGuardMilitaria.com

Red Cross Woman's Military Welfare Service uniform. **$385-$425 (£239-£264)**

AdvanceGuardMilitaria.com

Trousers, Skirts, Female

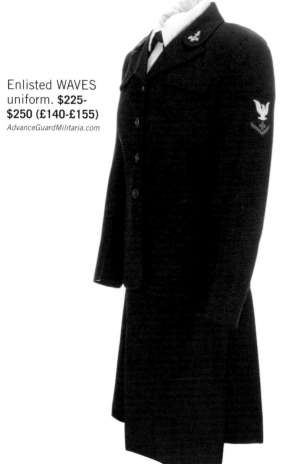

Enlisted WAVES uniform. **$225-$250 (£140-£155)**

AdvanceGuardMilitaria.com

4th Air Force woman's issue shirt and skirt. **$95-$135 (£59-£84)**

AdvanceGuardMilitaria.com

Footwear, Female

WAC/ANC issue service shoes. **$85-$125 (£50-£78)**
AdvanceGuardMilitaria.com

USMC Women's Reserve exercise shorts.
$75-$95 (£47-£59)
AdvanceGuardMilitaria.com

WAC/ANC trousers. **$35-$55 (£22-£34)**
AdvanceGuardMilitaria.com

"We loaded onto trucks for transport to the forward replacement depot, the headquarters of the Fifteenth Infantry Regiment, there to be relieved of all our baggage except as was recommended - only what you would carry into combat. We put on two of everything, wool shirts and pants, long-johns, socks, sweaters, our overcoats were turned in and we wore field jackets, one wool scarf, knit cap under the helmet and driving gloves."

—Early Maynard, 15th U.S. Infantry Regiment

Chapter 2

Headgear

One of the most popular areas of World War II collectibles is that of headgear. Whether German helmets, fatigue "boonie" hats, or dress visor caps, nothing seems to appeal more to collectors than a soldier's head covering.

Headgear collectors can be divided into three groups: helmet collectors, visor cap collectors, and a mixture of the two. Helmet collectors are by far the most numerous.

Helmets

Probably the most sought-after souvenir among British Tommies and American GIs (after Luger pistols) were German helmets. Images of jackboots and the steel-curtained helmets of the German soldier had permeated newsreels, magazines, and newspapers since 1934. Prior to World War II, boys (who would later serve as the soldiers in the global conflict) had played with the helmet trophies that their dads, brothers, and uncles brought home as souvenirs of the Great War. People recognized the basic shape, so it was no wonder soldiers of World War II clamored to bring home the Teutonic helmets.

It has only been during the last decade, however, that helmets of other participant nations have gained popularity. The steadily increasing prices for German helmets have directed many collectors to consider the headgear of Allied and Axis nations. Helmets of Japan, Bulgaria, and eastern European nations have all gained value in recent years.

Though German helmet prices have steadily increased since World War II, the meteoric rise has been in the prices of U.S. helmets. Surplus stocks of American M1 helmets kept prices low for years following the end of

World War II. Only as collectors sifted through the piles of surplus helmets to find the rare examples with some sort of camouflage or painted insignia did the hobby take notice of GI helmets.

The key to the value of any helmet is twofold: relative rarity and markings. An unmarked Model 36 Soviet helmet is rare because so few survived the war, having been mostly replaced by the Models 39 and Model 40. On the other hand, an American M1 helmet with a chinstrap on non-swiveling loops is relatively common. With liner, such a helmet will sell for $125-$250 (£78-155). In 1999, it was not uncommon to see one for $20 (£12)! The same helmet with the small, painted insignia of the 2nd Infantry Division, however, will jump to $800-$1,000 (£496-£620). Why? Because very few U.S. helmets were decorated with any sort of insignia, and those that were usually received a layer of paint when it was reissued during or after the war.

This phenomenon is not limited to U.S. helmets. It didn't take long for collectors to realize that the value of German helmets was not in the "shells" but rather the markings on the shell. A simple M40 steel helmet with liner and no decals or other insignia will sell for around $245-$345 (£152-£214). But if that same helmet has a single Army decal, add $300 (£186) to the price. If it has a single SS decal, add about $2,500 (£1,550): The same shell with three different configurations selling for three widely disparate prices.

Values based on markings, however, has led to a serious pitfall within the hobby. No single item is utilized as the basis for fakes more than the helmet. Unscrupulous dealers can't resist the temptation to "upgrade" a German helmet or paint something on an American shell. If you are fortunate enough to obtain a helmet with a trusted provenance, you will have a hard time convincing others of its validity. Similarly, if you want to buy a special helmet, you should buy only from a source that you trust and who offers a return policy should you later learn that the helmet is fake.

Visor Caps

When a military collector or dealer describes himself as a "visor cap collector," he usually means he collects Third Reich visor caps. The term could apply to the headgear worn by a variety of nationalities, but usually, within the hobby, if one says, "visor cap," he means "peaked cap worn by German military and paramilitary personnel."

Collectors of German visor caps approach their hobby with the same intensity as dagger collectors. They study and know the nuances of maker marks, celluloid plackets, lining material, and fabric samples. They will talk among themselves in a level of jargon that seems to purposefully exclude the non-headgear collector. Don't let that intimidate you, however. They have simply specialized in order to navigate a section of the hobby that is fraught with fakes.

Visor caps from the principal combatant nations are quite plentiful. Why? In simplest terms, visor caps were a part of dress uniforms. As such, they survived the war in the closets and trunks of the veterans.

Visor caps celebrate a soldier's military nature. Wearing one announced to others, "Here is a warrior. He walks erect and is smart in his bearing, decisions and prowess." Visor caps usually display some sort of national insignia and often will also convey (through colored piping or special insignia) the wearer's branch of service.

This is the sort of stuff a collector loves…a variety of material and enough clues to piece together some sort of understanding about the soldier who wore it. For example, a gray wool cap with a dark green band with a cockade in a wreath on the front, an eagle with a swastika in its talons above the wreath, and white piping around the crown tells the collector that this cap was intended for a German infantry soldier. Without knowing the soldier's name, the collector knows something about him. The collector is able to bond with history through the cap.

Because every branch of service in the German military had its own unique color and insignia combinations, this creates the other lure to a collector: variety. The visor caps of Germany are seemingly endless, so a collector can devote his entire career to this one form.

Visor caps of other nationalities have not been as quick to rise in value as German caps, though. American visor caps have remained stagnant for many years, though several attempts have been made to divide two basic cap forms (enlisted man's and officer's) into many groups. Other than the national seal on the front of either form, differences are limited to manufacturer, body color (basically, olive drab or khaki), and shape (the most desirable being the romantic "crusher" cap often associated with flight crews or other personnel who wore headphones over their caps). It doesn't take long for the collector to become bored and expand into different arenas.

Whatever the cap, condition plays a big role in its relative value. You might pull a Japanese Type 45 visor cap out of Grandpa's war trunk, but if it is mothed, crushed and smelly, you will have a hard time selling it to a collector. Likewise, if you are going to try to sell a U.S. enlisted man's visor, condition is about the only thing that will set it apart from the thousands of other examples on the market.

Collecting Hints

Pros:

- Headgear is extremely personal. The collector can determine some of a soldier's history from a single piece.

- Supply is plentiful. It is easy for a collector to find a level that is both affordable and enjoyable.

- Display is not difficult. A few shelves and hat stands will allow a collector to adequately and safely exhibit his items.

- Items are small enough that shipping is not a big issue, enabling a collector to buy from any source in the world.

Cons:

- In the arena of helmets, fakes abound. If a helmet displays any sort of decal or painted insignia, it is best to approach it with suspicion.

- Helmets are prone to shifts in humidity. Rust is the biggest threat to a helmet collection.

- It is easy to get carried away and acquire more headgear than one can enjoy or even afford. Supply is high, so a collector needs to exercise discipline and purchase wisely rather than wildly.

- If you decide to collect either helmets or visor caps, rare examples are going to run into the thousands of dollars.

Availability: ✪ ✪ ✪ ✪
Price: ✪ ✪
Reproduction Alert: ✪ ✪ ✪

Utility Headgear

"Utility" is a catch-all word to describe fatigue caps and hats, winter hoods, or other non-dress coverings. Not many collectors specialize in just utility headgear, but rather, obtain examples as parts of larger groupings. Utility headgear, by its very nature, generally does not display a variety of insignia, so collecting it usually is based on types of headgear – a single example of a particular variety sufficing the need to fill a hole in a collection. Therefore, the demand for utility headgear is not as high as it is for helmets or visor caps.

Values for utility headgear tend to be determined by function. An American GI's herringbone twill fatigue cap is going to run about $35-$55 (£22-£34) because so many were made, quite a few survived, and the demand is low. Ski troopers' mountain caps, on the other hand, will run $285-$385 (£177-£239) each because few were made and they were intended for a small group of "elite" soldiers and were not available to masses of U.S. soldiers.

Size Matters

When it comes to headgear (and uniforms, for that matter), size matters. If you have two German helmets with the same markings but one is a size 56 and the other a 64, the latter is going to command about a 30% higher price. How could size possibly matter, if it is the insignia on the helmet that is the primary price influencer? Size influencing price means only one thing: People intend to put them on their heads. The bigger the size, the higher the price. It is a dark fact of the hobby.

Camouflage is an Aesthetic Thing

Evaluating camouflaged helmets is a very difficult area. Because most camouflage was applied to helmets in the field and not at the factory, no two camouflaged helmets are alike. Therefore, one has to develop the sense of an art critic to be able to recognize a "pleasing" (that is, a desirable and expensive) camo job as opposed to a more "pedestrian" paint job. Whereas a mud-splattered M1 German M35 helmet is probably a good representation of camouflage helmets of the Eastern front, a four-colored, spray-painted example has a lot more eye appeal and, therefore, will command a higher price.

Consider camouflaged helmets carefully. It is just as easy to splatter paint on a helmet today as it was in 1944. The lure of high profit has pried open many paint cans in the last 20 years. Know your source before you hand over the cash for any camouflaged helmets. A good rule to follow: "It is fake until the dealer can convince me that it is not."

AUSTRALIA

Helmets, Flying

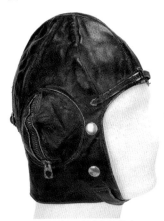 

Australian RAAF flying helmet. **$235-$285 (£146-£177)**
AdvanceGuardMilitaria.com

Australian RAAF flying helmet, 1942. **$255-$295 (£158-£183)**
AdvanceGuardMilitaria.com

Caps, Officers

Australian RAAF officer's visor cap. **$200-$265 (£124-£164)**
AdvanceGuardMilitaria.com

Australian RAAF officer's overseas cap, 1942. **$65-$100 (£40-£62)**
AdvanceGuardMilitaria.com

Caps and Hats, Enlisted

Australian tam o' shanter. **$55-$75 (£34-£47)**
AdvanceGuardMilitaria.com

RAAF Other Ranks overseas cap, 1942. **$75-$100 (£47-£62)**
AdvanceGuardMilitaria.com

Australian RAAF sidecap, no insignia, 1944. **$35-$55 (£22-£34)**
AdvanceGuardMilitaria.com

Australian RAAF Other Ranks overseas cap, 1942. **$75-$95 (£47-£59)**
AdvanceGuardMilitaria.com

Australian jungle hat. **$350-$400 (£217-£248)**
Charles D. Pautler collection

Australian slouch hat, 1941 dated. **$180 (£112)**
AdvanceGuardMilitaria.com

BELGIUM

Helmets

"Hot water was pretty hard to come by, although we could make a stove by filling a helmet with sand and adding gasoline from a jeep."

— Donald Nordlie, 2nd Marine Division

Model 1926/32 combat helmet with liner.
$85-$115 (£53-£71)
Peter Suciu

Belgian Model 1939 motorcycle troops helmet.
$295-$365 (£183-£226)
AdvanceGuardMilitaria.com

Belgian Model 1926 helmet, no liner.
$45-$75 (£28-£47)
AdvanceGuardMilitaria.com

BULGARIA

Helmets

Bulgarian M36 helmet, First Type.
$175-$195 (£109-£121)

AdvanceGuardMilitaria.com

Bulgarian M36 helmet, Second Type,
three-rivet variation. **$50-$65 (£31-£40)**

AdvanceGuardMilitaria.com

Bulgarian M36 helmet, Third Type, "short
visor" combat helmet. **$85-$150 (£53-£93)**

Peter Suciu

Bulgarian Model 1938 "Luftschutz" helmet.
$285-$350 (£177-£217)

Peter Suciu

Bulgarian M36
helmet, Third Type,
four-rivet variation,
identified. **$95 (£59)**

AdvanceGuardMilitaria.com

Caps, Enlisted

Bulgarian M43 cap. **$125-$185 (£78-£115)**

AdvanceGuardMilitaria.com

CANADA

Helmets, Flying

Canadian RCAF flying helmet.
$175-$200 (£109-£124)
AdvanceGuardMilitaria.com

Caps, Enlisted

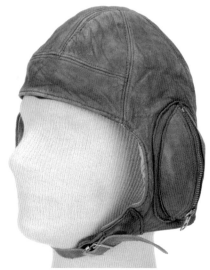

Canadian RCAF airman's visor cap, 1938.
$155-$175 (£96-£109)
AdvanceGuardMilitaria.com

Canadian RCAF Other Ranks sidecap.
$40-$65 (£25-£40)
AdvanceGuardMilitaria.com

Canadian Pattern 1943 general service cap.
$85-$95 (£53-£59)
Minnesota Military Museum

Canadian Army winter cap, Medical Corps.
$35-$55 (£22-£34)
AdvanceGuardMilitaria.com

Canadian Army winter cap, Women's Army Corps.
$45-$65 (£28-£40)
AdvanceGuardMilitaria.com

Canadian CWAC summer service dress cap.
$125-$145 (£78-£90)
AdvanceGuardMilitaria.com

Canadian RCAF Women's Division visor cap.
$150-$165 (£93-£102)
AdvanceGuardMilitaria.com

CHINA

Nationalist Chinese Army field cap.
$575-$650 (£357-£403)
Chris William

CZECHOSLOVAKIA

Czech Model 1932 combat helmet.
$300-$450 (£186-£279)
Peter Suciu

ENGLAND

Helmets

British MK II Combat helmet. **$45-$100**
Chris William

British MK II combat helmet, South Africa manufacture. **$145-$185 (£90-£115)**
Peter Suciu

British MK I Airborne helmet. **$1,200-$1,450 (£744-£899)**
Combat-helmets.com

British MK III helmet, 1939. **$100-$175 (£62-£109)**
Combat-helmets.com

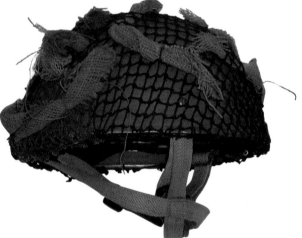

British MK II paratrooper helmet. **$1,250-$1,700 (£775-£1,054)**
Peter Suciu

British MK IV combat steel helmet. **$65-$125 (£40-£78)**
Peter Suciu

British dispatch rider's helmet. **$125-$225 (£78-£140)**
Peter Suciu

British pith helmet. **$75-$95 (£47-£59)**
AdvanceGuardMilitaria.com

British air raid protection helmet, First Aid Post.
$25-$45 (£16-£28)
AdvanceGuardMilitaria.com

British Army Wolseley Pattern pith helmet,
1942. **$75-$100 (£47-£62)**
AdvanceGuardMilitaria.com

British air raid protection helmet, First Aid Post.
$40-$55 (£25-£34)
AdvanceGuardMilitaria.com

British Army Wolseley Pattern pith
helmet, 1939. **$85-$125 (£53-£78)**
AdvanceGuardMilitaria.com

Air raid protection helmet, warden, 1938.
$85-$115 (£53-£71)
AdvanceGuardMilitaria.com

British air raid protection helmet, Light Rescue. **$75-$100 (£47-£62)**

AdvanceGuardMilitaria.com

British Homefront National Fire Service helmet, District 4. **$80-$110 (£50-£68)**

AdvanceGuardMilitaria.com

British air raid protection helmet, Heavy Rescue. **$75-$100 (£47-£62)**

AdvanceGuardMilitaria.com

British Homefront National Fire Service helmet, District 10. **$80-$110 (£50-£68)**

AdvanceGuardMilitaria.com

British air raid protection helmet, Repair Party, Electric. **$75-$100 (£47-£62)**

AdvanceGuardMilitaria.com

British Homefront Zuckerman helmet. **$95-$115 (£59-£71)**

AdvanceGuardMilitaria.com

British Homefront Fire Guard Zuckerman helmet. **$100-$135 (£62-£64)**
AdvanceGuardMilitaria.com

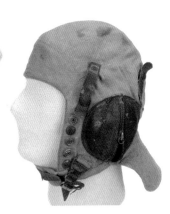

British RAF flying helmet, Type E.
$225-$265 (£140-£164)
AdvanceGuardMilitaria.com

RAF flying helmet, Type D. **$300-$350 (£186-£217)**
AdvanceGuardMilitaria.com

Helmets, Flying

Caps, Officers

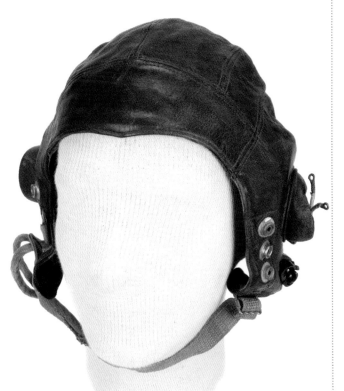

British RAF flying helmet, Type C.
$250-$325 (£155-£202)
AdvanceGuardMilitaria.com

British RAF other officer's visor cap.
$135-$165 (£64-£102)
AdvanceGuardMilitaria.com

British RAF group captain's visor cap.
$200-$265 (£124-£164)
AdvanceGuardMilitaria.com

British Royal Navy officer's fore-and-aft hat and metal storage case. **$170 (£105)**
AdvanceGuardMilitaria.com

Caps, Enlisted

British RAF officer's overseas cap. **$85-$145 (£53-£90)**
AdvanceGuardMilitaria.com

British Royal Dragoon Guards Service cap, Cutter's Pattern. **$45-$85 (£28-£53)**
AdvanceGuardMilitaria.com

British officer's Colored Field Service cap, Royal Regiment of Artillery. **$55-$85 (£34£-53)**
AdvanceGuardMilitaria.com

British Royal Scots tam o'shanter. **$65-$85 (£40-£53)**
AdvanceGuardMilitaria.com

British RAF commissioned officers of air rank visor cap. **$225-$265 (£140-£164)**
AdvanceGuardMilitaria.com

Lovat Scouts tam o' shanter, badge missing. **$35-$55 (£22-£34)**
AdvanceGuardMilitaria.com

British EM side cap, Middlesex Regiment.
$85-$115 (£53-£71)
AdvanceGuardMilitaria.com

British RAF Other Ranks overseas cap.
$65-$85 (£40-£53)
AdvanceGuardMilitaria.com

British Royal Army Service Corps slouch hat.
$185-$245 (£115-£152)
AdvanceGuardMilitaria.com

British ATS service dress cap.
$125-$145 (£78-£90)
AdvanceGuardMilitaria.com

British Army general service cap, 1943.
$40-$55 (£25-£34)
AdvanceGuardMilitaria.com

British WRNS petty officer tricorn hat.
$185-$225 (£115-£140)
AdvanceGuardMilitaria.com

British tam o' shanter, Argyll and Sutherland
Highlanders, no badge. **$35-$55 (£22-£34)**
AdvanceGuardMilitaria.com

British Royal Navy
hat with H.M.S.
Hood cap tally.
$195 (£121)
AdvanceGuardMilitaria.com

FINLAND

Helmets

Finland Reissue Hungarian helmet.
$235-$265 (£146-£164)
AdvanceGuardMilitaria.com

FRANCE

Helmets

Model 1926 infantry combat helmet.
$85-$125 (£53-£78)
Peter Suciu

Free French Foreign
Legion helmet.
$500-$650 (£310-£403)
Hermann-Historica.de

M42 German helmet used by Légion Des
Volontaires – LVF. **$3,500-$4,000 (£2,170-£2,480)**
Hermann-Historica.de

M1 helmet with 9th Colonial Infantry Division
insignia. **$750-$900 (£465-£558)**
Hermann-Historica.de

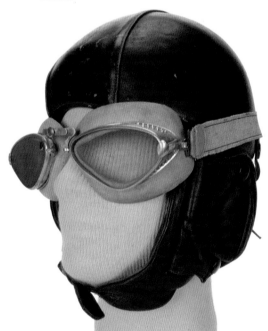

"Blitzkrieg" 1940 pilot's helmet and goggles.
$385-$465 (£239-£288)
AdvanceGuardMilitaria.com

Model 1931 Sun helmet, Auxiliary Police.
$150-$185 (£93-£115)
Peter Suciu

French Model 1931 Sun helmet, Marine
Infantry. **$185-$265 (£115-£164)**
Peter Suciu

Caps

French kepi for Quartermaster General 2nd
Class, 1930-1940. **$950-$1,300 (£589-£806)**
Hermann-Historica.de

French kepi for general officer of the Medical
Service, 1930-1940. **$1,000-1,400 (£620-£860)**
Hermann-Historica.de

French Mountain Troops officer's beret.
$85-125 (£53-£78)
AdvanceGuardMilitaria.com

Values at a Glance

Commonly encountered pieces of headgear:

• U.S. Army Officer's wool visor cap	$75
• USM1917A1 helmet	$185
• U.S. Army M1 helmet shell, swivel loops	$95
• British MK II combat helmet	$65
• British Air Raid Protection helmet	$45
• French Model 1926 Infantry helmet	$95
• Luftwaffe M40 single-decal helmet	$500
• German Army M40 single-decal helmet	$585
• German Army tropical helmet	$350
• Japanese Army Model 32 helmet	$700

GERMANY

Helmets

German 2nd Model paratrooper's helmet.
$5,500 (£3,410)
Hermann-Historica.de

Luftwaffe Fallschirmjäger helmet, Normandy camouflage. **$4,000-$6,000 (£2,480-£3,720)**
AdvanceGuardMilitaria.com

Luftwaffe Fallschirmjäger helmet, 2nd Model. **$5,500-$7,000 (£3,410-£4,340)**
Hermann-Historica.de

German Paratrooper's camouflaged helmet with hole from shell splinter. **$9,000 (£5,580)**
Hermann-Historica.de

Luftwaffe Fallschirmjäger helmet, no chinstrap assembly. **$2,975 (£1,845)**
AdvanceGuardMilitaria.com

Luftwaffe officer's parade helmet.
$4,500-$5,500 (£2,790-£3,410)
Hermann-Historica.de

Luftwaffe double-decal M35 helmet.
$1,000-$1,200 (£620-£744)
HistoryHunter.com

Luftwaffe M40 SD helmet, near mint. **$1,275 (£791)**
HistoryHunter.com

German Army reissue World War I Austrian
M17 helmet. **$900-$1,200 (£558-£744)**

AdvanceGuardMilitaria.com

Wehrmacht double-decal transitional
M16 helmet. **$800-$1,400 (£496-£860)**

HistoryHunter.com

German Army M18 transitional
double-decal helmet. **$760 (£471)**

HistoryHunter.com

German Army M36 double-decal parade
helmet. **$3,000-$3,500 (£1,860-£2,170)**

Hermann-Historica.de

German Army M18 double-decal helmet.
$2,000 (£1,240)

Hermann-Historica.de

German Army M35 double-decal helmet.
$1,325 (£822)

HistoryHunter.com

German Army M35 single-decal helmet.
$525 (£326)

AdvanceGuardMilitaria.com

German Army M35 single-decal helmet.
550-$650 (£341-£403)

Hermann-Historica.de

Army M35 single-decal helmet. **$775 (£481)**
AdvanceGuardMilitaria.com

Luftwaffe camouflaged M42 single-decal
helmet. **$2,680 (£1,662)**
Hermann-Historica.de

German M40 helmet. **$645 (£400)**
AdvanceGuardMilitaria.com

Luftwaffe camouflaged helmet.
$1,000-$1,4000 (£620-£860)
HistoryHunter.com

German Army M40 single-decal helmet.
$525 (£326)
AdvanceGuardMilitaria.com

German camouflaged M40 helmet.
$2,400 (£1,488)
AdvanceGuardMilitaria.com

Luftwaffe camouflaged M40 single-decal
helmet. **$1,625 (£1,008)**
HistoryHunter.com

German M42 helmet with wire
camouflage. **$625 (£388)**
AdvanceGuardMilitaria.com

German Army M40 single-decal helmet with US 29th Division insignia. **$795 (£493)**
AdvanceGuardMilitaria.com

German M40 helmet camouflaged with sand-colored paint. **$5,000 (£3,100)**
Hermann-Historica.de

German M42 painted helmet, Luftwaffe helper. **$1,300 (£806)**
Hermann-Historica.de

German Army M42 helmet, three-color camouflage. **$2,000-$2,800 (£1,240-£1,736)**
Hermann-Historica.de

German M42 painted camouflaged helmet. **$800-$1,000 (£496-£620)**
AdvanceGuardMilitaria.com

German M35 SS double-decal helmet. **$8,000-$11,000 (£4,960-£6,820)**
HistoryHunter.com

German M40 SS single-decal helmet. **$4,500-$6,000 (£2,790-£3,720)**
Hermann-Historica.de

German M42 helmet, former whitewash. **$745 (£462)**
AdvanceGuardMilitaria.com

"I take my baths in a helmet."

— Sgt. Wesley Slaymaker, Co. M, 129th Inf., 37th Division

German police M40 double-decal helmet.
$695-$1,000 (£431-£620)
HistoryHunter.com

German Red Cross helmet, unissued
condition. **$1,075 (£667)**
HistoryHunter.com

Kriegsmarine tropical pith helmet, Second
Pattern. **$685-$850 (£425-£527)**
AdvanceGuardMilitaria.com

Helmets, Flying/Crash

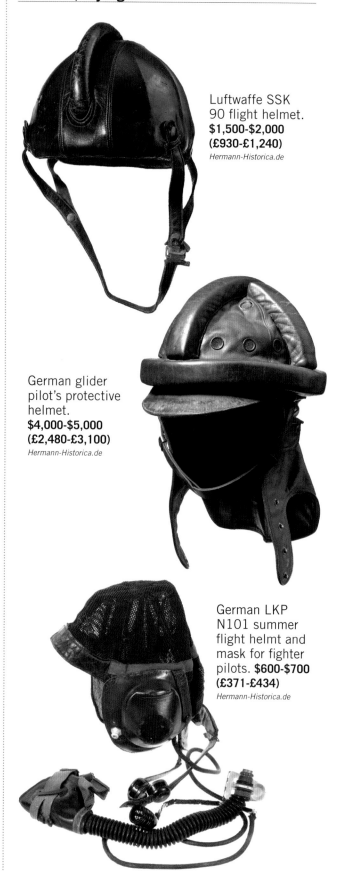

Luftwaffe SSK
90 flight helmet.
**$1,500-$2,000
(£930-£1,240)**
Hermann-Historica.de

German glider
pilot's protective
helmet.
**$4,000-$5,000
(£2,480-£3,100)**
Hermann-Historica.de

German LKP
N101 summer
flight helmt and
mask for fighter
pilots. **$600-$700
(£371-£434)**
Hermann-Historica.de

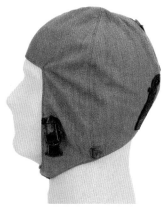

Luftwaffe leather LKpW101 flight helmet. **$150-$250 (£93-£155)**

AdvanceGuardMilitaria.com

Luftwaffe cloth flight helmet, FK34. **$200-$300 (£124-£186)**

AdvanceGuardMilitaria.com

Luftwaffe LKpN101 summer flight helmet with earphones and throat microphone. **$495 (£307)**

AdvanceGuardMilitaria.com

NSKK crash helmet. **$475-$650 (£295-£403)**

Hermann-Historica.de

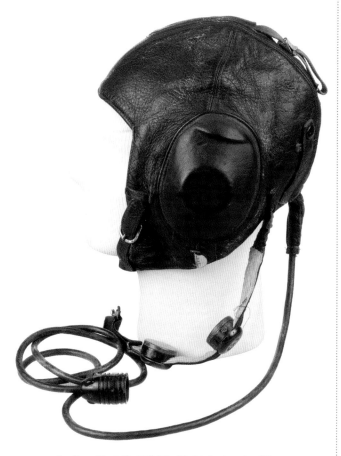

Luftwaffe LKpW101 flight helmet with earphones and throat microphone. **$400-$550 (£248-£341)**

Chris William

Luftwaffe leather LKpW101 flight helmet, complete set with earphones, microphone and goggles. **$700-$800 (£434-£496)**

AdvanceGuardMilitaria.com

Caps, Army

German Heer General officer's visor cap.
$10,000-$13,000 (£6,200-£8,060)
HistoryHunter.com

Rural police motorcycle
crash helmet. **$550-$685
(£341-£425)**
Hermann-Historica.de

Hoods and Helmet Covers

German Army officer's visor cap, Infantry
Regiment 17. **$535 (£332)**
Hermann-Historica.de

Third Reich
child's gas
protection hood.
$50-$100 (£31-£62)
AdvanceGuardMilitaria.com

German Army officer's visor cap,
Pioneers. **$500-$650 (£310-£403)**
Hermann-Historica.de

German SS camouflage cover for steel helmet, oak
leaf pattern. **$4,000-$5,000 (£2,480-£3,100)**
Hermann-Historica.de

German Army officer's visor cap, Signals.
$465-$575 (£288-£357)
Hermann-Historica.de

German Army officer's visor cap, Medical.
$495-$585 (£307-£363)
Hermann-Historica.de

"Crusher"-style visor cap for artillery
officer. **$1,200-$1,800 (£744-1,116)**
Hermann-Historica.de

German Army officer's visor cap, Cavalry.
$535-$665 (£332-£412)
Hermann-Historica.de

German Army officer's tropical visor cap.
$3,350 (£2,077)
Hermann-Historica.de

Panzer grenadier officer's visor cap.
$1,000-$1,500 (£620-£930)
Hermann-Historica.de

German Army officer's cap, Coastal
Artillery. **$1,500-$1,800 (£930-£1,116)**
Hermann-Historica.de

Panzer officer's visor cap.
$1,000-$1,200 (£620-£744)
Hermann-Historica.de

German Army Surgeon General's visor cap.
$4,000-$5,000 (£2,480-£3,100)
Hermann-Historica.de

German Army artillery officer's M38 overseas cap. **$595-$780 (£369-£484)**
AdvanceGuardMilitaria.com

German officer's papakha, Cossack Cavalry Corps XV. **$1,500-$2,275 (£930-£1,411)**
Hermann-Historica.de

Panzer officer's garrison cap. **$4,000-$5,000 (£2,480-£3,100)**
Hermann-Historica.de

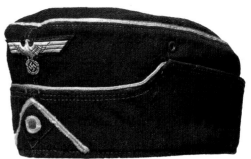

Panzer officer's garrison cap with soutache. **$4,500-$5,500 (£2,790-£3,410)**
Hermann-Historica.de

German enlisted/NCO visor cap for rail protection. **$750-$950 (£465-£589)**
Hermann-Historica.de

German Army Panzer enlisted/NCO garrison cap. **$850-$1,300 (£527-£806)**
Hermann-Historica.de

Panzer enlisted/NCO M43 field cap. **$1,250-$1,650 (£1,249-£1,023)**
Hermann-Historica.de

German Army enlisted/NCO M43 cap.
$450-$600 (£279-£372)
HistoryHunter.com

German Army enlisted/NCO M34 overseas
cap, unit marked. **$500-$650 (£310-£403)**
AdvanceGuardMilitaria.com

German Army Panzer grenadier's enlisted tropical
garrison cap (Schipfchen). **$700-$1,200 (£434-£744)**
Hermann-Historica.de

Panzer beret. **$7,500-$9,000 (£4,650-£5,580)**
HistoryHunter.com

Caps, Luftwaffe

Luftwaffe officer's visor cap by Halfar, named.
$1,525 (£946)
HistoryHunter.com

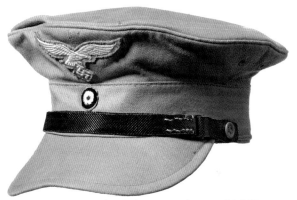

Luftwaffe tropical visor cap. **$4,000-$6,500
(£2,480-£4,030)**
Hermann-Historica.de

Luftwaffe enlisted/NCO visor cap, flying
personnel. **$450-$795 (£279-£493)**
Rick Fleury

Luftwaffe officer cadet's visor cap.
$600-$700 (£372-£434)
Hermann-Historica.de

Luftwaffe officer's M43 cap. **$900-$1,110
(£558-£682)**
Hermann-Historica.de

Luftwaffe enlisted/NCO M43 cap, double
button. **$395-$445 (£245-£276)**
AdvanceGuardMilitaria.com

Luftwaffe
officer's
overseas cap.
**$400-$600
(£248-£372)**
Hermann-Historica.de

Caps, Kriegsmarine

Kriegsmarine rear admiral's service cap.
$8,000-$9,000 (£4,960-£5,580)
Hermann-Historica.de

Kriegsmarine subaltern's cap.
$1,200-$1,650 (£744-£1,023)
Hermann-Historica.de

Kriegsmarine enlisted overseas cap for tropical
uniform. **$3,500-$4,250 (£2,170-£2,635)**
Hermann-Historica.de

Kriegsmarine Staboffiziere visor cap for tropical
uniform. **$1,850-$2,250 (£1,147-£1,395)**
Hermann-Historica.de

Helmet Myths

by Peter Suciu
**Adapted from an article that originally appeared in
Military Trader.**

One of the biggest misconceptions among militaria collectors is that "history" is fact. This is not exactly true. In fact – no pun intended – history didn't even really "happen." The past happened, and the events of the past become the history. For various reasons, history is not the absolute truth. Facts can be misinterpreted, details misunderstood, and information misread. All of this makes it very confusing in regards to the study of history, but it is just as big a problem for collectors of historic objects.

When it comes to militaria, where the prices keep rising, the facts can make it even more confusing, especially for new collectors. This is quite evident with helmets, where information ranges from confusing to downright wrong.

More importantly, because of the Internet, information – or far too often misinformation – is often spread, quoted and cited. While decades ago there were only a handful of books on the subject of helmets, and most of these were limited to German helmets from World War I and World War II, today there are dozens of books on the subject, but much information is still unclear. And except for American and German helmets, to this date very little has been written in length on international helmets, and much of what has been written on Italian, French, Polish or Japanese helmets has been in those languages.

All this has made the spread of militaria misinformation very common. Here is a look at some of the most common myths, fables, and downright lies about military helmets:

Lead paint is a true sign a German helmet is authentic.

The myth: The fakes today are so good it is sometimes hard to tell a real helmet from a bad one, but a surefire test is whether there is lead in the paint on the helmet.

The truth: "On the contrary," says advanced German helmet collector Ken Niewiarowcz, who adds that if there is lead found in the paint, something is wrong. "The fact is, if one takes a lead test strip (available through the EPA or at any hardware store) and tests the surface of any factory-painted helmet, it will indicate negative as far as the presence of lead. People assume that all old paint has lead. Though it is true that it was added as a binding agent to most latex and certain enamel paints, it was not added to the lacquers and enamels used by helmet-producing factories."

The exception to the rule: This answer does not apply to camo helmets, painted from a limitless variety of sources. A camouflage helmet with the so-called "Normandy Pattern" paint scheme might or might not contain lead.

German helmets had sand mixed into the paint.

The myth: The texture on German helmets, including those with camouflage paint, has a sandy texture.

The truth: German helmets painted according to 1940s specs have a texture compared to the pre-1940 smooth finishes, according to Niewiarowcz. People assume the texture is sand. "The actual material used was powdered aluminum oxide," he explains – a big difference and a telltale one at that.

German Model 1940 helmets should only have a single decal.

The myth: The German Wehrmacht realized that the pre-war "Apple Green" and "Parade Blue" helmets used respectively by the Army/SS and Luftwaffe weren't ideal for combat, and more importantly, the tri-color shield made it too easy for soldiers to be seen. The order was given to remove existing decals and that all future helmets would be issued with a single decal. Thus, only Model 1935 helmets should have two decals – "double-decal."

The truth: The truth is part of the myth. The Germans did change the color of the helmets from green to a darker gray color, and the decals were indeed ordered off. But that's where the truth ends and the myth begins. The order didn't strike at midnight on Jan. 1, 1940, and some Model 1940 helmets, with the modified vents, were produced with two decals. "At least two of the factories (ET and Q) continued for a short time to produce Heer (Army) and SS helmets in double-decal configuration after the switch to the Model 40 helmet shell and after the switch to 1940 specifications of the painted finish," Niewiarowcz stresses. "Of course, helmets supplied to the feldgendarmes continued to be adorned with two decals until the end of the war."

Germany made Spanish helmets.

The myth: This story is typically repeated on eBay: Germany, after World War II, produced the Spanish Model 1942 or Modelo Z helmets. The typical reason given by sellers is to help the German economy – as if

The Spanish Model 1942 or Modelo Z was clearly based on the German Model 1935 "Stahlhelm," but the rivet placement and liner are completely different. Unlike the German-designed helmet, the Modelo Z features a raw rim that isn't flared out, such as the later German Model 1942 helmet.
Peter Suciu

producing a few thousand helmets would eventually transform the nation to the most prosperous industrialized nation in Europe (something did, but it probably wasn't helmets).

The truth: The Spanish essentially copied the German design, but the helmet was not made in Germany or with German equipment. This is no doubt a story that sprang up to convince would-be collectors that the $50 helmet is somehow German in origin. There is nothing wrong with Spanish helmets, and the nation produced a variety of interesting helmets – and used a variety of other helmets from other nations, notably Czechoslovakia – but except for a few German helmets that may have made it to Spain, these weren't truly German.

The USMC EGA was on helmet covers during World War II.

The myth: USMC covers issued during World War II featured a stencil of the EGA on the front.

The truth: "The EGA was not worn on USMC covers during World War II," says American helmet collector Chris Armold, author of *Steel Pots: The History of America's Steel Combat Helmets*. Armold further states in his book that those surviving World War II covers with the EGA were likely a post-war addition.

The first pattern USMC cover does not feature any stenciled insignia.
Peter Suciu

Hinged chinstrap loops are a sign of a very late war or post-war M1 helmet.

The myth: American M1 helmets from World War II must be of the welded steel chinstrap loop (fixed bail) variety to have seen action.

The truth: The hinged chinstrap loop replaced the welded loop in the fall of 1943, and this style loop became the standard for all M1 helmets to follow. Thus, it is highly possible that helmets used following D-Day could be of the hinged-strap variety. "The hinged loop was created in 1943 and did see service in World War II, despite what collectors might think," confirms Armold.

The Soviet SSh-39/40 was a copy of the Italian Model 1933.

The myth: The Soviets copied the Italian steel helmets.

The truth: Just as the Romans may have borrowed the architecture of the Greeks, the Soviets may have "borrowed" from the designs of the Italians. But it is safe to say that the SSh-39/40 was not based solely on the Italian M-33, says Dr. Robert Clawson, author of *Russian Helmets: From Kaska to Stlashlyem 1916 – 2001*. "Many commentators have looked at the two and said that it obviously was a copy. I have had

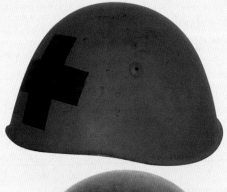

A comparison between the Italian Model 1933 (top) and the Soviet SSh-39/Model 1939 (bottom) shows that the designs are similar but hardly an outright copy.
Peter Suciu

independent design engineers look at the two without knowing the sequence, and every one of them said that the M-33 was a derivative of the SSh-39!" Dr. Clawson adds that it was likely that the Russians had looked at the M-33 and even designed one of their experimental models to look almost exactly like it but rejected it. "In the end it was an original design."

Japanese steel helmets were manufactured from American steel.

The myth: Japan bought up American scrap steel throughout the 1930s, and this is likely the metal used in Japanese helmets.

The truth: "Go prove it," says advanced headgear collector Jareth Holub. While it is true that the United States did sell scrap steel to the Japanese until an embargo was placed in October 1940, Holub says it is impossible to know whether this steel was used in a particular helmet. Japan was in the process of obtaining as much steel from any source possible, so it is impossible to say for certain whether a Japanese helmet is made of recycled American steel.

The Japanese didn't use camouflage helmets.

The myth: All the equipment issued to the average Japanese soldier was considered personal property of the emperor and, therefore, helmets wouldn't be camouflaged.

The truth: Within the myth lies much truth. Equipment was most certainly the personal property of the emperor, and according to Holub, "to be kept in the very best condition.

This helmet shows the subtle type of camouflage employed by the Japanese.
Jareth Holub

If a soldier was killed, his equipment was reissued." He adds that it is his opinion that painted camouflage patterns were discouraged or at least not encouraged, and that a use of camouflage could be considered a defacement of property. For this reason the Japanese preferred to use nets with foliage applied. However, camouflage helmets are encountered, and photographic evidence does confirm that these were used to a limited degree. "You see solid color over painted camos, but patterns are extremely scarce and were probably field enhancements done under desperate circumstances."

Caps, Political and Auxiliary

German SA Feldjägerkorps enlisted kepi. **$6,500-$8,000 (£4,030-£4,960)**
HistoryHunter.com

German Allgemeine SS and SS-Verfügungstruppe officer's visor cap, circa 1936. **$8,000-$10,000 (£4,960-£6,200)**
Hermann-Historica.de

German Allgemeine SS enlisted visor cap. **$4,500-$6,000 (£2,790-£3,720)**
AdvanceGuardMilitaria.com

German Waffen SS officer's visor cap, Cavalry. **$16,000-$19,000 (£9,920-£11,780)**
HistoryHunter.com

German SS NCO visor cap.
$10,000-$12,000 (£6,200-£7,440)
HistoryHunter.com

German Waffen SS enlisted/
NCO garrison cap. **$1,500-$2,500 (£930-£1,550)**
Hermann-Historica.de

German SS M43
Einheitsfeldmutze
Other Ranks Panzer
cap. **$2,500-$3,000
(£1,550-£1,860)**
HistoryHunter.com

German SS Waffen SS M43 camouflage field
cap. **$11,000-$14,000 (£6,820-£8,680)**
Hermann-Historica.de

German Waffen SS 13th
"Handschar" Division walking out
fez. **$750-$1,200 (£465-£744)**
Chris William

Caps, Auxiliary Formations

German SS M43 enlisted black cap,
classic two-button front. **$1,525 (£946)**
HistoryHunter.com

Hitler Youth 1936 Pattern cap.
$550-$700 (£341-£434)
Hermann-Historica.de

German SS-Verfügungstruppe enlisted/NCO
garrison cap. **$1,700-$2,250 (£1,054-£1,395)**
Hermann-Historica.de

German diplomat embassy assistant to the ministry
director visor cap. **$3,000-$4,000 (£1,860-£2,480)**
Hermann-Historica.de

German Reich Level NSDAP political leader's visor cap. **$1,625 (1,008)**
HistoryHunter.com

Hitler Youth summer cap.
$185-$265 (£115-£164)
AdvanceGuardMilitaria.com

German Kreisleitung political leader's visor cap. **$750-$950 (£465-£589)**
Hermann-Historica.de

German Reichsbahn railway worker's visor cap. **$225-$295 (£140-£183)**
AdvanceGuardMilitaria.com

German Red Cross First Pattern EM sidecap. **$265-$325 (£164-£202)**
AdvanceGuardMilitaria.com

German Organization Todt officer's M43 cap. **$650-$1,000 (£403-£620)**
Hermann-Historica.de

German SA enlisted kepi, Ostland.
$550-$675 (£341-£419)
AdvanceGuardMilitaria.com

German Fire Police officer's visor cap.
$1,000-$1,200 (£620-£744)
Hermann-Historica.de

HOLLAND

Helmets

Dutch M1928 Steel helmet. **$150-$185 (£93-£115)**
AdvanceGuardMilitaria.com

Caps

Dutch officer's Shako. **$185-$235 (£115-£177)**
AdvanceGuardMilitaria.com

HUNGARY

Helmets

Hungarian Model 1935/38 Army helmet. **$400-$485 (£248-£301)**
AdvanceGuardMilitaria.com

Hungarian M38 helmet. **$350-$400 (£217-£248)**
Combat-helmets.com

Caps

Hungarian Army Infantry sidecap, enlisted. **$175-$265 (£109-£164)**
AdvanceGuardMilitaria.com

ITALY

Helmets

Italian Model 1933 helmet, MVSN. **$900-$1,100 (£558-£682)**
Hermann-Historica.de

Italian Model 1941/1942 paratrooper helmet. **$2,500-$3,250 (£1,550-£2,015)**
Manions International

Italian M.33 helmet for auxiliary troops.
$50-$65 (£31-£40)
AdvanceGuardMilitaria.com

Italian North African campaign Bersaglieri pith helmet. **$200-$295 (£124-£183)**
AdvanceGuardMilitaria.com

Caps

Italian Army artillery officer's cap.
$200-$250 (£124-£155)
Chris Depere

Italian Infantry enlisted fatigue cap.
$65-$95 (£40-£59)
AdvanceGuardMilitaria.com

Italian Divisional General's visor cap.
$1,100-$1,450 (£682-£899)
Hermann-Historica.de

Italian Infantry officer's field cap.
$225-$265 (£140-£164)
AdvanceGuardMilitaria.com

Italian Nizza Cavalry Regiment officer's cap.
$300-$365 (£186-£226)
AdvanceGuardMilitaria.com

Italian Alpine officer's cap. **$225-$300 (£140-£186)**
Chris Depere

Mountain Engineer Officer Alpini hat. **$265 (£164)**
AdvanceGuardMilitaria.com

Italian Alpini Lieutenant Colonel's Model 1934 visor cap. **$250-$325 (£155-£202)**
AdvanceGuardMilitaria.com

Italian Alpini Lieutenant's visor cap. **$275 (£171)**
AdvanceGuardMilitaria.com

Italian Anti-Aircraft Artillery Colonel's visor cap. **$225 (£158)**
AdvanceGuardMilitaria.com

High Leader of MVSN cap. **$565 (£350)**
Hermann-Historica.de

JAPAN

Helmets

Japanese Army helmet. **$650-$950 (£403-£589)**
AdvanceGuardMilitaria.com

Japanese Army combat helmet with field cover. **$1,000-$1,600 (£620-£992)**
HistoryHunter.com

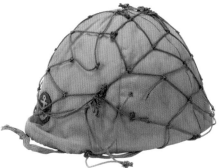

Japanese Naval Landing Force helmet, cover and net. **$1,600 (£992)**
HistoryHunter.com

Japanese Homeland Defense helmet. **$125-$165 (£78-£102)**
AdvanceGuardMilitaria.com

Japanese Naval Landing Force combat helmet. **$650-$1,200 (£403-£744)**
AdvanceGuardMilitaria.com

Japanese Home Guard helmet. **$200 (£124)**
AdvanceGuardMilitaria.com

Japanese World War II Army tanker helmet. **$600-$750 (£372-£465)**
HistoryHunter.com

Japanese Army tropical helmet, First Pattern. **$500-$650 (£310-£403)**
AdvanceGuardMilitaria.com

Japanese Homeland Defense helmet. **$125-$175 (£78-£109)**
AdvanceGuardMilitaria.com

Japanese Army tropical pith helmet, no insignia. **$400-$475 (£248-£295)**
AdvanceGuardMilitaria.com

Army tropical pith helmet with insignia. **$525-$600 (£326)**
AdvanceGuardMilitaria.com

Flight Helmets

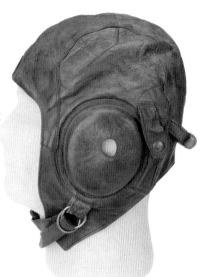

Japanese Army pilot's summer flight helmet. **$400-$500 (£248-£310)**
AdvanceGuardMilitaria.com

Japanese Army officer's tropical white pith helmet. **$450-$525 (£279-326)**
AdvanceGuardMilitaria.com

Japanese officer's private purchase tropical pith helmet. **$250-$300 (£155-£186)**
AdvanceGuardMilitaria.com

Japanese Navy summer issue flight helmet. **$650-$750 (£403-£465)**
AdvanceGuardMilitaria.com

Japanese Navy officer's pith helmet. **$500-$600 (£310-£372)**
AdvanceGuardMilitaria.com

Japanese Army fighter pilot's winter flying helmet. **$250-$400 (£155-£248)**
AdvanceGuardMilitaria.com

Caps

Japanese Army officer's field cap. **$150 (£93)**
AdvanceGuardMilitaria.com

Japanese Army officer's late war field cap.
$285-$325 (£177-£195)
AdvanceGuardMilitaria.com

Japanese Army officer's full dress kepi.
$350-$400 (£217-£248)
AdvanceGuardMilitaria.com

Japanese 1944-dated Army field service cap.
$285 (£177)
AdvanceGuardMilitaria.com

Japanese Naval officer's visor cap with
cover. **$300-$385 (£186-£239)**
AdvanceGuardMilitaria.com

Japanese Navy officer's visor cap. **$275-$350
(£171-£217)**
Chris William

Japanese Navy officer's white field cap.
$400-$500 (£248-£310)
Chris William

Japanese Navy officer field cap. **$385-$425 (£239-£264)**

AdvanceGuardMilitaria.com

Japanese Imperial Navy seaman's cap with cover. **$285-$325 (£177-£202)**

AdvanceGuardMilitaria.com

Japanese Navy petty officer black field cap. **$600-$700 (£372-£434)**

AdvanceGuardMilitaria.com

Japanese Imperial Navy enlisted seaman's hat with tally. **$235-$255 (£146-£158)**

AdvanceGuardMilitaria.com

Japanese Army enlisted field cap. **$245-$295 (£152-£183)**

Chris William

Japanese Navy petty officer field cap. **$260-$295 (£161-£183)**

AdvanceGuardMilitaria.com

Japanese Navy enlisted field cap. **$185-$210 (£115-£130)**

AdvanceGuardMilitaria.com

Japanese Army winter combat fur hat. **$290-$365 (£180-£226)**

AdvanceGuardMilitaria.com

Japanese Type 45 Army enlisted/NCO visor cap. **$145-$195 (£90-£121)**

AdvanceGuardMilitaria.com

POLAND

SOVIET UNION

Polish Model 1931 combat helmet.
$685-$800 (£424)

Peter Suciu

Helmets

Soviet Model 1936
helmet. **$625-$735
(£388-£456)**

AdvanceGuardMilitaria.com

Polish Infantry
officer's
"Rogatywka"
visor cap.
**$250-$365
(£155-£226)**

AdvanceGuardMilitaria.com

Polish issue
infantry enlisted
visor cap.
**$450-$550
(£279-£341)**

AdvanceGuardMilitaria.com

Soviet Model
1939 combat
helmet. **$500-$600
(£310-£372)**

AdvanceGuardMilitaria.com

Polish Infantry
enlisted
field cap.
**$1,000-$1,200
(£620-£744)**

AdvanceGuardMilitaria.com

Soviet Model 1940
combat helmet.
**$300-$375
(£186-£233)**

AdvanceGuardMilitaria.com

Caps

Soviet Model 1922 budenovka, Summer Pattern. **$465-$600 (£288-£372)**
AdvanceGuardMilitaria.com

Soviet German Occupation-era artillery officer's visor cap. **$300-$375 (£186-£233)**
AdvanceGuardMilitaria.com

Soviet M.35 enlisted visor cap, Air Force. **$200-$250 (£124-£155)**
AdvanceGuardMilitaria.com

Soviet M.35 Enlisted visor cap, Special Troops. **$235-$275 (£146-£171)**
AdvanceGuardMilitaria.com

Soviet "Pilotka" sidecap. **$35-$85 (£22-£53)**
AdvanceGuardMilitaria.com

Soviet ushanka fur cap. **$225-$285 (£140-£177)**
AdvanceGuardMilitaria.com

UNITED STATES

Helmets

U.S. early war M1917A1 helmet.
$175-$225 (£109-£140)
AdvanceGuardMilitaria.com

World War I M1917 helmets were upgraded with a new suspension and chinstrap. These are designated "M1917A1" helmets.
AdvanceGuardMilitaria.com

U.S. M1 helmet, fixed loops and liner. **$235-$295 (£146-£183)**
AdvanceGuardMilitaria.com

U.S. M1 helmet with Hawley fiber liner.
$600-$750 (£372-£465)
AdvanceGuardMilitaria.com

U.S. M1 helmet with Hawley liner, unit marked.
$1,230 (£763)
Manion's International

U.S. mid-war production M1 helmet, flexible loops and liner.
$195-$225 (£121-£140)
AdvanceGuardMilitaria.com

U.S. M1 helmet with name on shell and liner.
$325-$425 (£202-£264)
AdvanceGuardMilitaria.com

U.S. D-Day Utah Beach 1st Engineer Special Brigade NCO's painted helmet. **$4,000-$5,000 (£2,480-£3,100)**
AdvanceGuardMilitaria.com

U.S. Army paratrooper camouflaged
M1-C helmet. **$1,500 (£930)**
Manion's International

U.S. North Africa "Desert Pink"
camouflaged M1 helmet. **$1,850 (£1,147)**
AdvanceGuardMilitaria.com

U.S. M1 helmet with painted rank and
tactical marking on rear. **$495 (£307)**
AdvanceGuardMilitaria.com

U.S. M1 helmet with 2nd Pattern USMC
helmet cover. **$465-$565 (£288-£350)**
AdvanceGuardMilitaria.com

USMC M1 helmet and liner with
World War I-era EGA. **$595 (£369)**
AdvanceGuardMilitaria.com

U.S. Navy painted M1 helmet.
$400-$500 (£248-£310)
AdvanceGuardMilitaria.com

USMC M1 helmet with battle
damaged cover. **$495 (£307)**
AdvanceGuardMilitaria.com

Helmet Liners

U.S. early Hawley fiber helmet liner.
$300-$400 (£186-£248)
AdvanceGuardMilitaria.com

Rayon web suspension was typical of the Hawley M1 helmet liner.
AdvanceGuardMilitaria.com

Westinghouse M1 helmet liner.
$85-$125 (£53-£78)
AdvanceGuardMilitaria.com

St. Clair M1 helmet liner. **$195-$285 (£121-£177)**
AdvanceGuardMilitaria.com

Army Major's Saint Clair M1 helmet liner.
$315 (£195)
AdvanceGuardMilitaria.com

Helmets, Flak

U.S. AAF M3 flak helmet. **$115-$195 (£71-£121)**
AdvanceGuardMilitaria.com

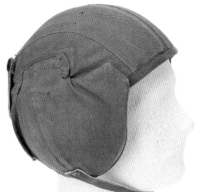

U.S. AAF M4A2 flak helmet.
$185-$235 (£115-£146)
AdvanceGuardMilitaria.com

U.S. AAF M5 anti-flak helmet.
$95-$165 (£59-£102)
AdvanceGuardMilitaria.com

Helmets, Tanker and Tropical

U.S. Armored Crewman "Tanker" helmet. **$215-$295 (£133-£183)**
AdvanceGuardMilitaria.com

USMC tropical pith helmet. **$65-$115 (£40-£71)**
AdvanceGuardMilitaria.com

USMC tropical pith helmet, olive drab. **$75-$125 (£47-£78)**
AdvanceGuardMilitaria.com

USMC World War II Pacific Theater "War Diary" trench art pith helmet. **$1,200 (£744)**
AdvanceGuardMilitaria.com

Helmet Covers

USMC First Pattern helmet cover sold with Korean War-era helmet. **$450 (£279)**
AdvanceGuardMilitaria.com

Helmets, Flying

USN/USMC leather flight helmet with Gosport communication system. **$225-$265 (£140-£164)**
AdvanceGuardMilitaria.com

Leather flight helmet with Gosport ear tubes. **$125-$165 (£78-£102)**
AdvanceGuardMilitaria.com

Navy/USMC pilot's heavily used M-450 flight helmet and goggles. **$250 (£155)**
AdvanceGuardMilitaria.com

AAF AN-H-15 flight helmet. **$85-$115 (£53-£71)**
AdvanceGuardMilitaria.com

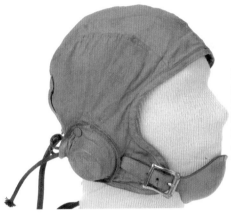

Navy/USMC pilot's M-450 flight helmet. **$225-$265 (£140-£164)**
AdvanceGuardMilitaria.com

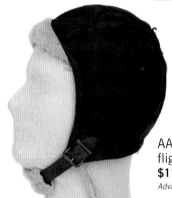

AAF B-6 fleece flight helmet. **$115-$150 (£71-£93)**
AdvanceGuardMilitaria.com

Caps and Hats, Officers, Male

U.S. Army officer's "Pink" visor cap. **$195-$265 (£121-£164)**
AdvanceGuardMilitaria.com

AAF A-11 flying helmet, Type A-14 oxygen mask, and a pair of AN-6530 flying goggles. **$435 (£370)**
AdvanceGuardMilitaria.com

General Doolittle's visor cap from Navy Relief Fund auction. **$7,170 (£4,445)**
HA.com

General Chennault's visor cap with signed card from Naval Relief Fund auction. **$5,078 (£3,148)**
HA.com

U.S. pre-war 344th Infantry officer's campaign hat. **$75-$125 (£47-£78)**
AdvanceGuardMilitaria.com

AAF Army officer's "Crusher" visor cap. **$200-$265 (£124-£164)**
AdvanceGuardMilitaria.com

U.S. Army major general's overseas cap attributed to Gen. Matthew B. Ridgway. **$836 (£518)**
HA.com

Air Transport Command visor "Crusher" cap. **$300-$345 (£186-£214)**
AdvanceGuardMilitaria.com

USN officer's visor cap, gray crown. **$100-$165 (£62-£102)**
AdvanceGuardMilitaria.com

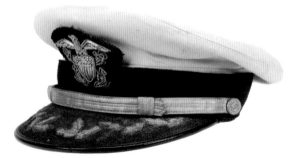

U.S. Army officer's summer cap owned and used by General Joseph W. "Vinegar Joe" Stilwell. **$3,585 (£2,223)**
HA.com

USN Navy officer's visor cap for Navy commander or captain. **$65-$95 (£40-£59)**
AdvanceGuardMilitaria.com

USN aviator's visor cap. **$65-$125 (£40-£78)**
AdvanceGuardMilitaria.com

U.S. Coast Guard Auxiliary yacht captain's visor cap. **$65-$95 (£40-£59)**
AdvanceGuardMilitaria.com

USMC officer's campaign hat, 1922 pattern. **$165-$275 (£102-£171)**
AdvanceGuardMilitaria.com

Caps and Hats, Enlisted

U.S. Army enlisted visor cap. **$45-$65 (£28-£40)**
AdvanceGuardMilitaria.com

U.S. Army enlisted campaign hat. **$45-$85 (£28-£53)**
AdvanceGuardMilitaria.com

USMC EM visor cap, khaki top. **$35-$65 (£22-£40)**
AdvanceGuardMilitaria.com

USMC EM visor cap, forest green top. **$45-$65 (£28-£40)**
AdvanceGuardMilitaria.com

USN flat hat. **$15-$25 (£9-£16)**
AdvanceGuardMilitaria.com

U.S. Army Signal Corps enlisted overseas cap.
$15-$20 (£9-£12)
AdvanceGuardMilitaria.com

AAF enlisted overseas cap. **$15-$20 (£9-£12)**
AdvanceGuardMilitaria.com

Civilian in the field overseas cap.
$20-$25 (£12-£16)
AdvanceGuardMilitaria.com

USMC khaki overseas cap with EGA.
$20-$25 (£12-£16)
AdvanceGuardMilitaria.com

USMC forest green wool overseas cap with
EGA. **$25-$30 (£16-£19)**
AdvanceGuardMilitaria.com

Caps and Hats, Utility

U.S. "Jeep" cap.
$65-$85 (£40-£53)
AdvanceGuardMilitaria.com

Lambskin lined
winter cap.
$85-$115 (£53-£71)
AdvanceGuardMilitaria.com

M1943 field cap.
$35-$45 (£22-£28)
AdvanceGuardMilitaria.com

U.S. Army brimmed fatigue hat with
personalized message. **$65 (£40)**
AdvanceGuardMilitaria.com

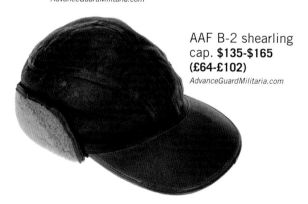

AAF B-2 shearling
cap. **$135-$165
(£64-£102)**
AdvanceGuardMilitaria.com

USMC Iceland
Detachment cold
weather cap.
**$200-$265
(£124-£164)**
AdvanceGuardMilitaria.com

WAC wool winter
issue cap, Type II.
$135-$165 (£64-£102)
AdvanceGuardMilitaria.com

USMC Model 1941
HBT utility cap.
$55-$75 (£34-£47)
AdvanceGuardMilitaria.com

Navy enlisted
WAVES cap.
$65-$85 (£40-£53)
Chris William

Caps and Hats, Female

Navy Nurse
Corps service
cap. **$125-$165
(£78-£102)**
Chris William

Army Nurses Corps
(ANC) officer's summer
service visor cap.
$145-$165 (£90-£102)
AdvanceGuardMilitaria.com

USMCWR
woman's summer
service cap.
$95-$125 (£59-£78)
AdvanceGuardMilitaria.com

ANC officer's visor
cap, 1943 Pattern.
$85-$115 (£53-£71)
AdvanceGuardMilitaria.com

USMCWR woman's
wool service cap.
$95-$135 (£59-£84)
AdvanceGuardMilitaria.com

AAF flight
nurse's K-1 cap.
$75-$85 (£47-£53)
AdvanceGuardMilitaria.com

Red Cross woman's
visor cap. **$65-$85
(£40-£53)**
AdvanceGuardMilitaria.com

WAAC khaki
summer issue cap.
$85-$115 (£53-£71)
AdvanceGuardMilitaria.com

Women's War
Volunteer Service
cap. **$265-$315
(£164-£195)**
Chris William

Chapter 3
Accoutrements

After World War II, many soldiers brought home pieces of their field gear. Often the intent was to continue to use their war materials in the pursuit of hobbies or careers. Today it is not uncommon to find an old Army shovel, pair of wire cutters, or some form of haversack or pouch amidst a stash of tools or outdoor gear.

Collecting and displaying accoutrements provide the World War II enthusiast with a feeling of direct connection to the soldier. These were, after all, the tools of the soldier's trade—the very trappings that he or she wore on campaign, in battle, on the drill field, and finally, the souvenirs of his or her time in the service.

Nearly every World War II combatant was issued some form of cartridge belt or carrier, a pack for his belongings, mess gear and canteen, and some form of tent or shelter. Regardless, all accoutrements have not survived at the same rate. Some of these items don't exist today. Cartridge belts, first aid pouches, and even knapsacks have survived by the hundreds of thousands, whereas specialty items such as gas detection brassards or special "paratrooper" first aid pouches are exceedingly rare.

Once sold as surplus material, a lot of accoutrements are still seeing hard service today. Reenacting the lives of the World War II soldier is a popular hobby in the United States, Great Britain, most of Europe and even Japan and Australia. Demand for the common trappings has driven prices up and even given birth to a widespread reproduction market. Some caution should be exercised when considering rare accoutrements, especially those designed for elite troops, such as paratroopers, commandos, or SS soldiers. The bulk of material that survived the war, however, has kept prices affordable for many of the more common pieces.

The abundance of some items (like cartridge belts or shovels) enables a collector to specialize in one particular accoutrement by seeking out variations and various makers' marks. Others find it satisfying to amass all of the trappings worn by a typical officer or enlisted man of various nations. Whatever the angle, though, there is plenty of material that survived the war to keep a collector busy for years.

AUSTRALIA

Australian folding wire cutters. **$35-$45 (£22-£28)**
AdvanceGuardMilitaria.com

BULGARIA

Bulgarian Ersatz canvas Luger holster. **$145-$165 (£90-£102)**
AdvanceGuardMilitaria.com

Bulgarian canteen. **$25-$35 (£16-£22)**
AdvanceGuardMilitaria.com

Values at a Glance

Commonly encountered accoutrements:

- German Army enlisted/NCO steel buckle and leather belt ....$145-$185 (£90-£115)
- Hitler Youth steel buckle .. $40-$65 (£25-£40)
- German M31 canteen with wool cover and cup ....$65-$100 (£40-£62)
- Italian Carcano rifle cartridge pouch set ....$20-$30 (£12-£19)
- Japanese Army Type 94 1st Pattern "Koh" canteen ....$75-$125 (£47-£78)
- Japanese Army mess kit..$55-$75 (£34-£47)
- U.S. rifleman's cartridge belt ....$75-$125 (£47-£78)
- U.S. Army pistol belt.........$15-$25 (£9-£16)
- U.S. canteen, cup, and cover set ....$25-$35 (£16-£22)
- U.S. Army 1942 Pattern wound dressing pouch..................................$5-$10 (£3-£6)

Bulgarian field
equipment.
**$225-$275
(£140-£171)**
AdvanceGuardMilitaria.com

CZECHOSLOVAKIA

Czech M25 rifle cartridge pouch. **$15-$20 (£9-£12)**
AdvanceGuardMilitaria.com

ENGLAND

Packs, Pouches

British Webley .455 revolver holster.
$45-$65 (£28-£40)
Chris William

CANADA

Canadian P37 entrenching tool. **$55-$85 (£34-£53)**
AdvanceGuardMilitaria.com

Canadian Navy binoculars. **$40-$65 (£25-£40)**
AdvanceGuardMilitaria.com

British Webley .38
revolver holster.
$25-$35 (£16-£22)
Chris William

British WAAF shoulder bag.
$165-$195 (£102-£121)
AdvanceGuardMilitaria.com

British first aid kit container. **$20-$30 (£12-£19)**
AdvanceGuardMilitaria.com

Chemical Warfare

British RAF portable oxygen cylinder.
$75-$100 (£47-£62)
AdvanceGuardMilitaria.com

Gloves/Mittens

ATS Palestinian Volunteer gauntlets and utility pouch. **$125 (£78)**
AdvanceGuardMilitaria.com

First Aid, Medical

FIRST FIELD DRESSING

TO OPEN | Outer Cover: Break thread holding flap. Inner Waterproof Cover: Tear apart at the uncemented corner (indicated by arrow)

CONTENTS | Two Dressings in Waterproof Covers, each consisting of a gauze pad stitched to a bandage, and a safety pin.

DIRECTIONS FOR USE. Take the folded ends of the bandage in each hand, and, keeping the bandage taut, apply the gauze pad to the wound and fix the bandage. One dressing to be used for each wound.
In the case of head wounds, when respirators have to be worn, care should be taken to adjust the pad so that it does not interfere with the fit of the face piece.
DO NOT HANDLE THE GAUZE OR WOUND

T. J. SMITH & NEPHEW, LTD. - HULL

Jan./June 1942

British soldier's wound dressing. **$5-$10 (£3-£6)**
AdvanceGuardMilitaria.com

British early war gas mask. **$100-$130 (£62-£81)**
AdvanceGuardMilitaria.com

Eyewear

British RAF flying goggles, MK VIII style.
$70-$135 (£43-£54)
AdvanceGuardMilitaria.com

British motorized goggles and case.
$85-$115 (£53-£71)
AdvanceGuardMilitaria.com

Compasses, Navigational Devices

British RAF
Azimuth compass.
**$100-$145
(£62-£90)**
AdvanceGuardMilitaria.com

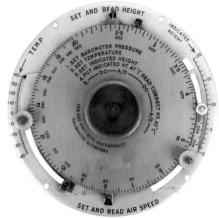

British RAF height and air speed computer,
Mark I. **$15-$25 (£9-£16)**
AdvanceGuardMilitaria.com

British
RAF course
and speed
calculator,
Mark II.
**$30-$45
(£19-£28)**
vanceGuardMilitaria.com

British No. 4A
mine detector
in wooden
transit chest.
**$200-$400
(£124-£248)**
HA.com

Flashlights

British No.1
electric lamp.
$25-$40 (£16-£25)
AdvanceGuardMilitaria.com

Optics

British No. 2 Mk II
binoculars and web case.
$75-$95 (£47-£59)
HA.com

Communications

British Fullerphone MK IV,
1943. **$40-$65 (£25-£40)**
AdvanceGuardMilitaria.com

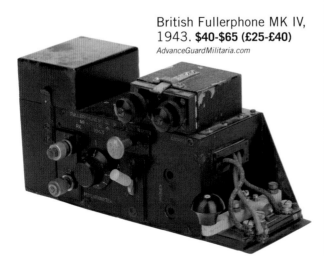

Collecting Hints

Pros:

- Fakes of common items are not as prevalent.

- Due to the volume of equipment produced, there is a wide variety of variations and manufacturers for most accoutrements. Therefore, assembling a wide study collection is fun.

- Accoutrements, by their very nature, have a personal feel to them. By collecting the complete trappings of a soldier, a collector can develop a keen sense of a typical World War II soldier's burden.

Cons:

- Leather and metal accoutrements can be hard to store properly. Leather requires special treatment and is prone to flaking and dryness. It should ideally be stored in a slightly humid environment. Metal items, especially tin-dipped iron such as canteens, are prone to rust and must be kept dry.

- Different types of accoutrements survived at disproportionate rates. As an example, U.S. cartridge belts have survived by the hundreds of thousands, but very few U.S. paratrooper first aid pouches have survived. Therefore, assembling a complete soldier's kit is costly, especially if one is depicting an "elite" soldier such as a paratrooper or British Commando.

- Because the bulk of accoutrements have entered the market through surplus channels, very few items have a known provenance. This can give accoutrements a bland feel because they do not have the same sorts of associated war stories as, say, a soldier's uniform with all of his medals displayed on it.

Availability: ✪ ✪ ✪ ✪
Price: ✪ ✪
Reproduction Alert: ✪ ✪

Favorite Find: USAAF Barter Kit

by Jim McCloskey

I have been collecting militaria for the past 40 years and have shifted my collecting interests numerous times. I remember buying my first ETO medal for $3 and still have it.

I was a career soldier and served 26 years in the Army (enlisted and officer), retiring in 2004. My career travels allowed me to see and purchase militaria from all over the world, including war zones.

One of my primary collecting specialties is anything related to World War II Army Air Forces. I was bitten by that bug one afternoon while walking home from high school, when I spotted a uniform in a box of trash. When I opened the box, there was a pile of OD wool and blue wool Class A uniforms, and at the bottom was a leather jacket. I grabbed as much as I could carry.

A career Air Force veteran had passed away with no next of kin, and the contents of his house went to the trash. I discovered the deceased vet was a fighter pilot in World War II and retired after 20 years in the modern Air Force. I was now in possession of a complete Army Air Force/U.S. Air Force grouping to include a named A-2 flight jacket. I now had the USAAF/USAF collecting bug bad.

Over the next 40 years, more books became available, revealing the uniforms and equipment used by the USAAF in World War II. Two books that provided me hours of informative reading and inspired countless hours of searching through piles of militaria were written by C.G Sweeting: *Combat Flying Clothing* and *Combat Flying Equipment*. I purchased both and set off to capture everything photographed in each book. Of course, I fell short of my goal, but not for lack of trying. Over the years I spent countless dollars and hours buying every jacket, flight helmet, specialty uniform — basically "you name it…I bought it" to fulfill my dream collection.

I met C.G. Sweeting at the Max Show one year and told him how his books had forever changed me. We discussed his work as curator of the USAAF exhibit at the Smithsonian Museum. I told him I found a relic mentioned in *Combat Flying Equipment*, but that it had no accompanying photograph that I could compare it to in order to get a step nearer to my goal.

The item is listed as a "Kit, Flyer, Trading Packet Spec No 40685." I had found the kit in an antiques mall in Chattanooga and took a chance that it was the one listed on page 193 of *Combat Flying Equipment*. Mr. Sweeting suggested I photograph the kit and send it to the Smithsonian because he had never seen the kit, and that it was only listed in the AAF class 13 catalog. He said the kit I possessed might be the only surviving example left since World War II. I could not believe that I possessed something that was listed in the books but was not photographed! Could it be?

I have to admit that when I first looked at the kit, I thought it was some phony items someone had put together. The box is labeled nicely, and inside are two plastic packets containing all sorts of beads and string and basically worthless junk. The only valuable items are seven silver coins from India.

I have been searching for a similar kit as the one I have, but so far have not found any or even a photo of one. I hope this article allows other collectors who possess a similar kit to share photos. If it is the "last survivor," I am delighted to share it with the militaria collecting community.

Parachutes/Life Preservers

British invasion
life belt.
**$75-$125
(£47-£78)**

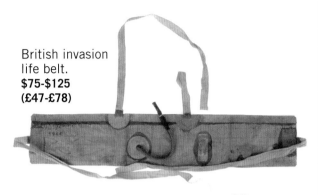

British RAF pilot's seat pack
parachute. **$295-$395 (£183-£245)**
AdvanceGuardMilitaria.com

British "Rupert"
D-Day dummy
paratrooper.
$3,346 (£2075)
HA.com

Aircraft/Vehicle Components

British RAF
aircraft time of
flight clock.
**$100-$135
(£62-£64)**
AdvanceGuardMilitaria.com

British RAF P8 aircraft
compass. **$125-$165
(£78-£102)**
AdvanceGuardMilitaria.com

FINLAND

Finnish World War II reissued World War I Russian
shovel with carrier. **$35-$50 (£22-£31)**
AdvanceGuardMilitaria.com

Finnish winter war enlisted belt buckle.
$45-$65 (£28-£40)
AdvanceGuardMilitaria.com

FRANCE

French Model 1892 revolver holster. **$90-$100 (£56-£62)**
Chris William

French M35 mess kit. **$20-$30 (£12-£19)**
AdvanceGuardMilitaria.com

French "Blitzkrieg" pilot's goggles. **$165-$225 (£102-£140)**
AdvanceGuardMilitaria.com

French Model 1935 ammunition pouch. **$15-$25 (£9-£16)**
AdvanceGuardMilitaria.com

French box flashlight. **$35-$50 (£22-£31)**
AdvanceGuardMilitaria.com

French flashlight. **$40-$55 (£25-£34)**
AdvanceGuardMilitaria.com

French M35 musette bag. **$35-$55 (£22-£34)**
AdvanceGuardMilitaria.com

French 1931 ANP gas mask. **$65-$95 (£40-£59)**
AdvanceGuardMilitaria.com

GERMANY

Bayonet Frogs

German tropical bayonet frog. **$135-$165 (£84-£102)**
AdvanceGuardMilitaria.com

Belts, Belt Plates, and Buckles

German Army enlisted/NCO steel buckle and leather belt. **$145-$185 (£90-£115)**
AdvanceGuardMilitaria.com

German Army enlisted/NCO aluminum buckle and leather tab. **$85-$125 (£53-£78)**
AdvanceGuardMilitaria.com

German Army tropical belt and buckle.
$275-$365 (£171-£226)
HistoryHunter.com

German Luftwaffe enlisted/NCO belt and buckle.
$165-$195 (£102-£121)
AdvanceGuardMilitaria.com

Hitler Youth steel buckle. **$40-$65 (£25-£40)**
AdvanceGuardMilitaria.com

Hitler Youth Kriegsmetall belt buckle.
$45-$65 (£28-£40)
AdvanceGuardMilitaria.com

Deutsche Jugend belt buckle. **$45-$95 (£28-£59)**
AdvanceGuardMilitaria.com

German SA belt and buckle. **$95-$135 (£59-£64)**
AdvanceGuardMilitaria.com

Deutsche Arbeitsfront (DAF) enlisted buckle and leather tab. **$125-$150 (£78-£93)**
Chris William

German SS enlisted buckle, aluminum.
$400-$500 (£248-£310)
Rick Fleury

NSDAP leader's belt buckle. **$165-$200 (£102-£124)**
Chris William

German SS officer's belt plate.
$1,500-$2,000 (£930-£1,240)
AdvanceGuardMilitaria.com

German Red Cross enlisted belt and plate. **$135-$165 (£64-£102)**
HistoryHunter.com

SS enlisted belt and plate. **$550-$650 (£341-£403)**
AdvanceGuardMilitaria.com

NSDAP officer's belt and buckle.
$200-$285 (£124-£177)
HistoryHunter.com

Reichsarbeitsdienst (RAD) enlisted buckle and leather tab. **$125-$150 (£78-£93)**
Chris William

Reichs Lufschutzbund enlisted buckle. **$195-$235 (£121-£146)**
Chris William

German Custom Services officer's brocade belt. **$1,500-$2,500 (£930-£1,550)**

German Army sword shoulder harness and hanger. **$145-$165 (£90-£102)**
AdvanceGuardMilitaria.com

German officer's field service belt and holster. **$145 (£90)**
AdvanceGuardMilitaria.com

Pouches, Ammunition

German MP 44 magazine pouch. **$1,500-$2,000 (£930-£1,240)**
Chris William

German K98 rifle ammunition pouch. **$25-$40 (£16-£25)**
AdvanceGuardMilitaria.com

Luftwaffe/police brown leather K98 rifle ammunition pouch. **$20-$35 (£12-£22)**
AdvanceGuardMilitaria.com

German G-43 double magazine pouch.
$600-$800 (£372-£496)
Chris William

Pouches, Packs and Bags, Personal Gear

NSDAP auxiliary
tornister with cloth
cover. **$45-$65 (£28-£40)**
AdvanceGuardMilitaria.com

Third Reich RAD
tornister. **$65-$95
(£40-£59)**
AdvanceGuardMilitaria.com

German Army 1934
Pattern tornister with
hair cover. **$17-$115
(£11-£71)**
AdvanceGuardMilitaria.com

German Heer
artillery rucksack.
$45-$65 (£28-£40)
AdvanceGuardMilitaria.com

German Army field-made rucksack. **$45 (£28)**
AdvanceGuardMilitaria.com

Suspenders, Combat

German Army 1939
Pattern tornister with
hair cover. **$55-$95
(£34-£59)**
AdvanceGuardMilitaria.com

Third Reich
political fur-covered
knapsack. **$45-$65
(£28-£40)**
AdvanceGuardMilitaria.com

German Army tropical "A" frame and assault
pack. **$575-$675 (£357-£419)**
AdvanceGuardMilitaria.com

German Army combat Y straps. **$125-$165 (£78-£102)**
AdvanceGuardMilitaria.com

Kriegsmarine lightweight Y straps. **$165-$225 (£102-£140)**
AdvanceGuardMilitaria.com

"I dropped down and checked out the gun placement with my captured German 6X field glasses."

— Alfred John Rocklitz, 104th Division

Bread Bags

German Army bread bag. **$40-$50 (£25-£31)**
AdvanceGuardMilitaria.com

German Army M31 bread bag and strap. **$85-$115 (£53-£71)**
AdvanceGuardMilitaria.com

German M31 canteen with wool cover and cup. **$65-$100 (£40-£62)**
AdvanceGuardMilitaria.com

Wehrmacht 1934 Pattern canteen and cup. **$65-$100 (£40-£62)**
AdvanceGuardMilitaria.com

Canteens

Third Reich political field canteen. **$25-$45 (£16-£28)**
AdvanceGuardMilitaria.com

Third Reich M31 canteen cup. **$25-$35 (£16-£22)**
AdvanceGuardMilitaria.com

Leggings

Heer M1940 Gamaschen. **$35-$65 (£22-£40)**
AdvanceGuardMilitaria.com

Mess Kits

German Army mess kit. **$35-$55 (£35-£34)**
AdvanceGuardMilitaria.com

Camouflage painted M31 mess kit. **$325 (£202)**
AdvanceGuardMilitaria.com

German NSDAP
political mess kit.
$35-$45 (£22-£28)
AdvanceGuardMilitaria.com

Wehrmacht
18-liter drinking
water backpack
container.
**$100-$135
(£62-£64)**
AdvanceGuardMilitaria.com

Entrenching Tools, Axes, and Hammers

German Heer folding
1938 Pattern
entrenching shovel
and carrier. **$265-$365
(£164-£226)**
AdvanceGuardMilitaria.com

Chemical Warfare

Wehrmacht gas mask M30 and carrier, second style. **$115-$165 (£71-£102)**
AdvanceGuardMilitaria.com

Luftwaffe Model 10-6701 oxygen mask (incorrect strap). **$295 (£183)**
AdvanceGuardMilitaria.com

Wehrmacht gas mask M30 and carrier, first style. **$95-$165 (£59-£102)**
AdvanceGuardMilitaria.com

Gloves/Mittens

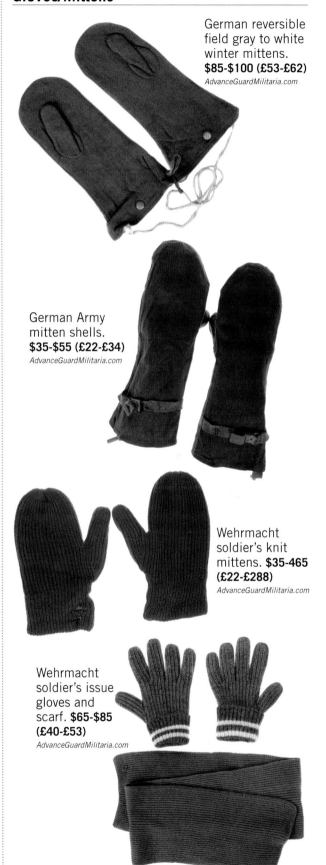

German reversible field gray to white winter mittens. **$85-$100 (£53-£62)**
AdvanceGuardMilitaria.com

German Army mitten shells. **$35-$55 (£22-£34)**
AdvanceGuardMilitaria.com

Wehrmacht soldier's knit mittens. **$35-465 (£22-£288)**
AdvanceGuardMilitaria.com

Wehrmacht soldier's issue gloves and scarf. **$65-$85 (£40-£53)**
AdvanceGuardMilitaria.com

Flashlights

Third Reich privately purchased field flashlight. **$45-$65 (£28-£40)**
AdvanceGuardMilitaria.com

Third Reich Pertrix flashlight. **$25-$45 (£16-£28)**
AdvanceGuardMilitaria.com

Wehrmacht field flashlight. **$40-$65 (£25-£40)**
AdvanceGuardMilitaria.com

Luftwaffe field lantern. **$145-$165 (£90-£102)**
AdvanceGuardMilitaria.com

Communications Gear

German people's radio, VE 301 Dyn. **$165-$225 (£102-£140)**
AdvanceGuardMilitaria.com

German air-ground receiver 52 a-1 "Köln." **$1,000-$1,500 (£620-£930)**

Philips Type 510A table model radio. **$165 (£102)**
AdvanceGuardMilitaria.com

Wehrmacht Communications desk telephone. **$75 (£47)**

AdvanceGuardMilitaria.com

Third Reich Communications T-1 telegraph key. **$75-$100 (£47-£62)**

AdvanceGuardMilitaria.com

Wehrmacht air raid siren. **$195-$265 (£121-£164)**

AdvanceGuardMilitaria.com

German Typewriter With "SS" Sig Runes key. **$600-$750 (£372-£465)**

German field radio "Feldfu.b1." **$950-$1,200 (£589-£744)**

Wehrmacht cypher machine, "Enigma I." **$40,200 (£24,924)**

Compasses

German Lensatic compass. $85-$125 (£53-£78)
AdvanceGuardMilitaria.com

Luftwaffe DR2 flight navigation computer.
$100-$135 (£62-£64)
AdvanceGuardMilitaria.com

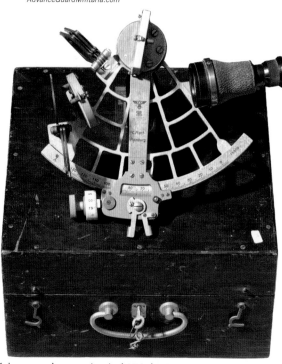

Kriegsmarine sextant. **$950-$1,200 (£589-£744)**
Hermann-Historica.de

Optics

Wehrmacht Zeiss 8x30 binoculars and carrying case. **$115-$145 (£71-£90)**
AdvanceGuardMilitaria.com

German Leitz 10x80 artillery ranging binoculars. **$300-$400 (£186-£248)**
HA.com

Wehrmacht 10x50 Dienstglas binoculars and case, Emil Busch. **$365-$435 (£226-£270)**
AdvanceGuardMilitaria.com

Wehrmacht 10x50 Dienstglas binoculars and case, M. Hensoldt & Sohne. **$365-$435 (£226-£270)**
AdvanceGuardMilitaria.com

Wehrmacht Entfernungsmesser on
80cm tripod. **$600-$850 (£372-£527)**
Hermann-Historica.de

Wehrmact Beobachtungs-Fernrohr, sog. Flakglas
D.F. 10 x 80. **$1,750-$2,200 (£1,085-£1,364)**
Hermann-Historica.de

Weapon Accessories

German Carl Zeiss P.Z.F. 1-2.5x28 scope.
$200 (£124)
HA.com

Pair of magazine pouches for Sturmgewehr 44.
$650-$800 (£403-£496)
Chris William

Holsters

TENO marked Walther
PP holster. **$175-$200
(£109-£124)**
AdvanceGuardMilitaria.com

German military P-38
holster. **$150-$170
(£93-£105)**
HA.com

Horse Equipment

German Heer cavalry stirrups. **$25-$45 (£16-£28)**
AdvanceGuardMilitaria.com

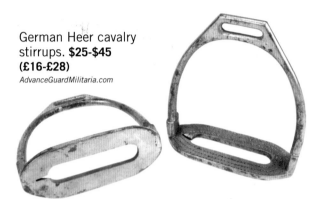

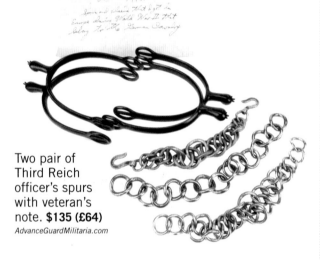

Two pair of Third Reich officer's spurs with veteran's note. **$135 (£64)**
AdvanceGuardMilitaria.com

Parachutes/Life Preservers

Luftwaffe pilot's seat pack parachute. **$225 (£140)**
AdvanceGuardMilitaria.com

Luftwaffe Model RH-28 parachute with bag. **$5,000-$7,500 (£3,100-£4,650)**
Hermann-Historica.de

Kapok-Schwimmweste Type 10-76 B. **$1,200-$1,500 (£744-£930)**
Hermann-Historica.de

Kriegsmarine U-boot inflatable life preserver. **$1,300-$1,500 (£806-£930)**
Hermann-Historica.de

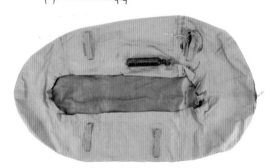

Luftwaffe inflatable one-man lifeboat. **$395-$495 (£245-£307)**
AdvanceGuardMilitaria.com

Aircraft/Vehicle Components

Luftwaffe Me109 pilot's seat. **$325-$450 (£202-£279)**
AdvanceGuardMilitaria.com

Luftwaffe cockpit airspeed indicator. **$75-$95 (£47-£59)**
AdvanceGuardMilitaria.com

Luftwaffe JU-87A Stuka steering yoke. **$950-$1,250 (£589-£775)**
AdvanceGuardMilitaria.com

Luftwaffe cockpit FK38 compass. **$145-$185 (£90-£115)**
AdvanceGuardMilitaria.com

Luftwaffe Me109 blind flying clock. **$135-$185 (£64-£115)**
AdvanceGuardMilitaria.com

Luftwaffe Lke 6 aircraft pilot's compass. **$85-$115 (£53-£71)**
AdvanceGuardMilitaria.com

Luftwaffe cockpit altimeter. **$155-$195 (£96-£121)**
AdvanceGuardMilitaria.com

HOLLAND

Dutch Infantry officer's equipment. **$395 (£248)**
AdvanceGuardMilitaria.com

Dutch Infantry bread bag. **$55-$75 (£34-£47)**
AdvanceGuardMilitaria.com

Dutch Army mess kit. **$45-$55 (£28-£34)**
AdvanceGuardMilitaria.com

Dutch Army gas mask. **$125-$155 (£78-£96)**
AdvanceGuardMilitaria.com

HUNGARY

ITALY

Pair of Hungarian Infantry cartridge pouches. **$95 (£59)**
AdvanceGuardMilitaria.com

Italian M91 carbine bandolier. **$55-$75 (£34-£47)**
AdvanceGuardMilitaria.com

Italian Infantry accoutrement lot. **$135 (£64)**
AdvanceGuardMilitaria.com

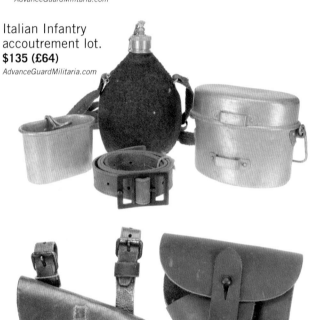

Hungarian Infantry entrenching tool and carrier. **$95-$135 (£59-£64)**
AdvanceGuardMilitaria.com

Hungarian Army camouflage shelter half. **$285-325 (£177-£202)**
AdvanceGuardMilitaria.com

Italian Model 1889 revolver holster. **$145-$175 (£90-£109)**
Chris William

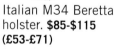

Italian M34 Beretta holster. **$85-$115 (£53-£71)**
AdvanceGuardMilitaria.com

Hungarian Infantry rucksack. **$85-$135 (£53-£64)**
AdvanceGuardMilitaria.com

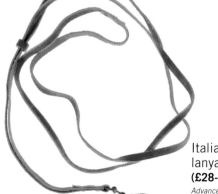

Italian pistol neck lanyard. **$45-$65 (£28-£40)**
AdvanceGuardMilitaria.com

Italian Alpini hose tops.
$65-$85 (£40-£53)
AdvanceGuardMilitaria.com

Italian two-liter
canteen. **$40-$50
(£25-£31)**
AdvanceGuardMilitaria.com

Italian one-liter
canteen. **$15-$25
(£9-£16)**
AdvanceGuardMilitaria.com

Italian Infantry
pickax and bayonet
set. **$185-$235
(£115-£146)**
AdvanceGuardMilitaria.com

Italian M31 gas mask with carrier.
$125-$135 (£78-£64)
AdvanceGuardMilitaria.com

Italian mess kit with
capture document.
$40 (£25)
AdvanceGuardMilitaria.com

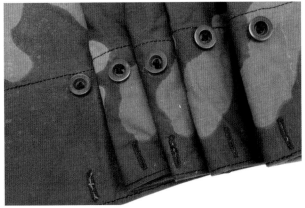

Italian camouflage shelter half. **$65-$95 (£40-£59)**
AdvanceGuardMilitaria.com

Italian Alpini mess kit. **$30-$40 (£19-£25)**
AdvanceGuardMilitaria.com

JAPAN

Belts, Belt Plates, and Buckles

Japanese officer's field service sword belt.
$155-$185 (£96-£115) *AdvanceGuardMilitaria.com*

Japanese naval officer
service dress sword belt.
$260-$325 (£161-£202)

AdvanceGuardMilitaria.com

Japanese Type 30 enlisted man's rubberized belt.
$165-$245 (£102-£152)

AdvanceGuardMilitaria.com

Japanese Army
officer of the
week sash.
**$100-$135
(£62-£64)**

AdvanceGuardMilitaria.com

Japanese Navy petty officer's belt buckle.
$55-$75 (£34-£47) *AdvanceGuardMilitaria.com*

Pouches, Ammunition

Japanese Type 96/99 machine gun magazine pouch
and strap. **$600-$665 (£372-£412)**

AdvanceGuardMilitaria.com

Japanese Type 30 rear ammunition pouch.
$400-$465 (£248-£288)

AdvanceGuardMilitaria.com

Japanese Infantry
front ammunition pouch.
$100-$125 (£62-£78)

AdvanceGuardMilitaria.com

Canteens and Mess Equipment

Japanese Army mess
kit. **$55-$75 (£34-£47)**
AdvanceGuardMilitaria.com

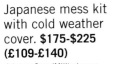

Japanese mess kit with cold weather cover. **$175-$225 (£109-£140)**

AdvanceGuardMilitaria.com

Japanese Army Type 94 1st Pattern "Koh" canteen. **$75-$125 (£47-£78)**

AdvanceGuardMilitaria.com

Japanese Army Type 94 2nd Pattern "Otsu" canteen. **$75-$125 (£47-£78)**

AdvanceGuardMilitaria.com

Japanese private purchase officer's canteen. **$85-$125 (£53-£78)**

AdvanceGuardMilitaria.com

Japanese officer's battle-damaged canteen. **$90 (£56)**

AdvanceGuardMilitaria.com

Japanese Navy canteen. **$95-$135 (£59-£64)**

AdvanceGuardMilitaria.com

Japanese Army officer later pattern mess tin. **$65-$90 (£40-£56)**

AdvanceGuardMilitaria.com

Japanese officer early pattern mess kit. **$65-$95 (£40-£59)**

AdvanceGuardMilitaria.com

Haversacks

Japanese 1940 Pattern Army haversack. **$75-$95 (£47-£59)**

AdvanceGuardMilitaria.com

Japanese 1945 Pattern Army haversack. **$45-$75 (£28-£47)**

AdvanceGuardMilitaria.com

Pouches and Packs, Personal Gear

Japanese
Army Type 99
knapsack.
**$165-$245
(£102-£152)**
AdvanceGuardMilitaria.com

Japanese
officer's leather
knapsack.
**$295-$335
(£183-£208)**
AdvanceGuardMilitaria.com

Japanese leather pouch and contents. **$285 (£177)**
AdvanceGuardMilitaria.com

Japanese waterproof cloth equipment straps
(reverse illustrated). **$35-$55 (£22-£34)**
AdvanceGuardMilitaria.com

Japanese student backpack. **$40-$65 (£25-£40)**
AdvanceGuardMilitaria.com

Map Cases

Japanese Army
officer map case.
$65-$85 (£40-£53)
AdvanceGuardMilitaria.com

Japanese Army officer map case with contents.
$95 (£59)
AdvanceGuardMilitaria.com

Medical Gear

Japanese soldier's individual wound dressing.
$40-$60 (£25-£37)
AdvanceGuardMilitaria.com

Japanese dental kit captured on Guadalcanal.
$1,075 (£667)
HA.com

Chemical Warfare

Japanese Type 95 gas mask.
$195-$285 (£121-£177)
AdvanceGuardMilitaria.com

Communications

Japanese aviator's throat microphone.
$115-$145 (£71-£90)
AdvanceGuardMilitaria.com

Japanese Type 92 field telephone.
$145-$175 (£90-£109)
HA.com

Japanese Type 95 telegraph set.
$200-$265 (£124-£164)
AdvanceGuardMilitaria.com

Japanese air raid siren. **$165-$225 (£102-£140)**

AdvanceGuardMilitaria.com

Japanese Army voltammeter. **$45-$65 (£28-£40)**

AdvanceGuardMilitaria.com

Eyewear

Japanese Navy pilot's goggles with "Man" maker's logo. **$300-$345 (£186-£214)**

AdvanceGuardMilitaria.com

Japanese aviator's goggles with box. **$345 (£214)**

AdvanceGuardMilitaria.com

Gloves/Mittens

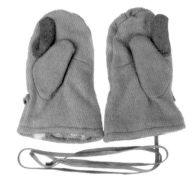

Japanese cold weather trigger finger mittens. **$55-$75 (£34-£47)**

AdvanceGuardMilitaria.com

Japanese Army tanker/pilot gloves. **$185-$225 (£115-£140)**

AdvanceGuardMilitaria.com

Japanese World War II cold weather "driver" mittens. **$100-$135 (£62-£64)**

AdvanceGuardMilitaria.com

Japanese pilot's winter issue flying gloves. **$300-$365 (£186-£226)**

AdvanceGuardMilitaria.com

Japanese Army mosquito mittens. **$30-$45 (£19-£28)**

AdvanceGuardMilitaria.com

Leggings

Japanese late war home defense puttees. **$25-$40 (£16-£25)**
AdvanceGuardMilitaria.com

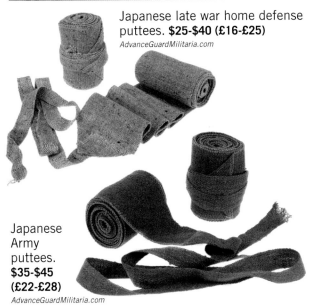

Japanese Army puttees. **$35-$45 (£22-£28)**
AdvanceGuardMilitaria.com

Optics

Japanese Type 93/50 trench periscope and case. **$365-$400 (£226-£248)**
Chris William

Japanese trench binoculars. **$200-$265 (£124-£164)**
AdvanceGuardMilitaria.com

Japanese binoculars and case. **$75-$115 (£47-£71)**
AdvanceGuardMilitaria.com

Tents

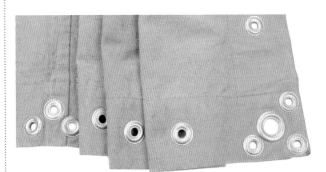

Japanese Army shelter half. **$195-$265 (£121-£164)**
AdvanceGuardMilitaria.com

Weapon Accessories

Japanese Type 99 4x sniper scope with case. **$2,500-$3,000 (£1,550-£1,860)**
Chris William

Japanese artillery fuse box. **$65-$85 (£40-£53)**
AdvanceGuardMilitaria.com

POLAND

SOVIET UNION

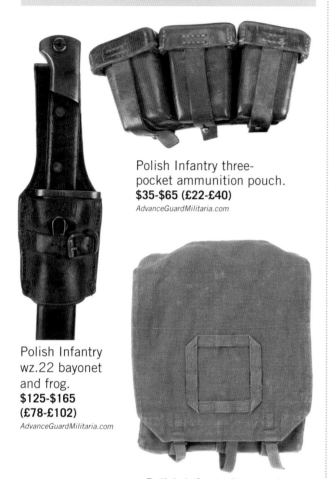

Polish Infantry three-pocket ammunition pouch.
$35-$65 (£22-£40)
AdvanceGuardMilitaria.com

Polish Infantry wz.22 bayonet and frog.
$125-$165 (£78-£102)
AdvanceGuardMilitaria.com

Polish Infantry knapsack.
$75-$95 (£47-£59)
AdvanceGuardMilitaria.com

Polish Army gas mask. **$95-$145 (£59-£90)**
AdvanceGuardMilitaria.com

Belts, Belt Plates, and Buckles

Soviet web and leather equipment belt.
$85-$100 (£53-£62)
AdvanceGuardMilitaria.com

Soviet officer's belt.
$85-$95 (£53-£59)
AdvanceGuardMilitaria.com

Soviet officer's M35 Sam Brown belt.
$100-$130 (£62-£81)
AdvanceGuardMilitaria.com

Pouches, Ammunition

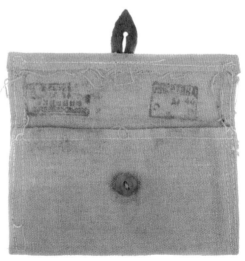

Soviet Infantry ammunition pouch, late war.
$25-45 (£16-£28)
AdvanceGuardMilitaria.com

Canteens and Mess Equipment

Soviet Army canteen and cover. **$65-$95 (£40-£56)**
AdvanceGuardMilitaria.com

Soviet Army mess kit. **$45-$65 (£28-£40)**
AdvanceGuardMilitaria.com

Soviet Army Model 26 mess kettle. **$125-$145 (£78-£90)**
AdvanceGuardMilitaria.com

Packs, Haversacks, Map Cases

Soviet M1936 knapsack. **$225-$265 (£140-£164)**
AdvanceGuardMilitaria.com

Soviet officer's map case. **$60-$80 (£37-£50)**
AdvanceGuardMilitaria.com

Soviet M1939 knapsack with kit pouches. **$300-$365 (£186-£226)**
AdvanceGuardMilitaria.com

Soviet Infantry Model 1930 assault pack. **$85-$135 (£53-£64)**
AdvanceGuardMilitaria.com

Chemical Warfare

Soviet Model 1938 gas mask. **$100-$200 (£62-£124)**
AdvanceGuardMilitaria.com

Holsters

Soviet Tokarev pistol holster. **$55-$85 (£34-£53)**
AdvanceGuardMilitaria.com

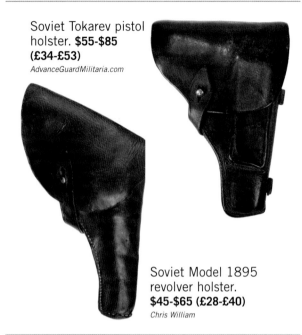

Soviet Model 1895 revolver holster. **$45-$65 (£28-£40)**
Chris William

Medical Gear

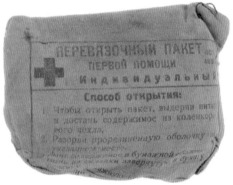

Soviet Army individual field dressing. **$15-$35 (£9-£22)**
AdvanceGuardMilitaria.com

Compasses

Soviet wrist compass. **$60-$80 (£37-£50)**
AdvanceGuardMilitaria.com

SWEDEN

Swedish Army entrenching shovel. **$55-$65 (£34-£40)**
AdvanceGuardMilitaria.com

UNITED STATES

Accoutrement Sets

U.S. GI accoutrement mixed lot. **$195 (£121)**
AdvanceGuardMilitaria.com

U.S. soldier's web equipment. **$225 (£140)**
AdvanceGuardMilitaria.com

U.S. BAR assistant gunner belt. **$45-$65 (£28-£40)**
AdvanceGuardMilitaria.com

USMC rifleman's cartridge belt. **$100-$145 (£61-£90)**
AdvanceGuardMilitaria.com

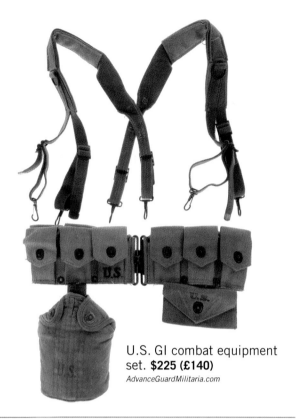

U.S. GI combat equipment set. **$225 (£140)**
AdvanceGuardMilitaria.com

Belts, Ammunition

U.S. rifleman's cartridge belt. **$75-$125 (£47-£78)**
AdvanceGuardMilitaria.com

U.S. rifleman's cartridge belt, British-made. **$115-$155 (£71-£96)**
AdvanceGuardMilitaria.com

U.S. BAR assistant gunner belt, M36 suspenders, and first aid. **$125 (£78)**
AdvanceGuardMilitaria.com

Belts, Pistol

U.S. Army pistol belt. **$15-$25 (£9-£16)**
AdvanceGuardMilitaria.com

U.S. pistol belt, 1944. **$15-$20 (£9-£12)**
AdvanceGuardMilitaria.com

USN M1936 pistol belt. **$25-$35 (£16-£22)**
AdvanceGuardMilitaria.com

Pouches, Ammunition

U.S. M1 carbine ammunition pouch and magazines. **$40-$55 (£25-£34)**
AdvanceGuardMilitaria.com

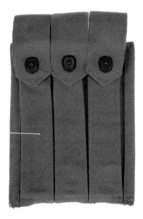

U.S. Army Thompson SMG three-magazine pouch. **$45-$75 (£28-£47)**
AdvanceGuardMilitaria.com

USMC Thompson SMG magazine pouch (reverse pictured). **$135-$165 (£64-£102)**
AdvanceGuardMilitaria.com

U.S. three-pocket grenade carrier. **$20-$25 (£12-£16)**
AdvanceGuardMilitaria.com

U.S. five-pocket grenade carrier. **$20-$30 (£12-£19)**
AdvanceGuardMilitaria.com

U.S. Thompson SMG five-magazine pouch. **$75-$115 (£47-£71)**
AdvanceGuardMilitaria.com

Suspenders

U.S. shotgun ammunition pouch. **$265-$325 (£164-£202)**
AdvanceGuardMilitaria.com

U.S. Paratrooper/Mountain Troops trouser suspenders. **$35-$45 (£22-£28)**
AdvanceGuardMilitaria.com

USMC combat suspenders. **$35-$45 (£22-£28)**
AdvanceGuardMilitaria.com

U.S. submachine gun ammunition magazine carrier with shoulder strap. **$125-$145**
AdvanceGuardMilitaria.com

U.S. Army M1 ammunition bag. **$50-$65 (£31-£40)**
AdvanceGuardMilitaria.com

U.S. Army M1936 combat suspenders. **$45-$55 (£28-£34)**
AdvanceGuardMilitaria.com

Canteens

USMC cross-flap canteen cover and black enamel canteen. **$110 (£68)**
AdvanceGuardMilitaria.com

British-made U.S. canteen set. **$85-$100 (£53-£62)**
AdvanceGuardMilitaria.com

USMC canteen and cover, Third Pattern, Second Type. **$55-$75 (£34-£47)**
AdvanceGuardMilitaria.com

USMC canteen and cover, Third Pattern, First Type. **$65-$85 (£40-£53)**
AdvanceGuardMilitaria.com

USMC canteen and cover, Second Pattern (reverse pictured). **$65-$85 (£40-£53)**
AdvanceGuardMilitaria.com

U.S. experimental plastic canteen. **$100-$135 (£62-£64)**
AdvanceGuardMilitaria.com

USMC 4th Marine Division marked canteen set. **$125 (£78)**
AdvanceGuardMilitaria.com

U.S. enameled canteen and cup set. **$235-$265 (£146-£164)**
AdvanceGuardMilitaria.com

Entrenching Tools, Axes

U.S. Army T-handle 1942 dated shovel and 1943 cover. **$145 (£90)**
AdvanceGuardMilitaria.com

U.S. Army issue hand axe and carrier. **$55-$95 (£34-£59)**
AdvanceGuardMilitaria.com

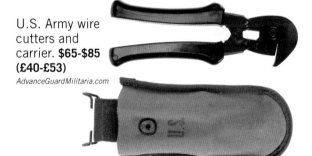

U.S. Army wire cutters and carrier. **$65-$85 (£40-£53)**
AdvanceGuardMilitaria.com

USMC wire cutter pouch. **$10-$20 (£6-£12)**
AdvanceGuardMilitaria.com

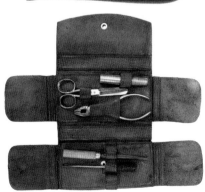

U.S. Signal Corps inspector's pocket kit. **$45-$75 (£28-£47)**
AdvanceGuardMilitaria.com

Holsters, Scabbards

U.S. .45 automatic pistol holster, belt, and magazine pouch. **$115 (£71)**
AdvanceGuardMilitaria.com

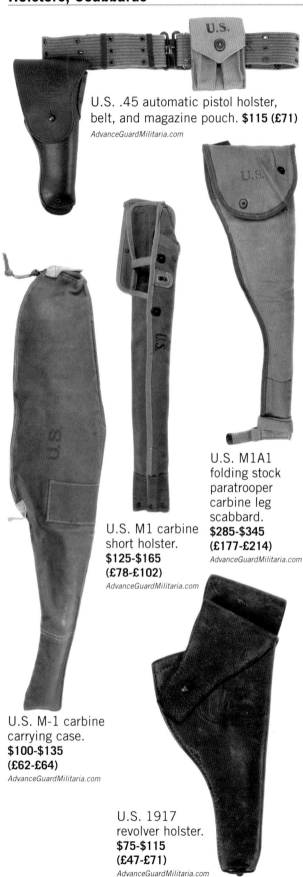

U.S. M-1 carbine carrying case. **$100-$135 (£62-£64)**
AdvanceGuardMilitaria.com

U.S. M1 carbine short holster. **$125-$165 (£78-£102)**
AdvanceGuardMilitaria.com

U.S. M1A1 folding stock paratrooper carbine leg scabbard. **$285-$345 (£177-£214)**
AdvanceGuardMilitaria.com

U.S. 1917 revolver holster. **$75-$115 (£47-£71)**
AdvanceGuardMilitaria.com

Packs/Haversacks

USAAF 5th Air Force NCO's painted B-4 suitcase. **$185 (£115)**
AdvanceGuardMilitaria.com

U.S. Army M1928 haversack. **$65-$125 (£40-£78)**
AdvanceGuardMilitaria.com

U.S. M1928 haversack, British-made. **$75-$135 (£47-£84)**
AdvanceGuardMilitaria.com

U.S. Army map case. **$65-$90 (£40-£56)**
AdvanceGuardMilitaria.com

Navy Atlantic Fleet Officer's seabag with five "Victory" German flags. **$150 (£93)**
AdvanceGuardMilitaria.com

"We had hot coffee and oatmeal, but as you ate it the rain filled up in the mess kit and it was cold in no time."

— Joseph Jones, Jr., U.S. Army, Purple Heart recipient

USMC Model 1941 haversack.
$95-$125 (£59-£78)
AdvanceGuardMilitaria.com

U.S. 43rd Division painted garment bag. **$95 (£59)**
AdvanceGuardMilitaria.com

USMC duffle bag with war diary. **$80 (£50)**
AdvanceGuardMilitaria.com

U.S. Army Pacific Theater camouflage jungle pack.
$200-$245 (£124-£152)
AdvanceGuardMilitaria.com

Female Accessories

USMC Women's Reserve issue utility bag-purse.
$250-$295 (£155-£183)
AdvanceGuardMilitaria.com

U.S. WAC issue utility bag-purse.
$145-$185 (£90)
AdvanceGuardMilitaria.com

Flashlights

USN flashlight. **$40-$50 (£25-£31)**
AdvanceGuardMilitaria.com

U.S. angle-head flashlight.
$25-$35 (£16-£22)
AdvanceGuardMilitaria.com

USAAF A-7 floating flashlight/survival signal light.
$10-$20 (£6-£12)
AdvanceGuardMilitaria.com

USAAF hand-energized flashlight.
$45-$80 (£28-£50)
AdvanceGuardMilitaria.com

Binoculars, Optics

USN Mark 33 binoculars.
$45-$75 (£28-£47)
AdvanceGuardMilitaria.com

USN 7x50 binoculars and case. **$85-$125 (£53-£78)**
AdvanceGuardMilitaria.com

USMC 7 x 50 Mark 40 binoculars.
$175-$235 (£109-£146)
AdvanceGuardMilitaria.com

USMC M9 binoculars.
$75-$125 (£47-£78)
AdvanceGuardMilitaria.com

U.S. Army Issue Type E 6 x 30 Power binoculars. **$50-$95 (£31-£59)**
AdvanceGuardMilitaria.com

Compasses and Navigational Tools

U.S. pocket clinometer.
$40-$60 (£25-£37)
AdvanceGuardMilitaria.com

USAAF Airman's British Escape compass.
$65-$75 (£40-£47)
AdvanceGuardMilitaria.com

USAAF sextant and case. **$135-$165 (£64-£102)**
AdvanceGuardMilitaria.com

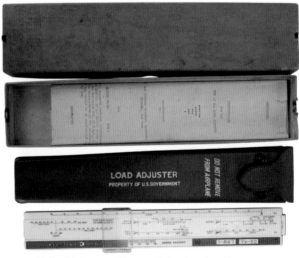

U.S. Airborne Waco glider load adjuster.
$75-$95 (£47-£59)
AdvanceGuardMilitaria.com

U.S. Paratrooper evasion and escape compass. **$125-$145 (£78-£90)**
AdvanceGuardMilitaria.com

US AAF navigation sextant. **$65-$95 (£40-£59)**
AdvanceGuardMilitaria.com

Gas Masks, Goggles

U.S. assault gas mask and waterproof carrier. **$65-$85 (£40-£53)**
AdvanceGuardMilitaria.com

Army lightweight service gas mask. **$65-$85 (£40-£53)**
AdvanceGuardMilitaria.com

U.S. Navy MK IV gas mask and carrier. **$35-$50 (£22-£31)**
AdvanceGuardMilitaria.com

Pre-World War II/early war U.S. Navy flying goggles. **$100-$200 (£62-£124)**
AdvanceGuardMilitaria.com

U.S. Army ski trooper goggles with case. **$25-$35 (£16-£22)**
AdvanceGuardMilitaria.com

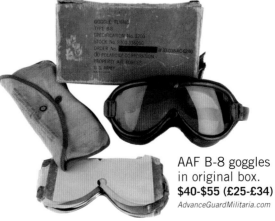

AAF B-8 goggles in original box. **$40-$55 (£25-£34)**
AdvanceGuardMilitaria.com

First Aid, Medical

U.S. Army jungle first
aid kit and contents.
$45-$65 (£28-£40)
AdvanceGuardMilitaria.com

U.S. Army medical
corpsman's field aid
pouch. **$45-$65
(£28-£40)**
AdvanceGuardMilitaria.com

U.S. Army medical corpsman's field aid pouch
insert, Type II. **$55-$65 (£34-£40)**
AdvanceGuardMilitaria.com

British-made U.S.
Army first aid
packet carrier.
$10-$15 (£6-£9)
AdvanceGuardMilitaria.com

USMC first aid
pouch. **$75-$95
(£47-£59)**
AdvanceGuardMilitaria.com

AAF/Airborne
aeronautic first
aid kit and
contents.
**$125-$150
(£78-£93)**
AdvanceGuardMilitaria.com

AAF pilot's
emergency
sustenance kit
and pouch.
**$235-$285
(£146-£177)**
AdvanceGuardMilitaria.com

USN individual
aviator's first
aid kit.
**$295-$365
(£183-£226)**
AdvanceGuardMilitaria.com

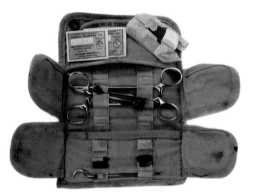

USN/USMC doctor's field surgical kit.
$55-$95 (£34-£59)
AdvanceGuardMilitaria.com

Weather, Clothing Protection

USMC/USN
leggings.
**$15-$25
(£9-£16)**
AdvanceGuardMilitaria.com

U.S. Army Mountain Troops ski leggings. **$25-$35 (£16-£22)**
AdvanceGuardMilitaria.com

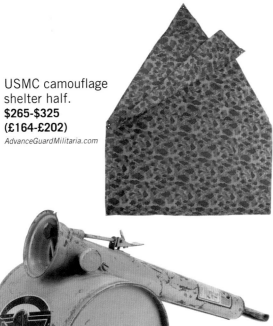

USMC camouflage shelter half. **$265-$325 (£164-£202)**
AdvanceGuardMilitaria.com

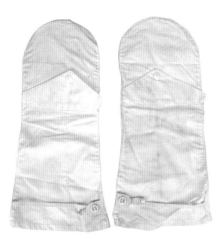

USN delousing insecticide sprayer. **$55-$75 (£34-£47)**
AdvanceGuardMilitaria.com

Gloves/Mittens

U.S. Army Mountain white over mittens. **$25-$35 (£16-£22)**
AdvanceGuardMilitaria.com

USN summer aviator's gloves. **$155-$195 (£96-£121)**
AdvanceGuardMilitaria.com

AAF Type A-9A aerial gunner's fleece mittens. **$85-$120 (£53-£74)**
AdvanceGuardMilitaria.com

AAF heated flying suit rheostat. **$20-$30 (£12-£19)**
AdvanceGuardMilitaria.com

Blankets

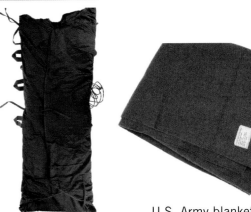

USAAF casualty heated blanket. **$95-$125 (£59-£78)**
AdvanceGuardMilitaria.com

U.S. Army blanket with 1942 contract tag. **$35-$65 (£22-£40)**
AdvanceGuardMilitaria.com

Parachutes/Life Preservers

U.S. Navy Kapok life jacket.
$350-$465 (£217-£288)

AdvanceGuardMilitaria.com

USAAF B-4 "Mae West" life preserver vest. **$135-$175 (£84-£109)**

AdvanceGuardMilitaria.com

USAAF AN-6512 back-type parachute. **$900-$1,100 (£558-£682)**

AdvanceGuardMilitaria.com

USAAF flyer's flak armor vest and apron (reverse illustrated).
$400-$500 (£248-£310)

AdvanceGuardMilitaria.com

U.S. invasion life preserver belt.
$100-$150 (£62-£93)

AdvanceGuardMilitaria.com

U.S. Army Paratrooper T-7 parachute harness.
$475-$575 (£295-£357)

AdvanceGuardMilitaria.com

U.S. paradummy decoy "Oscar."
$800-$1,000 (£496-£620)

AdvanceGuardMilitaria.com

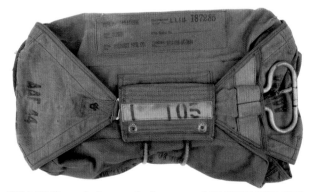

USAAF Type A-4 parachute cover. **$85-$125 (£53-£78)**

AdvanceGuardMilitaria.com

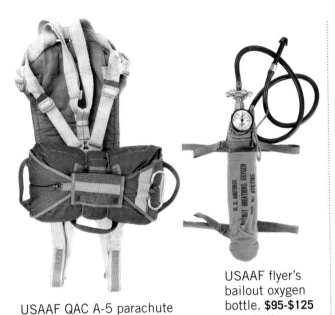

U.S. J-37 telegraph key with J-45 leg mount. **$65-$85 (£40-£53)**
AdvanceGuardMilitaria.com

U.S. field telephone. **$45-$60 (£28-£37)**
AdvanceGuardMilitaria.com

USAAF flyer's bailout oxygen bottle. **$95-$125 (£59-£78)**
AdvanceGuardMilitaria.com

USAAF QAC A-5 parachute harness with A-4 parachute. **$800-$1,000 (£496-£620)**
AdvanceGuardMilitaria.com

USN Navy type transmitter receiver unit. **$75-$125 (£47-£78)**
AdvanceGuardMilitaria.com

Radios, Communication Devices

U.S. Signal Corps BC-348-Q radio receiver. **$100-$165 (£62-£102)**
AdvanceGuardMilitaria.com

Army Signal Corps TP-9 portable telephone. **$65-$95 (£40-£59)**
AdvanceGuardMilitaria.com

1st Marine Division portable telephone. **$135 (£64)**
AdvanceGuardMilitaria.com

USAAF B-17 radio receiver unit. **$285-$350 (£177-£217)**
AdvanceGuardMilitaria.com

U.S. Army backpack for SCR-194/SCR-195 radio. **$30-$40 (£19-£25)**
AdvanceGuardMilitaria.com

U.S. ANH-B1 radio receiver headset. **$75-$95 (£47-£59)**
AdvanceGuardMilitaria.com

USN T-21/ARC-5 aircraft radio transmitter. **$75-$150 (£47-£93)**
AdvanceGuardMilitaria.com

Army carrier pigeon container PG-102/CB. **$135-$165 (£64-£102)**
HA.com

Weapon Accessories

U.S. gunner's quadrant and case. **$40-$55 (£25-£34)**
AdvanceGuardMilitaria.com

USAAF .50 caliber ammunition box. **$25-$35 (£16-£22)**
AdvanceGuardMilitaria.com

U.S. .50 caliber ammunition can. **$40-$70 (£25-£43)**
AdvanceGuardMilitaria.com

Aircraft and Ship Gauges, Parts

USAAF bomber master compass, Type D-12. **$100-$135 (£62-£64)**
AdvanceGuardMilitaria.com

USAAF aircraft directional gyro indicator. **$40-$60 (£25-£37)**
AdvanceGuardMilitaria.com

USAAF navigational master watch and carrying case. **$265-$365 (£164-£226)**
AdvanceGuardMilitaria.com

U.S. Army/Navy M-6 compass. **$60-$85 (£37-£53)**
AdvanceGuardMilitaria.com

USAAF Norden bombsight. **$1,100-$1,400 (£682-£860)**
AdvanceGuardMilitaria.com

U.S. World War II-era Sperry S-1 precision bombsight. **$1,175 (£729)**
HA.com

YUGOSLAVIA

Yugoslavian canteen and mess kit. **$95 (£59)**
AdvanceGuardMilitaria.com

Chapter 4

Medals

Medal collecting can become a hobby itself. Many medal collectors have never even considered branching out to other fields of militaria. To them, owning a fine German helmet is the same as owning a clay flowerpot—of little interest—and they certainly can't comprehend that it possesses any monetary value.

Medals are, by far, the most common military souvenirs from World War II. All the participant nations minted and awarded medals in one form or another. After the war, medals came home with soldiers who received them as commendations or recognition, but also as war trophies. Three factors made medals a popular souvenir: Medals are small; they are embodied with the mystique of valor, bravery or merit; and they exude the aura of monetary worth, perhaps because of their similarity to coinage or their perceived precious metal content. These three factors are at the heart of the popularity of medal collecting.

Medals seem to be a fairly sound investment. Prices have steadily increased over the years, and as supply of popular examples (like those of the Third Reich) become less, the popularity of medals increases (like those of the Soviet Union). The end result is, even the most common medals have held their values over the years and few, if any, have dropped in value.

Because medals are an attractive collecting arena, the field has attracted its share of unscrupulous dealers. It takes little effort to swap a ribbon, grind away or add a hallmark, or simply clean and embellish a medal. Reproductions of many medals and awards emerged on the market even *during* World War II! It is an old, tired saying, but your best defense, should you decide to collect medals, is to arm yourself with as many good books as possible. Study examples in reputable collection. Remember: The *real story of any medal is usually found on the back.* Turn it over, consider how it was meant to be worn, and examine the minting quality. All of these can be signs of reproductions, forgery, or simply spurious material.

Collecting Hints

Pros:

- Medals are extremely personal. The collector can determine some of a soldier's history from a single piece.
- Supply is plentiful. It is easy for a collector to find a level that is both affordable and enjoyable.
- Display is not difficult. Hundreds of medals can be inexpensively and safely exhibited.
- Variety of medals is wide, enabling a collector to pick an area in which to specialize.
- Medals are a sound investment.
- Items are small enough that shipping is not a big issue, enabling a collector to buy from any source in the world.

Cons:

- A lot medals—especially those of the Germany's Third Reich—have been reproduced.
- Many medals contain metals that react to the environment. May require specialized storage and handling.
- It is easy to get carried away and acquire more than one can enjoy or even afford. Supply is high, so a collector needs to exercise discipline and purchase wisely rather than wildly.
- Advanced collections will cost thousands of dollars.
- It is easy to fake name and/or serial number engraving on a medal, so identified groupings must be regard with a degree of skepticism.

Availability: ✪ ✪ ✪ ✪
Price: ✪ ✪ ✪
Reproduction Alert: ✪ ✪ ✪

Badge, Medal, Order, or Decorations— What Term is Right?

Go to any military show in the United States or Great Britain, and you will hear the terms "badge," "medal," "order," and "decoration" used interchangeably. The diehard dealer and collectors will know when to use which expression, but for the general militaria collector, all of these words will be used to describe the same object, depending on the mood of the speaker. However, learning the terminology will give you an edge when interacting with a dealer. It could be the difference in being perceived as a rube from the sticks or an informed customer. And you know how that difference is measured—in dollars or pounds, of course!

An **order** dates back to the days of knighthood. Generally, an order is associated with nobility or religious belief. Today, orders are generally conferred to citizens for some act performed during peace or war. It is not uncommon, however, to find military medal groupings that contain an order.

Decoration refers to an award other than an order. Decorations are presented to soldiers for some act of distinction against an enemy in combat. An example of a decoration would be the U.S. Silver Star, German Iron Cross, I Class, or the United Kingdom's Victoria Cross.

A term you probably won't encounter in your collecting, but that does come up in descriptions is **collar**. A "collar" is the highest class of some orders. A collar may often be a chain from which the order is suspended.

The most common term in the field—and the most encompassing—is **medal**. Properly, "medal" is used to describe any award that hangs from a ribbon. A medal will generally not be enameled (a characteristic of an order). A medal will commemorate a range of activities such as campaigns, long service, good conduct, or commemoration, or significant dates such as independence or a ruler's rise to power. Examples of medals include the United Kingdom's 1939-45 Star, Germany's Civil Service Honor Award, or the United States' Victory Medal. "Medal" is the term most commonly used to refer to the entire field of orders, decorations, and medals. If you are going to use just one word, this is the one to choose. A more experienced collector will not consider it a gaffe if you casually refer to a Medal of Honor as a medal (more correctly, it should be called a decoration). However, should you call a Rumanian Anti-Communist Campaign Medal a decoration, this will reveal your unfamiliarity (and therefore, vulnerability) with the hobby. When in doubt, refer to those orders, decorations, and badges as "medals." For the purposes of this chapter, the term "medal" will be used interchangeably with "order" and "decoration."

A **badge** is an outward symbol of a soldier having received a "passing grade" in a particular skill (and is not covered in this chapter). Badges include parachute or pilot wings and marksmanship awards. However, medal collectors reserve the word "badge" for an order that hangs from a ribbon. Yes, it is confusing. However, most diehard medal collectors are not going to be interacting regularly with general militaria collectors or dealers. So, for the purpose of *this* book, the term "badge" will generally imply that the item is a medal intended to be pinned directly to the wearer's uniform without an intervening ribbon.

Named, Named, Named

Across the hobby of World War II collecting and even more so in the medals field, three factors determine the highest price for any medal: named, named, and named! The highest prices are being paid for any medal that can be directly—and conclusively—linked to the name of the soldier who originally received it. Many medals were inscribed with a soldier's name or number. This presents the collector with the opportunity to learn more about the circumstances surrounding the award of that actual medal. Collectors pay top price for that opportunity (and some actually will do the research and learn the story of the award).

The next level of "value added" is a medal that is accompanied by the original award certificate or documentation. This is a bit harder to sell. Consider for a moment the German Knight's Cross to the Iron Cross. Best estimates indicate that nearly 7,500 examples of Knight's Crosses were awarded. However, none were engraved with the recipient's name or other identifying mark. Therefore, it is very hard to conclusively prove that a Knight's Cross belonged to a specific individual. A dealer has only condition and maker's marks to use to determine pricing. However, if the original award document (naming the recipient) accompanies the Knight's Cross, this is a clear advantage and will add hundreds, perhaps thousands, of dollars to the price. But unfortunately, nothing *conclusively* links the document to that particular example, so one is going to have to rely on instincts and trust of the dealer. Remember, the lure of adding significantly to the value of a medal by placing it with an award document is very strong. An "assembled" medal/document combination should not command the same price as a set that has been together since the war.

Copies, Restrikes, Reproductions and Fakes

When it comes to evaluating the authenticity of a medal, resist the urge to use common sense.

German II Class Iron Crosses were produced and distributed in the hundreds of thousands during World War II. Common sense would suggest that a reproducer would not waste his time on such a common medal—right?

When it comes to evaluating the authenticity of a medal, resist the urge to use common sense. In the case of the Iron Cross, some soldiers wanted something a bit more special, so they would visit a jeweler or other non-military associated business to purchase finer example (perhaps made with real silver) than what the military had given them. These medals, though purchased and worn during the war, were not authorized examples provided by the military establishment. One of these would be best referred to as a **copy**.

After Germany's surrender, the market was hungry for souvenirs. The tooling that stamped the medals during the war still existed and was put right back into action to stamp out yet more Iron Crosses.

These post-war crosses that were made from the original dies are best referred to as **restrikes**.

Since the supply of originals, copies and restrikes didn't meet the demand for Iron Crosses, factories decided to make **reproductions** of the originals, either by creating new tooling or making a mold to produce castings that were then finished to look as close as possible to the original crosses. When sold as reproductions, some of the demand is adequately met.

And finally, some folks just can't resist the lure of easy money. They will do whatever it takes to inexpensively produce an item that they can sell to an unsuspecting customer as an original. Whether they alter and misrepresent an original, copy, restrike or reproduction, they are producing a **fake**. It is illegal to do so but very difficult to prove intent. Therefore, a lot of people sell spurious medals. Use caution out there!

Note about pricing:

• *The following pricing does not address medals authorized after 1946.*

• *Many medals have a miniature counterpart. The following prices do not cover any miniatures, though rarity of miniatures is roughly proportionate to the rarity of full-sized examples.*

• *The values of medals for which no recent report sales were reported are denoted with "n/a" (not available) for price.*

BELGIUM

Croix de Guerre, Type II (1940-45). **$30 (£18)**
Armed Resistance Medal. **$20 (£12)**
Volunteers Medal. **$20 (£12)**
Maritime Medal. **$25 (£16)**
War Commemorative Medal. **$25 (£16)**
Merit Cross for Military Chaplains. **$390 (£242)**
Abyssinia Campaign Medal with bar. **$25 (£16)**
Abyssinia Campaign without bar. **$20 (£12)**
Africa Service Medal without bar. **$20 (£12)**
Africa Service Medal with Nigerie bar. **$25 (£16)**
Africa Service Medal with Moyen Orient bar. **$25 (£16)**
Africa Service Medal with Madagascar bar. **$25 (£16)**
Africa Service Medal with Birmaniae bar. **$25 (£16)**

BRAZIL

Expeditionary Cross, First Class. **$85 (£53)**
Expeditionary Cross, Second Class. **$60 (£37)**
South Atlantic Anti-Submarine Patrol Medal. **$60 (£37)**

BULGARIA

Bulgaria Military Order for Bravery, 4th Class, 1st Grade. **$150-$200 (£93-£124)**
Hermann-Historica.de

Bulgarian Military Service Order, Commander. **$535 (£332)**
Hermann-Historica.de

Bulgarian Pilot's Badge, 1935-1944. **$580-$650 (£360-£403)**
Hermann-Historica.de

Bulgarian Military Merit Order, Grand Officer (2nd Class) and Commander's Cross (3rd Class). **$845 (£524)**
Hermann-Historica.de

Bulgarian Military Merit Order, Commander's Cross (3rd Class) with Swords. **$845 (£524)**
Hermann-Historica.de

Military Order of Bravery, III Class, Grade 1. **$130 (£80)**
Military Order of Bravery, III Class, Grade 2. **$127 (£78)**
Military Order of Bravery, IV Class, Grade 1. **$106 (£65)**
Military Order of Bravery, IV Class, Grade 1 without swords. **$114 (£70)**
Military Order of Bravery, IV Class, Grade 2. **$82 (£50)**
Military Order of Bravery, IV Class, Grade 2 without swords. **$106 (£65)**
Military Merit Order, Grand Cross. **$505 (£310)**
Military Merit Order, Grand Cross with war decoration. **$546 (£335)**
Military Merit Order, Grand Cross breast star. **$481 (£295)**
Military Merit Order, Grand Cross breast star with war decoration. **$505 (£310)**
Military Merit Order, Grand Officer. **$342 (£210)**
Military Merit Order, Grand Officer with war decoration. **$399 (£245)**
Military Merit Order, Grand Officer breast star. **$277 (£170)**
Military Merit Order, Grand Officer breast star with war decoration. **$342 (£210)**
Military Merit Order, Commander. **$383 (£235)**
Military Merit Order, Commander with war decoration. **$318 (£195)**
Military Merit Order, Officer. **$302 (£185)**
Military Merit Order, Officer with war decoration. **$318 (£195)**
Military Merit Order, Knight. **$236 (£145)**
Military Merit Order, Knight with crown and war decoration. **$155 (£95)**
Military Merit Order, Knight without crown. **$122 (£75)**
Military Merit Order, Knight with war decoration. **$114 (£70)**
Military Merit Order, Merit Cross with crown. **$73 (£45)**
Military Merit Order, Merit Cross without crown. **$65 (£40)**
Pilot's Badge. **$570 (£350)**
Observer's Badge. **$530 (£325)**

Favorite Find: German Cross

by "Denny from the Sun Coast of Florida"

After receiving my real estate license in the late 1970s, I joined a small company in a suburb of Toledo, Ohio. One of the fledgling realtors (along with myself) was a wonderful lady named Jean. Her husband had been a fighter pilot with the 8th Air Force in Europe in 1944 and 1945 and had the opportunity to send back a footlocker full of German war souvenirs. They were apparently liberated from Schloss Klessheim near Salsburg.

Jean's husband died at a very young age. Many years passed before she decided to sell some of her husband's war booty. I became the very happy recipient of a German Cross in silver in its original case and still packaged in the original cellophane.

I think of Jean often, and the sacrifices both she and her husband made during the war years.

CHINA

Order of the Cloud and Banner, IV Class. **$693 (£425)**
Order of the Cloud and Banner, V Class. **$611 (£375)**
Order of the Cloud and Banner, VI Class. **$530 (£325)**
Order of the Cloud and Banner, VII Class. **$391 (£240)**
Order of the Cloud and Banner, VIII Class. **$350 (£215)**
Order of the Cloud and Banner, IX Class. **$285 (£175)**
Order of Victory. **$489 (£300)**
Decoration for American Troops, Type I, numbered. **$106 (£65)**
Decoration for American Troops, Type II, unnumbered. **$57 (£35)**
Decoration for American Troops, Type III, U.S.-made. **$16 (£10)**

CROATIA (also see YUGOSLAVIA)

Croatian Golden Badge of Honor for aircraft pilots.
$700-$800 (£434-£496)
Hermann-Historica.de

Order of the Crown of Zvonimir, Grand Cross. **$733 (£450)**
Order of the Crown of Zvonimir, Grand Cross with swords. **$774 (£475)**
Order of the Crown of Zvonimir, Grand Cross with oak leaves. **$799 (£490)**
Order of the Crown of Zvonimir, Grand Cross breast star. **$693 (£425)**
Order of the Crown of Zvonimir, Grand Cross breast star with swords. **$733 (£450)**
Order of the Crown of Zvonimir, Grand Cross breast star with oak leaves. **$758 (£465)**
Order of the Crown of Zvonimir, Grand Cross, I Class (with star). **$652 (£400)**
Order of the Crown of Zvonimir, Grand Cross, I Class with swords (with star). **$693 (£425)**
Order of the Crown of Zvonimir, Grand Cross, I Class with oak leaves (with star). **$652 (£400)**
Order of the Crown of Zvonimir, Grand Cross, I Class (without star). **$571 (£350)**
Order of the Crown of Zvonimir, Grand Cross, I Class with swords (without star). **$611 (£375)**
Order of the Crown of Zvonimir, Grand Cross, I Class with oak leaves (without star). **$571 (£350)**
Order of the Crown of Zvonimir, Grand Cross, I Class, breast star. **$652 (£400)**
Order of the Crown of Zvonimir, Grand Cross, I Class breast star with swords. **$693 (£425)**
Order of the Crown of Zvonimir, Grand Cross, I Class breast star with oak leaves. **$595 (£365)**
Order of the Crown of Zvonimir, Grand Cross, II Class. **$448 (£275)**
Order of the Crown of Zvonimir, Grand Cross, II Class with swords. **$489 (£300)**
Order of the Crown of Zvonimir, Grand Cross, II Class with oak leaves. **$513 (£315)**
Order of the Crown of Zvonimir, Grand Cross, III Class. **$408 (£250)**
Order of the Crown of Zvonimir, Grand Cross, III Class with swords. **$432 (£265)**
Order of the Crown of Zvonimir, Grand Cross, III Class with oak leaves. **$448 (£275)**
Order of the Crown of Zvonimir, Grand Cross, Silver Medal. **$326 (£200)**
Order of the Crown of Zvonimir, Grand Cross, Silver Medal with oak leaves. **$350 (£215)**

Order of the Crown of Zvonimir, Grand Cross, Bronze Medal. **$285 (£175)**
Order of the Crown of Zvonimir, Grand Cross, Bronze Medal with oak leaves. **$309 (£190)**
Order of the Crown of Zvonimir, Grand Cross, Iron Medal. **$147 (£90)**
Order of the Crown of Zvonimir, Grand Cross, Iron Medal with oak leaves. **$122 (£75)**
Order of the Iron Trefoil, I Class. **$652 (£400)**
Order of the Iron Trefoil, I Class with oak leaves. **$693 (£425)**
Order of the Iron Trefoil, II Class. **$571 (£350)**
Order of the Iron Trefoil, II Class with oak leaves. **$611 (£375)**
Order of the Iron Trefoil, III Class. **$432 (£265)**
Order of the Iron Trefoil, III Class with oak leaves. **$478 (£290)**
Order of the Iron Trefoil, IV Class. **$350 (£215)**
Order of the Iron Trefoil, IV Class with oak leaves. **$391 (£240)**
Croatia Order of Merit, Grand Cross (Christian). **$611 (£375)**
Croatia Order of Merit, Grand Cross (Muslim). **$1,141 (£700)**
Croatia Order of Merit, Grand Cross, breast star (Christian). **$611 (£375)**
Croatia Order of Merit, Grand Cross, breast star (Muslim). **$1,141 (£700)**
Croatia Order of Merit, I Class, with star (Christian). **$448 (£275)**
Croatia Order of Merit, I Class, with star (Muslim). **$774 (£475)**
Croatia Order of Merit, I Class, (Christian). **$432 (£265)**
Croatia Order of Merit, I Class, (Muslim). **$758 (£465)**
Croatia Order of Merit, I Class, breast star (Christian). **$448 (£275)**
Croatia Order of Merit, I Class, breast star (Muslim). **$774 (£475)**
Croatia Order of Merit, II Class (Christian). **$367 (£225)**
Croatia Order of Merit, II Class (Muslim). **$571 (£350)**
Croatia Order of Merit, III Class (Christian). **$350 (£215)**
Croatia Order of Merit, III Class (Muslim). **$489 (£300)**
Medal For Bravery, Gold. **$448 (£275)**
Medal For Bravery, Silver. **$350 (£215)**
Medal For Bravery, Silver, next-of-kin, officer. **$245 (£150)**
Medal For Bravery, Bronze. **$139 (£85)**
Wound Medal, Gold. **$155 (£95)**
Wound Medal, Iron. **$106 (£65)**
Independence Commemorative Medal. **$179 (£110)**
Incorporation of Dalmatia Medal. **n/a**
Labor Service Sports Badge. **$220 (£135)**
Army Legion Badge. **$318 (£195)**
Naval Legion Badge. **$375 (£230)**
Air Force Legion Badge. **$375 (£230)**
Pilot's Badge. **$571 (£350)**
Air Crew Radio Operator Badge. **$478 (£290)**
Croat Legion Badge. **$522 (£320)**

Values at a Glance

Commonly encountered medals:

• German Iron Cross, II Class	$95
• German Wound Badge, black	$30
• German War Merit Cross, II Class	$25
• U.S. Bronze Star	$25
• U.S. Purple Heart (not named)	$65
• Japanese Manchurian Incident Medal	$25
• British 1939-45 Star	$25

CZECHOSLOVAKIA (also see SLOVAKIA)

Czechoslovakian Order of the White Lion, Merit Medal, I Class. **$163-$236 (£100-£145)**
George S. Cuhaj

Czechoslovakian Bravery Medal. **$106-$139 (£65-£85)**
George S. Cuhaj

Czechoslovakian War Cross, 1939. **$16-$24 (£10-£15)**
George S. Cuhaj

Czechoslovakian Campaign Medal, 1939-45, with bar. **$33-$41 (£20-£25)**
George S. Cuhaj

Czechoslovakian Merit Medal, I Class. **$41-$49 (£25-£30)**
George S. Cuhaj

Czechoslovakian Merit Medal, II Class. **$24-$29 (£15-£18)**
George S. Cuhaj

Order of Charles IV, Grand Cross. **$530 (£325)**
Order of Charles IV, Grand Cross breast star. **$562 (£345)**
Order of Charles IV, Commander, neck badge. **$440 (£270)**
Order of Charles IV, Commander with swords. **$465 (£285)**
Order of Charles IV, Officer. **$432 (£265)**
Order of Charles IV, Officer with swords. **$277 (£170)**
Order of Charles IV, Knight. **$122 (£75)**
Order of Charles IV, Knight with swords. **$98 (£60)**
Order of Charles IV, Merit Medal. **$82 (£50)**
Military Order of the White Lion, I Class breast star with gold swords. **$1,141 (£700)**
Military Order of the White Lion, II Class breast star with silver swords. **$978 (£600)**
Military Order of the White Lion, III Class breast badge. **$375 (£230)**
Military Order of the White Lion, Merit Medal, I Class. **$236 (£145)**
Military Order of the White Lion, Merit Medal, II Class. **$196 (£120)**
Officer's Order of Jan Ziska, I Class. **$1,459 (£895)**
Officer's Order of Jan Ziska, II Class. **$807 (£495)**
Officer's Order of Jan Ziska, II Class. **$375 (£230)**
Military Order for Liberty, II Class. **$375 (£230)**
Military Order for Liberty, II Class. **$277 (£170)**
Bravery Medal. **$139 (£85)**
Merit Medal, I Class. **$49 (£30)**
Merit Medal, II Class. **$29 (£18)**

Slovak Commemorative Medal. **$49 (£30)**
War Cross, 1939. **$24 (£15)**
Campaign Medal, 1939-45. **$29 (£18)**
Campaign Medal, 1939-45 with bar. **$40 (£25)**
Cross for Political Prisoners. **$73 (£45)**

DENMARK

Order of the Dannebrog, Type VII, Grand Cross. **$1,223 (£750)**
Order of the Dannebrog, Type VII, Grand Cross breast star. **$1,223 (£750)**
Order of the Dannebrog, Type VII, Commander. **$815 (£500)**
Order of the Dannebrog, Type VII, Commander breast star. **$693 (£425)**
Order of the Dannebrog, Type VII, Commander. **$408 (£250)**
Order of the Dannebrog, Type VII, Knight. **$122 (£75)**
Christian X's War Participation Medal. **$310 (£190)**

ENGLAND

Note: *Attribution greatly affects the prices of U.K. medals. Many medals have the recipient's name on the rim or reverse, that, in turn, can be researched. Prices reflect the base prices of named but unresearched examples.*

British Order of the Empire, Fifth Class. **$140-$175 (£87-£109)**
AdvanceGuardMilitaria.com

British Military Cross. **$600-$750 (£372-£465)**
AdvanceGuardMilitaria.com

British World War II Efficiency Medal: Highland Light Infantry. **$95-$125 (£59-£78)**
AdvanceGuardMilitaria.com

British 1937-48 Army Long Service and Good Conduct Medal. **$100-$135 (£62-£84)**
AdvanceGuardMilitaria.com

British New Zealand Service Medal (reverse illustrated). **$30-$40 (£19-£25)**
AdvanceGuardMilitaria.com

Indian Army Long Service and Good Conduct Medal, 11th Sikh Regiment. **$120-$145 (£74-£90)**
AdvanceGuardMilitaria.com

British Atlantic Star with France and Germany clasp. $80-$95 (£50-£59)

AdvanceGuardMilitaria.com

British 1939-1945 Star. $20-30 (£12-£18)

Colin R. Bruce II

British France and Germany Star. $20-$30 (£12-£18)

AdvanceGuardMilitaria.com

British Africa Service Medal. $35-$40 (£22-£25)

AdvanceGuardMilitaria.com

British Royal Naval Reserve Long Service and Good Conduct Medal (reverse illustrated). $85-$100 (£53-£62)

AdvanceGuardMilitaria.com

British Special Constabulary Long Service Medal. $45-$65 (£28-£40)

AdvanceGuardMilitaria.com

British World War II War Medal (reverse illustrated). $10-$15 (£6-£9)

AdvanceGuardMilitaria.com

British India Service Medal (reverse illustrated). $15-$20 (£9-£12)

AdvanceGuardMilitaria.com

Irish Emergency Medal, Local Defence Force. $40-$55 (£25-£34)

AdvanceGuardMilitaria.com

Victoria Cross. **$244,500 (£150,000)**
George Cross, Service Award. **$40,750 (£25,000)**
Distinguished Service Order. **$2,445 (£1,500)**
Imperial Service Order, Male. **$490 (£300)**
Imperial Service Order, Female. **$1,956 (£1,200)**
Imperial Service Medal. **$32 (£20)**
Indian Order of Merit, Reward for Gallantry, I Class. **n/a**
Indian Order of Merit, Reward for Gallantry, II Class. **$1,223 (£750)**
Indian Order of Merit, For Bravery. **$4,075 (£2,500)**
Royal Red Cross, I Class. **$571 (£350)**
Royal Red Cross, II Class. **$408 (£250)**
Distinguished Service Cross. **$1,223 (£750)**
Military Cross. **$734 (£450)**
Military Cross, one bar. **$1,141 (£700)**
Distinguished Flying Cross. **$2,934 (£1,800)**
Distinguished Flying Cross, one bar. **$3,260 (£2,000)**
Air Force Cross. **$1,630 (£1,000)**
Air Force Cross, one bar. **$2,608 (£1,600)**
Order of British India, I Class. **$1,630 (£1,000)**
Order of British India, II Class. **$1,630 (£1,000)**
Order of Burma. **$6,520 (£4,000)**
Kaisar-I-Hind Medal, I Class. **$1,956 (£1,200)**
Kaisar-I-Hind Medal, II Class. **$571 (£350)**
Albert Medal, Gold, Sea, civilian. **$16,300 (£10,000)**
Albert Medal, Gold, Sea, service. **$19,560 (£12,000)**
Albert Medal, Bronze, Sea, civilian. **$13,040 (£8,000)**
Albert Medal, Bronze, Sea, service. **$14,670 (£9,000)**
Albert Medal, Gold, Land, civilian. **$16,300 (£10,000)**
Albert Medal, Gold, Land, service. **$19,560 (£12,000)**
Albert Medal, Bronze, Land, civilian. **$13,040 (£8,000)**
Albert Medal, Bronze, Land, service. **$13,040 (£8,000)**
Union of South Africa King's Medal for Bravery, gold. **$3,260 (£2,000)**
Union of South Africa King's Medal for Bravery, silver. **$2,445 (£1,500)**
Distinguished Conduct Medal. **$6,520 (£4,000)**
Conspicuous Gallantry Medal, Navy/Royal Marines. **$16,300 (£10,000)**
Conspicuous Gallantry Medal, Royal Air Force. **$16,300 (£10,000)**
George Medal, civilian. **$4,890 (£3,000)**
George Medal, Service. **$5,710 (£3,500)**
Indian Distinguished Service Medal. **$1,550 (£950)**
Burma Gallantry Medal. **$5,705 (£3,500)**
Distinguished Service Medal. **$1,386 (£850)**
Military Medal, Corps. **$1,630 (£1,000)**
Military Medal, Regiment. **$2,445 (£1,500)**
Distinguished Flying Medal. **$3,260 (£2,000)**
Air Force Medal. **$3,260 (£2,000)**
King's Medal for Courage in the Cause of Freedom. **$408 (£250)**
King's Medal for Service in the Cause of Freedom. **$408 (£250)**
King's Medal for Native Chiefs, gilt. **$1,630 (£1,000)**
King's Medal for Native Chiefs, silver. **$978 (£600)**
1939-45 Star. **$16 (£10)**
1939-45 Star with Battle of Britain clasp. **$2,445 (£1,500)**
Atlantic Star. **$49 (£30)**

British Indian Recruiting Badge. $65-$85 (£40-£53)

AdvanceGuardMilitaria.com

British Africa Star Medal with North Africa clasp. $40-$50 (£25-£31)

AdvanceGuardMilitaria.com

Atlantic Star with Air Crew Europe clasp. **$106 (£65)**
Atlantic Star with France and Germany clasp. **$90 (£55)**
Air Crew Europe Star. **$408 (£250)**
Air Crew Europe Star with Atlantic clasp. **$505 (£310)**
Air Crew Europe Star with France and Germany Class. **$440 (£270)**
Africa Star. **$20 (£12)**
Africa Star with 8th Army clasp. **$52 (£32)**
Africa Star with 1st Army clasp. **$52 (£32)**
Africa Star with North Africa 1942-43 clasp. **$52 (£32)**
Pacific Star. **$57 (£35)**
Pacific Star with Burma clasp. **$122 (£75)**
Burma Star. **$25 (£15)**
Burma Star with Pacific clasp. **$90 (£55)**
Italy Star. **$20 (£12)**
France and Germany Star. **$30 (£18)**
France and Germany Star with Atlantic clasp. **$127 (£78)**
Defence Medal, cupro-nickel. **$26 (£16)**
Defence Medal, silver (Canadian). **$40 (£25)**
War Medal, 1939-45, cupro-nickel. **$16 (£10)**
War Medal, 1939-45, named (Australian or South African). **$32 (£20)**
War Medal, 1939-45, silver (Canadian). **$41 (£25)**
King's Badge for War Service. **$25 (£15)**
Irish Emergency Service Medal, Local Defence. **$57 (£35)**
India Service Medal. **$20 (£12)**
British Indian Recruiting Badge. **$65 (£40)**
Canadian Volunteer Service Medal. **$49 (£30)**
Canadian Volunteer Service Medal with Maple Leaf clasp. **$49 (£30)**
Canadian Volunteer Service Medal with Dieppe clasp. **$57 (£35)**
Canadian Volunteer Service Medal with Hong Kong clasp. **$57 (£35)**
Canadian Memorial Cross. **$196 (£120)**
Africa Service Medal. **$41 (£25)**
Australia Service Medal. **$65 (£40)**
New Zealand Service Medal. **$40 (£25)**
New Zealand Memorial Cross. **$147 (£90)**
South African Medal for War Service. **$57 (£35)**
Southern Rhodesia War Service Medal. **$424 (£260)**
Newfoundland Volunteer War Service Medal. **$734 (£450)**
Royal Marines Meritorious Service Medal. **$978 (£600)**
Army Meritorious Service Medal, crowned profile. **$1,386 (£850)**
Army Meritorious Service Medal, coinage profile. **$408 (£250)**
Indian Army Meritorious Service Medal. **$139 (£85)**
Royal Household Faithful Service Medal. **$571 (£350)**
Royal Naval Long Service and Good Conduct Medal. **$114 (£70)**
Royal Naval Reserve Decoration. **$245 (£150)**
Royal Naval Reserve Long Service and Good Conduct Medal. **$90 (£55)**
Royal Naval Volunteer Reserve Decoration. **$228 (£140)**
Royal Naval Volunteer Reserve Long Service and Good Conduct Medal. **$82 (£50)**
Royal Fleet Reserve Long Service and Good Conduct Medal. **$73 (£45)**
Royal Naval Auxiliary Sick Berth Reserve Long Service and Good Conduct Medal. **$163 (£100)**
Royal Naval Auxiliary Reserve Long Service and Good Conduct Medal. **$408 (£250)**
Rocket Apparatus Volunteer Long Service Medal, Board of Trade. **$155 (£95)**
Rocket Apparatus Volunteer Long Service Medal, Rocket Apparatus. **$155 (£95)**
Army Long Service and Good Conduct Medal. **$82 (£50)**
Army Long Service and Good Conduct Medal with Commonwealth bar. **$122 (£75)**
Efficiency Decoration. **$139 (£85)**
Efficiency Medal. **$82 (£50)**
Indian Army Long Service and Good Conduct Medal (Indian). **$90 (£55)**
King's African Rifles Long Service and Good Conduct Medal. **$408 (£250)**
South Africa Permanent Force Long Service and Good Conduct Medal. **$236 (£145)**
Efficiency Medal (South Africa). **$106 (£65)**
Voluntary Medical Service Medal, silver. **$40 (£25)**
Voluntary Medical Service Medal, cupro-nickel. **$25 (£15)**
Service Medal of the Order of St. John, silver. **$33 (£20)**
Service Medal of the Order of St. John, base metal. **$25 (£15)**

Royal Air Force Long Service and Good Conduct Medal. **$82 (£50)**
Air Efficiency Award. **$245 (£150)**
Special Constabulary Long Service Medal. **$25 (£15)**
Colonial Police Long Service Medal. **$122 (£75)**
Hong Kong Royal Naval Dockyard Police Long Service Medal. **$652 (£400)**
Colonial Fire Brigade Long Service Medal. **$489 (£300)**
Ceylon Fire Brigade Long Service and Good Conduct Medal. **$489 (£300)**
South African Prison Service Faithful Service Medal. **$65 (£40)**

FINLAND

Order of the Liberty Cross, Type II, Grand Cross. **$571 (£350)**
Order of the Liberty Cross, Type II, Grand Cross with swords and diamonds. **$652 (£400)**
Order of the Liberty Cross, Type II, Grand Cross breast star. **$1,100 (£675)**
Order of the Liberty Cross, Type II, Grand Cross breast star with swords. **$1,345 (£825)**
Order of the Liberty Cross, Type II, I Class. **$473 (£290)**
Order of the Liberty Cross, Type II, I Class with swords. **$530 (£325)**
Order of the Liberty Cross, Type II, I Class breast star. **$611 (£375)**
Order of the Liberty Cross, Type II, I Class breast star with swords. **$693 (£425)**
Order of the Liberty Cross, Type II, II Class. **$245 (£150)**
Order of the Liberty Cross, Type II, II Class with swords. **$228 (£140)**
Order of the Liberty Cross, Type II, II Class with red cross. **$489 (£300)**
Order of the Liberty Cross, Type II, III Class. **$163 (£100)**
Order of the Liberty Cross, Type II, III Class with swords. **$188 (£115)**
Order of the Liberty Cross, Type II, III Class with red cross. **$408 (£250)**
Order of the Liberty Cross, Type II, IV Class. **$245 (£150)**
Order of the Liberty Cross, Type II, IV Class with swords. **$163 (£100)**
Order of the Liberty Cross, Type II, IV Class with red cross. **$367 (£225)**
Order of the Liberty Cross, Type II, Liberty Medal I Class. **$65 (£40)**
Order of the Liberty Cross, Type II, Liberty Medal I Class with red cross. **$163 (£100)**
Order of the Liberty Cross, Type II, Liberty Medal II Class. **$49 (£30)**
Order of the Liberty Cross, Type II, Liberty Medal II Class with red cross. **$122 (£75)**
Order of the Liberty Cross, Type II, Merit Medal I Class. **$40 (£25)**
Order of the Liberty Cross, Type II, Merit Medal II Class. **$33 (£20)**
Order of the Liberty Cross, Type II, Merit Medal III Class. **$25 (£15)**
Order of the Liberty Cross, Type III, I Class. **$571 (£350)**
Order of the Liberty Cross, Type III, I Class with swords. **$652 (£400)**
Order of the Liberty Cross, Type III, I Class with oak leaves and swords. **$717 (£440)**
Order of the Liberty Cross, Type III, I Class breast star. **$611 (£375)**
Order of the Liberty Cross, Type III, I Class breast star with swords. **$652 (£400)**
Order of the Liberty Cross, Type III, I Class breast star with oak leaves and swords. **$1,100 (£675)**
Order of the Liberty Cross, Type III, II Class breast badge. **$245 (£150)**
Order of the Liberty Cross, Type III, II Class breast badge with swords. **$285 (£175)**
Order of the Liberty Cross, Type III, II Class breast badge with oak leaves and swords. **$310 (£190)**
Order of the Liberty Cross, Type III, III Class. **$188 (£115)**
Order of the Liberty Cross, Type III, III Class with swords. **$204 (£125)**
Order of the Liberty Cross, Type III, III Class with red cross. **$367 (£225)**
Order of the Liberty Cross, Type III, III Class with oak leaves and swords. **$220 (£135)**

Order of the Liberty Cross, Type III, IV Class. **$204 (£125)**
Order of the Liberty Cross, Type III, IV Class with swords.
 $106 (£65)
Order of the Liberty Cross, Type III, IV Class with red cross.
 $391 (£240)
Order of the Liberty Cross, Type III, IV Class with oak leaves and
 swords. **$269 (£165)**
Order of the Liberty Cross, Type III, Liberty Medal I Class.
 $40 (£25)
Order of the Liberty Cross, Type III, Liberty Medal I Class with red
 cross. **$187 (£115)**
Order of the Liberty Cross, Type III, Liberty Medal II Class.
 $33 (£20)
Order of the Liberty Cross, Type III, Liberty Medal II Class with
 red cross. **$147 (£90)**
Order of the Liberty Cross, Type III, Merit Medal I Class. **$57 (£35)**
Order of the Liberty Cross, Type III, Merit Medal I Class next of
 kin. **$41 (£25)**
Order of the Liberty Cross, Type III, Merit Medal II Class.
 $33 (£20)
Order of the Liberty Cross, Type III, Merit Medal III Class.
 $16 (£10)
Campaign Medal, 1939-40. **$16 (£10)**
Campaign Medal, 1939-40 with swords. **$25 (£15)**
Campaign Medal for Foreign Volunteers. **$33 (£20)**
Kainuu Cross, 1939-40. **$41 (£25)**
Keski-Kannas Cross, 1939-40. **$41 (£25)**
Kolvisto Cross, 1939-40. **$41 (£25)**
Kollaa Cross, 1939-40. **$57 (£35)**
Lappland Cross, 1939-40. **$57 (£35)**
Ladoga Medal, 1939-40. **$57 (£35)**
Lansi-Kannas Cross, 1939-40. **$41 (£25)**
Ladoga Medal, 1939-40. **$41 (£25)**
Mohia Cross, 1939-40. **$41 (£25)**
Pitkaranta Cross, 1939-40. **$41 (£25)**
Summa Cross, 1939-40. **$41 (£25)**
Taipale Cross, 1939-40. **$41 (£25)**
Tolvajarvi Cross, 1939-40. **$41 (£25)**
War Wound Badge, 1939-40. **$65 (£40)**
War Wound Badge, 1939-40 and 1941-44. **$122 (£75)**
War with USSR 1941-45. **$12 (£7)**

FRANCE

French Order of the
Legion of Honor.
$65-$80 (£40-£50)
AdvanceGuardMilitaria.com

French Croix de
Guerre, 1939-45.
$25-$35 (£16-£22)
AdvanceGuardMilitaria.com

French Medal for
Voluntary Service
in Free France.
$15-$25 (£9-£16)
AdvanceGuardMilitaria.com

French medal for
deportees and
interned resisters.
$25-$35 (£16-£22)
AdvanceGuardMilitaria.com.

Ordre National
du Travail Medal,
Vichy Period.
$2,010 (£1,246)
Hermann-Historica.de

Médaille Coloniale
de l'Etat Francais,
Vichy Period.
$1,630 (£1,010)
Hermann-Historica.de

Favorite Find: German Order Medal

by Mike Morris, Texas Weapon Collector Gun Shows

The German Order Medal traveled to the Fort Worth, Texas, Gun Show in a shoebox full of medals. A garage sale picker brought them in for me. He wanted $400 for each medal, which was high for some and low for others. He wanted $500 for a Spanish Cross with Swords, though. I offered $400, like all the others, when he decided to call his wife. She said, "Just bring it back," which he did.

I did buy this German Order Medal with pinback suspension, however. I contacted a prominent collector about it and sent him scans as I had never seen one before. Apparently it is one of five made. He offered me over $10,000 for it!

I'm still a very devoted collector after 50 years, so I decided to hang onto it for a while. It's like a new

Corvette—ya gotta drive it a while.

After some research, I learned there was only one pinback medal awarded! This piece has enough legitimate wear that it could very well be the one described. If only the picker had acquired some provenance when he bought the shoebox of medals!

Croix de Compagnon de la Libération. **$200-$300 (£124-£186)**
Hermann-Historica.de

Médaille du Levant with Levant 1941 bar, Vichy Period. **$100-$165 (£62-£102)**
Hermann-Historica.de

Vichy Croix de Guerre "1939-1940," double ring suspension, three stars. **$95-$125 (£59-£78)**
Hermann-Historica.de

Order of Military Merit, Commander. **$147 (£90)**
Order of Military Merit, Officer. **$41 (£25)**
Order of Military Merit, Knight. **$33 (£20)**
Croix de Guerre, undated. **$25 (£15)**
Croix de Guerre, 1939. **$33 (£20)**
Croix de Guerre, 1939-45. **$33 (£20)**
Combat Cross. **$12 (£7)**
Escaped Prisoners Medal. **$12 (£7)**
Combat Volunteers Cross. **$16 (£10)**
Resistance Medal, I Class. **$16 (£10)**
Resistance Medal, II Class. **$12 (£7)**
Wound Medal, combat. **$12 (£7)**
Wound Medal, non-combat. **$8 (£5)**
Deportees Medal. **$8 (£5)**
Medal for Internees. **$8 (£5)**
Reconnaissance Francaise, Type II, I Class. **$41 (£25)**
Reconnaissance Francaise, Type II, II Class. **$25 (£15)**
Reconnaissance Francaise, Type II, III Class. **$16 (£10)**
Volunteers Medal. **$8 (£5)**
Cross of Voluntary Military Service, Army/Navy. **$8 (£5)**
Cross of Voluntary Military Service, Air Force. **$12 (£7)**
Colonial Medal, large type. **$25 (£15)**
Colonial Medal, small type. **$12 (£7)**
Free French Cross. **$12 (£7)**
Prisoner of War Medal. **$12 (£7)**
World War II Commemorative Medal. **$8 (£5)**
Medal of Liberated France. **$41 (£25)**
Italian Campaign 1943-44. **$33 (£20)**
Military Chaplain's Cross. **$204 (£125)**

FRANCE, VICHY

Croix de Guerre. **$65 (£40)**
Combat Cross, 1939-40. **$163 (£100)**
Black Africa Merit Medal. **$228 (£140)**
Levant Medal. **$41 (£25)**
Colonial Medal. **$41 (£25)**

GERMANY

Note: Prices are affected by maker's marks and material of construction. Prices represent the lowest price on the spectrum, i.e., unmarked and lowest quality of material.

Civil Awards

Croix de la 1re Armée de France, Vichy Period. **$940 (£583)**
Hermann-Historica.de

Vichy Railway Service Medal. **$65-$85 (£40-£53)**
Colin R. Bruce II

Ordre de la Francisque Gallique, Vichy Period. **$300-$400 (£186-£248)**
Hermann-Historica.de

Légion des Volontaires Francais (LVF) Croix de Guerre, Vichy Period, second model, with palm. **$1,000-$1,650 (£620-£1,023)**
Hermann-Historica.de

TeNo (Technischen Nothilfe) Honor Badge 1922, cased. **$800-$1,000 (£496-£620)**
Hermann-Historica.de

Order of the German Eagle, IV Class. **$1,500-$1,800 (£930-£1,116)**
Hermann-Historica.de

Order of the German Eagle, V Class with swords.
$1,000-$1,300
(£620-£806)
Hermann-Historica.de

Annexation of the Sudetenland 1.
Oktober 1938 in case.
$100-$125 (£62-£78)
HistoryHunter.com

German Olympic Games Commemorative Medal in case.
$335-$400 (£208-£248)
HistoryHunter.com

Germanic Proficiency Runes, SS in silver with sales carton.
$16,750 (£10,385)
Hermann-Historica.de

German Olympic Decoration, II Class with award document.
$2,145 (£1,330)
Hermann-Historica.de

SA Defense Badge for War Disabled. $300-$400 (£186-£248)
Chris William

German Horse Driver's Badge, bronze. $185-$200 (£115-£124)
HistoryHunter.com

Gendarmerie Alpine Award. $3,000-$3,400 (£1,860-£2,108)
Hermann-Historica.de

Police Ski Leader Badge. $3,000-$3,400 (£1,860-£2,108)
Hermann-Historica.de

Hitler Youth Achievement Badge, silver. $95-$135 (£59-£84)
Chris William

German Red Cross Honor Badge Cross, 3rd Model. $1,610 (£998)
Hermann-Historica.de

Hitler Youth Leader Sports Badge. $400 (£248)
Hermann-Historica.de

Police Mountain Guide Badge. $4,200-$4,700 (£2,604-£2,914)
Hermann-Historica.de

Anti-Partisan War Badge in gold, half-hollow issue. $10,050 (£6,231)
Hermann-Historica.de

Type II National Sports Badge, III Class. $45-$65 (£28-£40)
AdvanceGuardMilitaria.com

BDM Achievement Badge, bronze. $150-165 (£93-£102)
Chris William

NSDAP Long Service Cross, 25 years. $45-$65 (£28-£40)
AdvanceGuardMilitaria.com

Gendarmerie High Mountain Guide Badge. $3,200-$3,400 (£1,984-£2,108)
Hermann-Historica.de

SS Long Service Award, 3rd Class for eight years. $900-$1,100 (£558-£682)
Chris William

SS Long Service Award, 4th Class for four years. $650-$850 (£403-£527)
Chris William

NSDAP Long Service Decoration, Special Class "50." $50-$425 (£31-£264)
HistoryHunter.com

German Youth Achievement Badge, black. **$195-$225 (£121-£140)**
Chris William

Third Reich Mother's Cross, silver. **$65-$75 (£40-£47)**
AdvanceGuardMilitaria.com

Victors' Badge, National Trade Competition, 2nd Model, Kreissieger, 1938. **$285-$300 (£177-£186)**
Chris William

Hitler Youth Achievement Badge, bronze. **$85-$125 (£53-£78)**
Chris William

Hitler Youth Shooting Badge. **$75-$95 (£47-£59)**
Chris William

Third Reich Annexation of Austria, March 13, 1938, Medal. **$75-$100 (£47-£62)**
AdvanceGuardMilitaria.com

Order of the German Eagle, Grand Cross. **$12,000 (£7,400)**
Order of the German Eagle, Grand Cross with swords. **$13,500 (£8,370)**
Order of the German Eagle, Grand Cross breast star. **$9,000 (£5,580)**
Order of the German Eagle, Grand Cross breast star with swords. **$11,000 (£6,820)**
Order of the German Eagle, I Class. **$9,500 (£5,890)**
Order of the German Eagle, I Class with swords. **$11,500 (£7,130)**
Order of the German Eagle, I Class breast star. **$7,000 (£4,340)**
Order of the German Eagle, I Class breast star with swords. **$8,000 (£4,960)**
Order of the German Eagle, II Class. **$2,700 (£1,674)**
Order of the German Eagle, II Class with swords. **$3,000 (£1,860)**
Order of the German Eagle, II Class breast star. **$4,700 (£2,914)**
Order of the German Eagle, II Class breast star with swords. **$5,500 (£3,410)**
Order of the German Eagle, III Class. **$2,700 (£1,674)**
Order of the German Eagle, III Class with swords. **$3,000 (£1,860)**
Order of the German Eagle, IV Class pinback. **$1,800 (£1,116)**
Order of the German Eagle, IV Class pinback with swords. **$2,000 (£1,240)**
Order of the German Eagle, Silver Merit Medal, Gothic. **$810 (£502)**
Order of the German Eagle, Silver Merit Medal, Gothic with swords. **$950 (£589)**
Order of the German Eagle, Silver Merit Medal, Roman. **$810 (£502)**
Order of the German Eagle, Silver Merit Medal, Roman with swords. **$950 (£589)**
Order of the German Eagle, Bronze Merit Medal. **$540 (£335)**
Order of the German Eagle, Bronze Merit Medal with swords. **$675 (£419)**
Honor Cross with swords. **$10 (£6)**

Honor Cross without swords. **$15 (£9)**
Honor Cross for next-of-kin (blackened iron). **$30 (£18)**
Lifesaving Medal. **$400 (£248)**
Mother's Cross, Type I, gold. **$2,700 (£1,674)**
Mother's Cross, Type I, silver. **$2,700 (£1,674)**
Mother's Cross, Type I, bronze. **$2,700 (£1,674)**
Mother's Cross, Type II, gold. **$70 (£43)**
Mother's Cross, Type II, silver. **$55 (£34)**
Mother's Cross, Type II, bronze. **$35 (£22)**
Fire Service Cross, I Class pinback. **n/a**
Fire Service Cross, I Class on ribbon. **$880 (£546)**
Fire Service cross, II Class. **$245 (£152)**
Mine Rescue Service Badge, I Class. **$1,500 (£930)**
Mine Rescue Service Badge, II Class. **$375 (£232)**
Air Raid Service Decoration, I Class. **$1,220 (£756)**
Air Raid Service Decoration, II Class. **$95 (£59)**
Civilian Faithful Service Cross, 50 years. **$340 (£211)**
Civilian Faithful Service Decoration, 40 years. **$100 (£62)**
Civilian Faithful Service Decoration, 40 years with oak leaves. **$500 (£310)**
Civilian Faithful Service Decoration, 25years. **$35 (£22)**
Police Long Service, I Class, 25 years. **$230 (£143)**
Police Long Service, II Class, 18 years. **$200 (£124)**
Police Long Service, III Class, 8 years. **$120 (£74)**
Customs Service Decoration. **$340 (£211)**
Labor Service, I Class. **$540 (£335)**
Labor Service, II Class. **$470 (£291)**
Labor Service, III Class. **$160 (£99)**
Labor Service, IV Class. **$135 (£84)**
Labor Service, I Class female. **$675 (£419)**
Labor Service, II Class female. **$540 (£335)**
Labor Service, III Class female. **$270 (£167)**
Labor Service, IV Class female. **$200 (£124)**
Olympic Decoration, I Class. **$2,700 (£1,674)**
Olympic Decoration, II Class. **$1,150 (£713)**
Olympic Medal. **$200 (£124)**
National Sports Badge, Type I, I Class. **$95 (£59)**
National Sports Badge, Type I, II Class. **$70 (£43)**
National Sports Badge, Type I, III Class. **$35 (£22)**
National Sports Badge, Type II, I Class. **$135 (£84)**
National Sports Badge, Type II, II Class. **$95 (£59)**
National Sports Badge, Type II, III Class. **$40 (£25)**
National Youth Sports Badge, Type I,. **$55 (£34)**
National Youth Sports Badge, Type I, female. **$70 (£43)**
National Youth Sports Badge, Type II, . **$55 (£34)**
National Youth Sports Badge, Type II, female. **$80 (£50)**
German Rider's Badge, gold. **$340 (£211)**
German Rider's Badge, silver. **$240 (£149)**
German Rider's Badge, bronze. **$135 (£84)**
German Youth Rider's Badge. **$160 (£99)**
German Horse Driver's Badge, gold. **$610 (£378)**
German Horse Driver's Badge, silver. **$400 (£248)**
German Horse Driver's Badge, bronze. **$200 (£124)**
German Master Rider Badge. **$4,700 (£2,914)**
Badge for Horse Care, gold. **$950 (£589)**
Badge for Horse Care, silver. **$540 (£335)**
Badge for Horse Care, bronze. **$270 (£167)**
Motor Sports Badge, gold. **$4,700 (£2,914)**
Motor Sports Badge, silver. **$2,700 (£1,674)**
Motor Sports Badge, bronze. **$2,000 (£1,240)**
SA Sports Badge, gold. **$365 (£226)**
SA Sports Badge, silver. **$230 (£123)**
SA Sports Badge, bronze. **$75 (£47)**
SA Defense Badge for War Disabled. **$400 (£248)**
Naval SA Sports Badge, Gold. **$2,700 (£1,674)**
Naval SA Sports Badge, Silver. **$2,200 (£1,364)**
Naval SA Sports Badge, Bronze. **$1,900 (£1,178)**
SA Master Riding Badge. **$4,700 (£2,914)**
Germanic Proficiency Runes, silver. **$5,400 (£3,348)**
Germanic Proficiency Runes, bronze. **$4,700 (£2,914)**
Gendarmerie High Alpine Award. **$3,400 (£2,108)**
Gendarmerie Alpine Award. **$3,400 (£2,108)**
Police Expert Skier Award. **$3,400 (£2,108)**
Police Expert Mountain Climber Award. **$4,700 (£2,914)**

DLV Pilot Badge. **$540 (£335)**
DLV Radioman's Badge. **$540 (£335)**
DLV Balloon Pilot, gold. **$2,000 (£1,240)**
DLV Balloon Pilot, silver. **$1,900 (£1,178)**
DLV Balloon Pilot, bronze. **$1,750 (£1,085)**
NSFK Powered Flight Pilot's Badge, Type I. **$1,350 (£837)**
NSFK Powered Flight Pilot's Badge, Type II. **$2,000 (£1,240)**
NSFK Radioman's Badge. **$270 (£167)**
NSFK Free Balloon Badge. **$2,000 (£1,240)**
NSFK Large Glider Pilot's Badge. **$1,600 (£992)**
NSFK Areo-Modeling Proficiency Badge, Class A. **$540 (£335)**
NSFK Areo-Modeling Proficiency Badge, Class B. **$400 (£248)**
NSFK Areo-Modeling Proficiency Badge, Class C. **$340 (£211)**
Blood Order, Type I. **$12,000 (£7.440)**
Blood Order, Type II. **$8,500 (£5,270)**
Golden Party Badge, large (30mm). **$4,000 (£2,480)**
Golden Party Badge, small (24mm). **$2,000 (£1,240)**
Party Badge. **$65 (£40)**
Party Badge for Foreigners. **$2,200 (£1,364)**
Frontbann Badge. **$610 (£378)**
Coburg Decoration. **$4,000 (£2,480)**
Nuremburg Party Day Badge. **$175 (£109)**
Brunswick SA Rally Badge, Type I. **$245 (£152)**
Brunswick SA Rally Badge, Type II. **$190 (£118)**
NSDAP Long Service Cross, 25 years. **$2,700 (£1,674)**
NSDAP Long Service Cross, 15, years. **$610 (£378)**
NSDAP Long Service Cross, 10 years. **$190 (£118)**
Hitler Youth Badge, gold with oak leaves. **$1,350 (£837)**
Hitler Youth Badge, gold. **$200 (£124)**
Hitler Youth Badge. **$45 (£28)**
Hitler Youth Expert Skiing Badge. **$5,400 (£3,348)**
Hitler Youth Leader Sports Badge. **$450 (£279)**
Hitler Youth Achievement Badge, silver. **$95 (£59)**
Hitler Youth Achievement Badge, bronze. **$95 (£59)**
Hitler Youth Achievement Badge, black. **$95 (£59)**
HJ Shooting Badge, Master Shooter. **$675 (£419)**
HJ Shooting Badge, Sniper. **$200 (£124)**
HJ Shooting Badge. **$90 (£59)**
BDM Achievement Badge, silver. **$200 (£124)**
BDM Achievement Badge, bronze. **$160 (£99)**
DJ Achievement Badge, silver. **$95 (£59)**
DJ Achievement Badge, black. **$200 (£124)**
DJH Shooting Badge. **$110 (£63)**
SS Long Service, 25 years. **$5,000 (£3,100)**
SS Long Service, 12 years. **$3,500 (£2,170)**
SS Long Service, 8 years. **$1,100 (£682)**
SS Long Service, 4 years. **$880 (£546)**

Military Awards

Narvik Shield.
**$400-$500
(£248-£310)**
Chris William

Cholm Shield.
**$1,600-$2,150
(£992-£1,333)**
Hermann-Historica.de

20. Juli 1944 Wound Badge, black, in original case.
$42,880 (£26,586)
Hermann-Historica.de

Close Combat Clasp, silver.
**$600-$975
(£372-£605)**
Hermann-Historica.de

Knight's Cross of the Iron Cross.
**$5,500-$13,500
(£3,410-£8,370)**
Hermann-Historica.de

Oak Leaves to the Knight's Cross.
**$4,000-$15,000
(£2,480-£9,300)**
Hermann-Historica.de

Oberst Werner Mölders Oak Leaves with Swords and Diamonds to the Knight's Cross of the Iron Cross.
$348,400 (£216,008)
Hermann-Historica.de

War Merit Cross, Knight's Cross with Swords. **$1,350-$5,400
(£837-£3,348)**
Hermann-Historica.de

Third Reich Iron Cross, I Class.
**$200-$400
(£124-£248)**
AdvanceGuardMilitaria.com

1939 Clasp to the Iron Cross, I Class.
**$500-$1,200
(£310-£744)**
HistoryHunter.com

German Cross in gold.
**$2,300-$3,000
(£1,426-£1,860)**
Hermann-Historica.de

Tank Battle Badge, 25 engagements sold for **$800 (£496)**
Hermann-Historica.de

General Assault Badge. **$135-$270
(£84-£167)**
HistoryHunter.com

General Assault Badge with number "25." **$1,300-$1,650
(£806-£1,023)**
Hermann-Historica.de

Army Flak Badge.
**$675-$950
(£419-£589)**
Chris William

Infantry Assault Badge, bronze.
$120-$220 (£74-£126)
Chris William

Spanish Cross in silver with swords.
**$1,600-$2,250
(£992-£1,395)**
HistoryHunter.com

Spanish Cross in bronze with swords.
**$1,000-$1,250
(£620-£775)**
Hermann-Historica.de

War Merit Cross, I Class with swords, silver "900".
$750-$825 (£465-£512)
HistoryHunter.com

Third Reich War Merit Cross, II Class without swords. $30-$40 (£19-£25)
AdvanceGuardMilitaria.com

Third Reich War Merit Medal. $20-$25 (£12-£16)
AdvanceGuardMilitaria.com

Third Reich Winter Campaign in Russia Medal. $35-$45 (£22-£28)
AdvanceGuardMilitaria.com

Spanish Volunteer Medal, gray metal planchet. $75-$100 (£47-£62)
AdvanceGuardMilitaria.com

West Wall Medal. $35-$55 (£22-£34)
AdvanceGuardMilitaria.com

Third Reich Italian-German Campaign Medal. $65-$80 (£40-£50)
AdvanceGuardMilitaria.com

20. Juli 1944 Wound Badge, silver, in original case. $64,320 (£39,878)
Hermann-Historica.de

Third Reich 1939 Wound Badge, gold. $200-$265 (£124-£164)
AdvanceGuardMilitaria.com

Third Reich 1939 Wound Badge, silver. $65-$100 (£40-£62)
AdvanceGuardMilitaria.com

Third Reich 1939 Wound Badge, black. $30-$55 (£19-£34)
AdvanceGuardMilitaria.com

Army Paratrooper Badge. $1,350-$2,700 (£837-£1,674)
Hermann-Historica.de

Honor Roll Clasp, Navy. $1,800-$2,200 (£1,116-£1,364)
Hermann-Historica.de

Luftwaffe Pilot's Badge. $540-$1,200 (£335-£744)
Hermann-Historica.de

Combined Pilot/ Observer Badge, 2nd Model. $2,680 (£1,662)
Hermann-Historica.de

Luftwaffe Observer's Badge. $540-1,900 (£335-£1,178)
Hermann-Historica.de

"Oberst Werner Mölders" Combined Pilot/Observer Badge in gold with diamonds. $128,640 (£79,757-£)
Hermann-Historica.de

Luftwaffe Air Gunner's Badge with Lightning bundle. $470-$810 (£291-£502)
Hermann-Historica.de

Luftwaffe Ground Assault Badge. $300-$400 (£186-£248)
Chris William

Luftwaffe Anti-Aircraft Badge. $335-$425 (£208-£264)
AdvanceGuardMilitaria.com

Luftwaffe Paratrooper's Badge. $600-$1,100 (£372-£682)
Hermann-Historica.de

German High Seas Fleet War Badge. $270-$610 (£167-£378)
Hermann-Historica.de

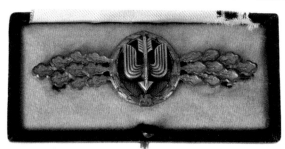

Destroyers and Air to Ground Support Pilots Clasp, gold. $1,100-$1,350 (£682-£837)
HistoryHunter.com

Luftwaffe Reconnaissance Operational Flying Clasp, silver. $540-$675 (£335-£419)
HistoryHunter.com

Heavy & Medium Dive Bomber Operational Flying Clasp, gold with star hanger. **$900-$1,000 (£558-£620)**

Hermann-Historica.de

Heavy & Medium Dive Bomber Operational Flying Clasp, gold. **$540-$675 (£335-£419)**

HistoryHunter.com

Heavy & Medium Dive Bomber Operational Flying Clasp, silver. **$400-$475 (£248-£295)**

Hermann-Historica.de

Destroyers and Air to Ground Support Pilots Clasp, gold with numbered hanger. **$1,200-$1,600 (£744-£992)**

Hermann-Historica.de

Air to Ground Support Squadron Operational Flying Clasp, gold with numbered hanger. **$1,400-$1,500 (£868-£930)**

Hermann-Historica.de

Luftwaffe Day Fighter Operational Flying Clasp, silver. **$675-$800 (£419-£496)**

Hermann-Historica.de

U-Boat Combat Clasp, bronze. **$750-$950 (£465-£589)**

Hermann-Historica.de

Balloon Observer Badge. **$3,500-$4,500 (£2,170-£2,790)**

Rock Island Auction Co.

German Destroyer Badge. **$340-$540 (£211-£335)**

Hermann-Historica.de

Blockade Runner Badge. **$340-$470 (£211-£291)**

Chris William

German E-Boat War Badge, Type I. **$810-$1,800 (£502-£1,116)**

Hermann-Historica.de

German E-Boat War Badge, Type II. **$675-$810 (£419-£502)**

Hermann-Historica.de

German Auxiliary Cruiser War Badge. **$400-$1,100 (£248-£682)**

Hermann-Historica.de

German Minesweeper Badge. **$150-$340 (£93-£211)**

Chris William

U-Boat War Badge. **$400-$880 (£248-£546)**

Hermann-Historica.de

German Coastal Artillery Badge. **$200-$610 (£124-£378)**

Hermann-Historica.de

Spanish Cross, gold with diamonds. **$100,000 (£62,000)**
Spanish Cross, gold with swords. **$3,500 (£2,170)**
Spanish Cross, silver with swords. **$2,200 (£1,364)**
Spanish Cross, silver without swords. **$3,400 (£2,108)**
Spanish Cross, bronze with swords. **$1,100 (£682)**
Spanish Cross, bronze without swords. **$1,100 (£682)**
Spanish Cross for next of kin. **$3,400 (£2,108)**
Condor Legion Tank Badge, silver. **$5,400 (£3,348)**
Annexation of Austria 13. März 1938. **$70 (£43)**
Annexation of the Sudetenland 1. Oktober 1938. **$35 (£22)**
Memel Return Medal. **$270 (£167)**
West Wall Medal. **$25 (£15)**
Knight's Cross with oak leaves and swords. **$38,000 (£23,560)**
Knight's Cross with oak leaves. **$20,000 (£12,400)**
Knight's Cross. **$12,800 (£7,936)**
Iron Cross, I Class, pinback, flat. **$350 (£217)**
Iron Cross, I Class, pinback, vaulted. **$465 (£288)**
Iron Cross, I Class, screwback. **$400 (£248)**
Iron Cross, II Class. **$95 (£59)**
1939 Clasp to the Iron Cross, I Class. **$365 (£226)**
1939 Clasp to the Iron Cross, II Class. **$200 (£124)**
War Merit Cross, Knight's Cross with swords. **$16,500 (£10,230)**
War Merit Cross, Knight's Cross without swords. **$8,000 (£4,960)**
War Merit Cross, I Class with swords, pinback. **$160 (£99)**
War Merit Cross, I Class with swords, screwback. **$190 (£118)**
War Merit Cross, I Class without swords, pinback. **$160 (£99)**
War Merit Cross, I Class without swords, screwback. **$240 (£149)**
War Merit Cross, II Class with swords. **$35 (£22)**
War Merit Cross, II Class without swords. **$30 (£19)**
War Merit Medal. **$25 (£16)**
German Cross in gold. **$2,300 (£1,426)**
German Cross in silver. **$3,000 (£1,860)**
Honor Roll Clasp, Army. **$1,600 (£992)**
Honor Roll Clasp, Navy. **$2,200 (£1,364)**
Honor Roll Clasp, Luftwaffe. **$2,200 (£1,364)**
Winter Campaign in Russia Medal. **$35 (£22)**
Spanish Volunteer Medal. **$165 (£102)**
Italian-German Campaign Medal. **$65 (£40)**
1936/39 Wound Badge, silver. **$500 (£310)**
1936/39 Wound Badge, black. **$230 (£143)**
1939 Wound Badge, gold. **$270 (£167)**
1939 Wound Badge, silver. **$90 (£56)**
1939 Wound Badge, black. **$35 (£22)**
20. Juli 1944 Wound Badge, gold. **$85,000 (£52,700)**
20. Juli 1944 Wound Badge, silver. **$45,000 (£27,900)**
20. Juli 1944 Wound Badge, black. **$38,000 (£23,560)**
Eastern People's Award, I Class, gold with swords. **$400 (£248)**
Eastern People's Award, I Class, gold without swords. **$340 (£211)**
Eastern People's Award, I Class, silver with swords. **$340 (£211)**
Eastern People's Award, I Class, silver without swords. **$270 (£167)**
Eastern People's Award, II Class, gold with swords. **$200 (£124)**
Eastern People's Award, II Class, gold without swords. **$220 (£136)**
Eastern People's Award, II Class, silver with swords. **$150 (£93)**
Eastern People's Award, II Class, silver without swords. **$160 (£99)**
Eastern People's Award, II Class, bronze with swords. **$100 (£62)**
Eastern People's Award, II Class, bronze without swords.**$135 (£84)**
Army & Navy Long Service Award I Class with oak leaves, 40 years. **$300 (£186)**
Army & Navy Long Service Award I Class, 25 years. **$270 (£167)**

Army & Navy Long Service Award II Class, 18 years. $160 (£99)
Army & Navy Long Service Award III Class, 12 years. $150 (£93)
Army & Navy Long Service Award IV Class, 4 years. $60 (£37)
Luftwaffe Long Service Award, I Class with oak leaves, 40 years. $300 (£186)
Luftwaffe Long Service Award, I Class, 25 year. $170 (£105)
Luftwaffe Long Service Award, II Class, 18 years. $160 (£99)
Luftwaffe Long Service Award, III Class, 12 years. $150 (£93)
Luftwaffe Long Service Award, IV Class, 4 years. $70 (£43)
Narvik Shield, silver. $540 (£335)
Narvik Shield, gold. $800 (£496)
Cholm Shield. $1,700 (£1,054)
Crimea Shield. $170 (£105)
Demjansk Shield. $350 (£217)
Kuban Shield. $260 (£161)
Lapland Shield. $345 (£214)
Lorient Shield. $1,500 (£930)
Kreta Cuff Title. $450 (£279)
Afrika Cuff Title. $340 (£211)
Kurland Cuff Title. $800 (£496)
Driver's Badge, gold. $95 (£59)
Driver's Badge, silver. $70 (£43)
Driver's Badge, bronze. $50 (£31)
Mountain Guard Executive Breast Badge. $3,400 (£2,108)
Close Combat Clasp, gold. $2,000 (£1,240)
Close Combat Clasp, silver. $610 (£378)
Close Combat Clasp, bronze. $400 (£248)
Infantry Assault Badge, silver. $95 (£59)
Infantry Assault Badge, bronze. $100 (£62)
General Assault Badge, 100 engagements. $5,400 (£3,348)
General Assault Badge, 75 engagements. $3,500 (£2,170)
General Assault Badge, 50 engagements. $2,200 (£1,364)
General Assault Badge, 25 engagements. $1,600 (£992)
General Assault Badge. $135 (£84)
Tank Battle Badge, Silver, 100 engagements. $5,500 (£3,410)
Tank Battle Badge, Silver, 75 engagements. $3,500 (£2,170)
Tank Battle Badge, Silver, 50 engagements. $1,500 (£930)
Tank Battle Badge, Silver, 25 engagements. $1,550 (£961)
Tank Battle Badge Silver. $355 (£220)
Tank Battle Badge, Bronze, 100 engagements. $6,000 (£3,720)
Tank Battle Badge, Bronze, 75 engagements. $3,800 (£2,356)
Tank Battle Badge, Bronze, 50 engagements. $2,450 (£1,519)
Tank Battle Badge, Bronze, 25 engagements. $1,700 (£1,054)
Tank Battle Badge, Bronze. $340 (£211)
Army Flak Badge. $50 (£31)
Single-Handed Destruction of a Tank Badge, gold. $2,700 (£1,674)
Single-Handed Destruction of a Tank Badge, silver. $810 (£502)
Airplane Destruction Badge, gold. n/a
Airplane Destruction Badge, silver. n/a
Army Paratrooper Badge. $2,700 (£1,674)
Balloon Observer Badge, gold. $5,000 (£3,100)
Balloon Observer Badge, silver. $4,000 (£2,480)
Balloon Observer Badge, bronze. $3,500 (£2,170)
U-Boat Combat Clasp, silver. $1,750 (£1,085)
U-Boat Combat Clasp, bronze. $950 (£589)
U-Boat War Badge with diamonds. $27,000 (£16,740)
U-Boat War Badge. $525 (£326)
Destroyer Badge. $335 (£208)
Minesweeper Badge. $225 (£140)
Auxiliary Cruiser War Badge with diamonds. $34,000 (£21,080)
Auxiliary Cruiser War Badge. $475 (£295)
High Seas Fleet War Badge with diamonds. $34,000 (£21,080)
High Seas Fleet War Badge. $340 (£211)
E-Boat War Badge, Type I with diamonds. n/a
E-Boat War Badge, Type I. $1,000 (£620)
E-Boat War Badge, Type II with diamonds. $34,000 (£21,080)
E-Boat War Badge, Type II. $674 (£418)
Coastal Artillery Badge. $200 (£124)
Blockade Runner Badge. $340 (£211)
Naval Combat Clasp. $340 (£211)
Naval Combat Badge for Small Battle Units, Grade I. n/a
Naval Combat Badge for Small Battle Units, Grade II. n/a
Naval Combat Badge for Small Battle Units, Grade III. n/a
Naval Combat Badge for Small Battle Units, Grade IV. n/a

Naval Combat Badge for Small Battle Units, Grade V. n/a
Naval Combat Badge for Small Battle Units, Grade VI. n/a
Naval Combat Badge for Small Battle Units, Grade VII. n/a
Day Fighter Operational Flying Clasp, gold with diamonds. n/a
Day Fighter Operational Flying Clasp, gold with hanger and number. $1,600 (£992)
Day Fighter Operational Flying Clasp, gold with hanger. $1,350 (£837)
Day Fighter Operational Flying Clasp, gold. $880 (£546)
Day Fighter Operational Flying Clasp, silver. $675 (£419)
Day Fighter Operational Flying Clasp, bronze. $540 (£335)
Night Fighter Operational Flying Clasp, gold with hanger and number. $1,650 (£1,023)
Night Fighter Operational Flying Clasp, gold with hanger. $1,500 (£930)
Night Fighter Operational Flying Clasp, gold. $1,100 (£682)
Night Fighter Operational Flying Clasp, silver. $950 (£589)
Night Fighter Operational Flying Clasp, bronze. $810 (£502)
Long Range Fighter & Night Intruder Operational Flying Clasp, gold with hanger and number. $1,600 (£992)
Long Range Fighter & Night Intruder Operational Flying Clasp, gold with hanger. $1,500 (£930)
Long Range Fighter & Night Intruder Operational Flying Clasp, gold. $1,100 (£682)
Long Range Fighter & Night Intruder Operational Flying Clasp, silver. $950 (£589)
Long Range Fighter & Night Intruder Operational Flying Clasp, bronze. $810 (£502)
Heavy & Medium Dive Bomber Operational Flying Clasp, gold with hanger and number. $1,000 (£620)
Heavy & Medium Dive Bomber Operational Flying Clasp, gold with hanger. $950 (£589)
Heavy & Medium Dive Bomber Operational Flying Clasp, gold. $540 (£335)
Heavy & Medium Dive Bomber Operational Flying Clasp, silver. $400 (£248)
Heavy & Medium Dive Bomber Operational Flying Clasp, bronze. $340 (£211)
Reconnaissance Operational Flying Clasp, gold with hanger and number. $1,220 (£756)
Reconnaissance Operational Flying Clasp, gold with hanger. $1,150 (£713)
Reconnaissance Operational Flying Clasp, gold. $810 (£502)
Reconnaissance Operational Flying Clasp, silver. $540 (£335)
Reconnaissance Operational Flying Clasp, bronze. $340 (£211)
Transport Squadron Operational Flying Clasp, gold with hanger and number. $1,150 (£713)
Transport Squadron Operational Flying Clasp, gold with hanger. $1,100 (£682)
Transport Squadron Operational Flying Clasp, gold. $675 (£419)
Transport Squadron Operational Flying Clasp, silver. $540 (£335)
Transport Squadron Operational Flying Clasp, bronze. $340 (£211)
Destroyers and Air to Ground Support Pilots Clasp, gold with hanger and number . $1,500 (£930)
Destroyers and Air to Ground Support Pilots Clasp, gold with star hanger. $1,000 (£620)
Destroyers and Air to Ground Support Pilots Clasp, gold. $950 (£589)
Destroyers and Air to Ground Support Pilots Clasp, silver. $700 (£434)
Destroyers and Air to Ground Support Pilots Clasp, bronze . $450 (£279)
Air to Ground Support Squadron Operational Flying Clasp, gold with diamonds. n/a
Air to Ground Support Squadron Operational Flying Clasp, gold with hanger and number. $1,500 (£930)
Air to Ground Support Squadron Operational Flying Clasp, gold with hanger. $1,420 (£880)
Air to Ground Support Squadron Operational Flying Clasp, gold. $1,100 (£682)
Air to Ground Support Squadron Operational Flying Clasp, silver. $950 (£589)
Air to Ground Support Squadron Operational Flying Clasp, bronze. $810 (£502)
Luftwaffe Anti-Aircraft Badge. $330 (£205)

Luftwaffe Ground Assault Badge. **$300 (£186)**
Luftwaffe Close Combat Clasp, gold. **n/a**
Luftwaffe Close Combat Clasp, silver. **n/a**
Luftwaffe Close Combat Clasp, bronze. **n/a**
Luftwaffe Tank Battle Badge, silver, 100 Engagements. **n/a**
Luftwaffe Tank Battle Badge, silver, 75 Engagements. **n/a**
Luftwaffe Tank Battle Badge, silver, 50 Engagements. **n/a**
Luftwaffe Tank Battle Badge, silver, 25 Engagements. **n/a**
Luftwaffe Tank Battle Badge, silver. **$4,000 (£2480)**
Luftwaffe Tank Battle Badge, black, 100 Engagements. **n/a**
Luftwaffe Tank Battle Badge, black, 75 Engagements. **n/a**
Luftwaffe Tank Battle Badge, black, 50 Engagements. **n/a**
Luftwaffe Tank Battle Badge, black, 25 Engagements. **n/a**
Luftwaffe Tank Battle Badge, black. **$4,000 (£2480)**
Luftwaffe Pilot's Badge. **$540 (£335)**
Luftwaffe Observer's Badge. **$400 (£248)**
Luftwaffe Pilot's and Observer's Badge, gold with diamonds.
  $100,000 (£62,000)
Luftwaffe Pilot's and Observer's Badge. **$1,100 (£682)**
Luftwaffe Air Gunner's Badge with Lightning. **$470 (£291)**
Luftwaffe Air Gunner's Badge without Lightning. **$470 (£291)**
Luftwaffe Air Gunner's Badge with black wreath . **$610 (£378)**
Luftwaffe Paratrooper's Badge. **$610 (£378)**
Luftwaffe Glider Pilot's Badge. **$1,350 (£837)**
Luftwaffe Former Flyer's Commemorative Badge. **$1,600 (£992)**
Anti-Partisan War Badge, gold. **$4,700 (£2,914)**
Anti-Partisan War Badge, silver. **$3,400 (£2,108)**
Anti-Partisan War Badge, Bronze. **$2,600 (£1,612)**

GREECE

Order of the Redeemer, Grand Cross badge. **$650 (£403)**
Order of the Redeemer, Grand Cross breast star. **$550 (£341)**
Order of the Redeemer, Commander Cross, I Class. **$425 (£264)**
Order of the Redeemer, Commander Cross, I Class breast star.
  $425 (£264)
Order of the Redeemer, Commander Cross, II Class. **$400 (£248)**
Order of the Redeemer, Officer. **$245 (£152)**
Order of the Redeemer, Knight. **$125 (£78)**
Order of George I, Grand Cross. **$400 (£248)**
Order of George I, Grand Cross with swords. **$650 (£403)**
Order of George I, Grand Cross breast star. **$550 (£341)**
Order of George I, Commander Cross, I Class. **$375 (£233)**
Order of George I, Commander Cross, I Class with swords.
  $425 (£264)
Order of George I, Commander Cross, I Class breast star.
  $375 (£233)
Order of George I, Commander Cross, I Class breast star with
  swords. **$425 (£264)**
Order of George I, Commander Cross, II Class. **$375 (£233)**
Order of George I, Commander Cross, II Class with swords.
  $425 (£264)
Military Merit Cross, I Class. **$65 (£40)**
Military Merit Cross, II Class. **$65 (£40)**
Military Merit Cross, III Class. **$50 (£31)**
Military Merit Cross, IV Class. **$30 (£18)**
Merchant Marine Service Medal, I Class. **$30 (£18)**
Merchant Marine Service Medal, II Class. **$25 (£16)**
Naval Good Shooting Medal. **$65 (£40)**
Long Service & Good Conduct Medal, I Class, 20 years. **$40 (£25)**
Long Service & Good Conduct Medal, II Class, 15 years. **$25 (£16)**
Long Service & Good Conduct Medal, III Class, 10 years.
  $20 (£12)
Medal for Outstanding Acts. **$55 (£34)**
Royal Navy Cross. **$85 (£53)**
Valor Cross in Flight. **$250 (£155)**
Distinguished Flying Cross. **$275 (£171)**
Air Force Cross, non-combatant. **$175 (£109)**
Air Force Cross, non-combatant, NCO. **$180 (£111)**
Air Force Merit Medal. **$150 (£93)**
Distinguished Service Medal, Air Force. **$165 (£102)**
Convoy Escort Medal. **$175 (£109)**
Commemorative Medal, 1940-41, Army. **$25 (£16)**

Commemorative Medal, 1940-41, Navy. **$25 (£16)**
Commemorative Medal, 1941-45, Army. **$25 (£16)**
Commemorative Medal, 1941-45, Navy. **$25 (£16)**
War Cross, I Class. **$50 (£31)**
War Cross, II Class. **$40 (£25)**
War Cross, III Class. **$25 (£16)**

HOLLAND

Bronze Lion Decoration. **$122 (£75)**
Cross for Merit. **$82 (£50)**
Bronze Cross for Gallantry. **$106 (£65)**
Flying Cross. **$245 (£150)**
Resistance Cross, Europe. **$122 (£75)**
East Asia Resistance Star. **$82 (£50)**
Air Raid Service Medal. **$33 (£20)**
Commemorative Cross. **$25 (£15)**
War Commemorative Cross. **$25 (£15)**
Officer's Long Service Cross, 40 years. **$187 (£115)**
Officer's Long Service Cross, 35 years. **$82 (£50)**
Officer's Long Service Cross, 30 years. **$65 (£40)**
Officer's Long Service Cross, 25 years. **$57 (£35)**
Officer's Long Service Cross, 20 years. **$41 (£25)**
Officer's Long Service Cross, 15 years. **$25 (£15)**
Officer's Long Service Cross, 5 years. **$11 (£7)**
Long Service Medal, Army, gold, large, 50 years. **$571 (£350)**
Long Service Medal, Army, gold, small, 35 years. **$367 (£225)**
Long Service Medal, Army, silver, 24 years. **$41 (£25)**
Long Service Medal, Army, bronze. **$33 (£20)**
Long Service Medal, Navy. **$41 (£25)**
Long Service Medal, Coast Guard, military issue. **$49 (£30)**
Long Service Medal, Coast Guard, naval issue. **$65 (£40)**

HUNGARY

Hungarian Order of Merit,
Commanders Cross awarded
to Knight's Cross winner
von Nostitz-Wallwitz.
$2,814 (£1,745)
Hermann-Historica.de

Order of Merit, collar. **n/a**
Order of Merit, Grand Cross
  with cross. **$1,630 (£1,000)**
Order of Merit, Grand Cross with crown and swords. **$868 (£1,400)**
Order of Merit, Grand Cross. **$1,019 (£625)**
Order of Merit, Grand Cross with swords. **$1,100 (£675)**
Order of Merit, Grand Cross with swords and war decoration.
  $1,223 (£750)
Order of Merit, Grand Cross breast star with crown. **$1,712 (£1,050)**
Order of Merit, Grand Cross breast star with crown and swords.
  $2,038 (£1,250)
Order of Merit, Grand Cross breast star. **$611 (£375)**
Order of Merit, Grand Cross breast star with swords. **$552 (£415)**
Order of Merit, Grand Cross breast star with swords and war
  decoration. **$717 (£440)**
Order of Merit, Commander. **$432 (£265)**
Order of Merit, Commander with swords. **$473 (£290)**
Order of Merit, Commander with swords and war decoration.
  $530 (£325)
Order of Merit, Officer pinback cross. **$432 (£265)**
Order of Merit, Officer pinback cross with swords. **$473 (£290)**
Order of Merit, Officer pinback cross with swords and war
  decoration. **$513 (£315)**

Order of Merit, Knight. **$310 (£190)**
Order of Merit, Knight with swords. **$367 (£225)**
Order of Merit, Knight with swords and war decoration. **$391 (£240)**
Silver Merit Cross. **$147 (£90)**
Order of the Holy Crown, Grand Cross. **$978 (£600)**
Order of the Holy Crown, Grand Cross with swords. **$1,100 (£675)**
Order of the Holy Crown, Grand Cross with swords and war decoration. **$1,223 (£750)**
Order of the Holy Crown, Grand Cross breast star. **$815 (£500)**
Order of the Holy Crown, Grand Cross, breast star with swords. **$897 (£550)**
Order of the Holy Crown, Grand Cross, breast star with swords and war decoration. **$1,019 (£625)**
Order of the Holy Crown, Commander. **$693 (£425)**
Order of the Holy Crown, Commander with swords. **$733 (£450)**
Order of the Holy Crown, Commander with swords and war decoration. **$733 (£450)**
Order of the Holy Crown, Commander breast star. **$693 (£425)**
Order of the Holy Crown, Commander breast star with swords. **$693 (£425)**
Order of the Holy Crown, Commander breast star with swords and war decoration. **$733 (£450)**
Order of the Holy Crown, Officer, pinback cross. **$676 (£415)**
Order of the Holy Crown, Officer, pinback cross with swords. **$717 (£440)**
Order of the Holy Crown, Officer, pinback cross with swords and war decoration . **$733 (£450)**
Order of the Holy Crown, Knight. **$269 (£165)**
Order of the Holy Crown, Knight with swords. **$310 (£190)**
Order of the Holy Crown, Knight with swords and war decoration. **$350 (£215)**
Order of the Holy Crown, Gold Merit Cross. **$228 (£140)**
Order of the Holy Crown, Gold Merit Cross with swords. **$269 (£165)**
Order of the Holy Crown, Gold Merit Cross with swords and war decoration. **$310 (£190)**
Order of the Holy Crown, Silver Merit Cross. **$122 (£75)**
Order of the Holy Crown, Silver Merit Cross with swords. **$147 (£90)**
Order of the Holy Crown, Silver Merit Cross, with swords and war decoration. **$187 (£115)**
Order of the Holy Crown, Bronze Merit Cross. **$106 (£65)**
Order of the Holy Crown, Bronze Merit Cross with swords. **$122 (£75)**
Order of the Holy Crown, Bronze Merit Cross with swords and war decoration. **$147 (£90)**
Mathias Corvin Decoration, I Class. **$4,483 (£2,750)**
Mathias Corvin Decoration, II Class. **$1,223 (£750)**
Mathias Corvin Decoration, III Class. **$1,019 (£625)**
Merit Medal, Silver. **$65 (£40)**
Merit Medal, Bronze. **$40 (£25)**
National Defense Service Cross. **$33 (£20)**
Medal for Bravery, gold. **$245 (£150)**
Medal for Bravery, silver, large. **$122 (£75)**
Medal for Bravery, silver, small. **$82 (£50)**
Medal for Bravery, bronze. **$65 (£40)**
Frontline Combat Cross, I Class. **$40 (£25)**
Frontline Combat Cross, I Class, 1941. **$40 (£25)**
Frontline Combat Cross, I Class, 1942. **$40 (£25)**
Frontline Combat Cross, I Class, 1943. **$40 (£25)**
Frontline Combat Cross, I Class with extra award bar. **$65 (£40)**
Frontline Combat Cross, II Class. **$33 (£20)**
Frontline Combat Cross, II Class, 1941. **$33 (£20)**
Frontline Combat Cross, II Class, 1942. **$33 (£20)**
Frontline Combat Cross, II Class, 1943. **$33 (£20)**
Frontline Combat Cross, II Class with extra award bar. **$40 (£25)**
Frontline Combat Cross, III Class. **$25 (£15)**
Frontline Combat Cross, III Class, 1941. **$25 (£15)**
Frontline Combat Cross, III Class, 1942. **$25 (£15)**
Frontline Combat Cross, III Class, 1943. **$25 (£15)**
Civil Merit Cross, gold. **$82 (£50)**
Civil Merit Cross, silver. **$57 (£35)**
Civil Merit Cross, bronze. **$33 (£20)**
Officers' Long Service Decoration, I Class 35-40 years. **$65 (£40)**

Officers' Long Service Decoration, II Class 25-30 years. **$49 (£30)**
Officers' Long Service Decoration, III Class 15-20 years. **$40 (£25)**
Enlisted Men's Long Service Award, I Class 20 years. **$33 (£20)**
Enlisted Men's Long Service Award, II Class 10 years. **$25 (£15)**
Enlisted Men's Long Service Award, III Class 6 years. **$11 (£7)**
Enlisted Men's Long Service Honor Medal, 35 years. **$73 (£45)**
South Hungary Commemorative Medal. **$33 (£20)**

ITALY

Italian Order of the Roman Eagle, Star to the Grand Cross in gold with swords. **$6,000-$6,700 (£3,720-£4,154)**
Hermann-Historica.de

Order of the Roman Eagle, Star to the Grand Cross. **$6,000-$6,700 (£3,720-£4,154)**
Hermann-Historica.de

Military Order of Savoy Military Merit, Grand Cross, II Class. **$800-$1,000 (£496-£620)**
Hermann-Historica.de

Military Order of Savoy, Commander, Knight, **$385-$450 (£239-£279)**
Hermann-Historica.de

Italian Aeronautical Valor Medal, bronze. **$80-$90 (£50-£56)**
AdvanceGuardMilitaria.com

Italian Campaign Medal, Occupation of Greece. **$40-$75 (£25-£47)**
AdvanceGuardMilitaria.com

Italian Fiume Expedition Medal. **$120-$150 (£74-£93)**
AdvanceGuardMilitaria.com

Italian Fascist Youth GIL Cross of Merit, Red (Girls'). **$200-$275 (£124-£171)**
Chris William

Italian Fascist Youth GIL Cross of Merit, Blue (Boys', 14-18). **$200-$235 (£124-£146)**
Chris William

Order of Annunciation, large collar. **n/a**
Order of Annunciation, small collar. **$20,000 (£12,400)**
Order of Annunciation, breast star. **$5,000 (£3,100)**
Order of Sts. Maurice & Lazarus, Grand Cross. **$1,250 (£775)**
Order of Sts. Maurice & Lazarus, Grand Cross breast star. **$900 (£558)**
Order of Sts. Maurice & Lazarus, Commander I Class. **$550 (£341)**
Order of Sts. Maurice & Lazarus, Commander I Class breast star. **$550 (£341)**
Order of Sts. Maurice & Lazarus, Commander II Class. **$525 (£326)**
Order of Sts. Maurice & Lazarus, Commander Officer. **$425 (£264)**

Order of Sts. Maurice & Lazarus, Commander Knight. **$325 (£202)**
Military Order of Savoy, Grand Cross badge. **$3,000 (£1,860)**
Military Order of Savoy, Grand Cross breast star. **$2,000 (£1,240)**
Military Order of Savoy, Commander, I Class. **$1,200 (£744)**
Military Order of Savoy, Commander, I Class breast star.
 $1,200 (£744)
Military Order of Savoy, Commander, II Class. **$1,000 (£620)**
Military Order of Savoy, Commander, Officer. **$800 (£496)**
Military Order of Savoy, Commander, Knight. **$650 (£403)**
Civil Order of Savoy, Badge of the Order. **$500 (£310)**
Order of the Crown of Italy, Grand Cross. **$550 (£341)**
Order of the Crown of Italy, Grand Cross breast star. **$500 (£310)**
Order of the Crown of Italy, Grand Officer. **$400 (£248)**
Order of the Crown of Italy, Grand Officer breast star. **$300 (£186)**
Order of the Crown of Italy, Commander. **$245 (£152)**
Order of the Crown of Italy, Officer. **$125 (£78)**
Order of the Crown of Italy, Knight. **$65 (£40)**
Order of Merit in Labor badge. **$350 (£217)**
Colonial Merit Order, Grand Cross. **$450 (£279)**
Colonial Merit Order, Grand Cross breast star. **$450 (£279)**
Colonial Merit Order, Grand Officer. **$300 (£186)**
Colonial Merit Order, Grand Officer breast star. **$300 (£186)**
Colonial Merit Order, Commander. **$200 (£124)**
Colonial Merit Order, Officer. **$150 (£93)**
Colonial Merit Order, Knight. **$125 (£78)**
Order of the Roman Eagle, Grand Cross. **$850 (£527)**
Order of the Roman Eagle, Grand Cross with swords. **$950 (£589)**
Order of the Roman Eagle, Grand Cross gold breast star.
 $500 (£310)
Order of the Roman Eagle, Grand Cross gold breast star with
 swords. **$575 (£357)**
Order of the Roman Eagle, Grand Cross silver breast star.
 $800 (£496)
Order of the Roman Eagle, Grand Cross silver breast star with
 swords. **$875 (£543)**
Order of the Roman Eagle, Grand Officer. **$650 (£403)**
Order of the Roman Eagle, Grand Officer with swords. **$700 (£434)**
Order of the Roman Eagle, Grand Officer breast star. **$550 (£341)**
Order of the Roman Eagle, Grand Officer breast star with swords.
 $650 (£403)
Order of the Roman Eagle, Commander. **$650 (£403)**
Order of the Roman Eagle, Officer. **$425 (£264)**
Order of the Roman Eagle, Officer with swords. **$475 (£295)**
Order of the Roman Eagle, Knight. **$400 (£248)**
Order of the Roman Eagle, Knight with swords. **$425 (£264)**
Order of the Roman Eagle, Medal. **$125 (£78)**
Order of the Roman Eagle, Medal with swords. **$175 (£109)**
Military Valor Medal, gold. **$90 (£56)**
Military Valor Medal, silver. **$75 (£47)**
Military Valor Medal, bronze. **$50 (£31)**
Military Valor Cross, 1941. **$35 (£22)**
Military Valor Cross, 1942. **$35 (£22)**
Civil Valor Medal, gold. **$20 (£12)**
Civil Valor Medal, silver. **$15 (£9)**
Civil Valor Medal, bronze. **$10 (£6)**
Aeronautical Valor Medal, gold. **$50 (£31)**
Aeronautical Valor Medal, silver. **$40 (£28)**
Aeronautical Valor Medal, bronze. **$20 (£12)**
Campaign Medal, Albania. **$35 (£22)**
Campaign Medal, French Campaign. **n/a**
Campaign Medal, Occupation of Greece. **$75 (£47)**
Campaign Medal, North Africa Service. **$25 (£16)**
Fiume Expedition Medal. **$150 (£93)**
Long Service Cross, gold with crown. **$50 (£31)**
Long Service Cross, gold without crown. **$35 (£22)**
Long Service Cross, silver with crown. **$25 (£16)**
Long Service Cross, silver without crown. **$15 (£9)**
National Fire Service Medal. **$25 (£16)**
Fascist Militia Long Service Cross, 25 years. **$50 (£31)**
Fascist Militia Long Service Cross, 10 years. **$35 (£22)**
Colonial Police Long Serve Cross, gold with crown 40 years. **$45 (£28)**
Colonial Police Long Serve Cross, gold without crown 25 years.
 $30 (£19)
Colonial Police Long Serve Cross, silver with crown 25 years.
 $25 (£16)

Colonial Police Long Serve Cross, silver without crown 16 years.
 $20 (£12)
Colonial Police Long Serve Cross, bronze with crown 20 years.
 $15 (£9)
Colonial Police Long Serve Cross, bronze without crowns 10 years.
 $10 (£6)
Fire Serve Cross, 15 years. **$15 (£9)**
Navy Long Service Medal, gold 20 years. **$50 (£31)**
Navy Long Service Medal, silver 15 years. **$30 (£19)**
Navy Long Service Medal, bronze 10 years. **$15 (£9)**
Air Force Long Service Medal, gold 30 years . **$50 (£31)**
Air Force Long Service Medal, silver 15 years. **$25 (£16)**
Air Force Long Service Medal, bronze 10 years . **$15 (£9)**
Army Long Service Medal, gold 30 years . **$40 (£25)**
Army Long Service Medal, silver 20 years. **$25 (£16)**
Army Long Service Medal, bronze 15 years. **$15 (£9)**
Customs Long Service Medal, gold 30 years. **$35 (£22)**
Customs Long Service Medal, silver 20 years. **$20 (£12)**
Customs Long Service Medal, bronze 10 years. **$10 (£6)**
Medal of the Italian Family. **$15 (£9)**
Medal for Aeronautical Pioneer. **$25 (£16)**
National Balilla Merit Medal, gold. **$75 (£47)**
National Balilla Merit Medal, silver. **$50 (£31)**
National Balilla Merit Medal, bronze. **$25 (£16)**
Medal of Merit, Fascist Workers Recreation Service, gold. **$35 (£22)**
Medal of Merit, Fascist Workers Recreation Service, silver.
 $20 (£12)
Medal of Merit, Fascist Workers Recreation Service, bronze.
 $15 (£9)
Fascist Youth GIL Cross of Merit, red. **$200 (£124)**
Fascist Youth GIL Cross of Merit, blue. **$200 (£124)**
Fascist Party Loyalty Medal. **$35 (£22)**

ITALY, SOCIAL REPUBLIC (1943-1945)

Order of the Roman Eagle, Officer. **$636 (£390)**
Order of the Roman Eagle, Officer with swords. **$514 (£315)**
Order of the Roman Eagle, Knight. **$171 (£275)**
Order of the Roman Eagle, Knight with swords. **$489 (£300)**
Order of the Roman Eagle, Medal. **$350 (£215)**
Order of the Roman Eagle, Medal with swords. **$367 (£225)**

JAPAN (also see MANCHUKO)

Japanese Order of the
Rising Sun, VI Class.
$185-$215 (£115-£133)
AdvanceGuardMilitaria.com

Japanese Order of the
Rising Sun, IV Class.
$300-$360 (£186-£223)
AdvanceGuardMilitaria.com

Japanese Order
of the Sacred
Treasure, IV Class.
$160-$175
(£99-£109)
AdvanceGuardMilitaria.com

Japanese Order of
the Sacred Treasure,
VIII Class. **$30-$40**
(£19-£25)
AdvanceGuardMilitaria.com

Japanese Order
of the Sacred
Treasure, VI Class.
$85-$115 (£53-£71)
AdvanceGuardMilitaria.com

Japanese Order of
the Golden Kite,
V Class. **$600-$675**
(£372-£419)
AdvanceGuardMilitaria.com

Japanese Order of the
Golden Kite, IV Class.
$685-$750 (£424-£465)
AdvanceGuardMilitaria.com

Japanese Order of
the Golden Kite,
Vii Class. **$150-$165**
(£93-£102)
AdvanceGuardMilitaria.com

Japanese Order of
the Sacred Treasure,
III Class. **$520-$675**
(£322-£419)
AdvanceGuardMilitaria.com

Japanese Order of the
Rising Sun, VII Class.
$50-$65 (£31-£40)
AdvanceGuardMilitaria.**com**

Japanese Order of the
Rising Sun, VIII Class.
$15-$20 (£9-£12)
AdvanceGuardMilitaria.**com**

Japanese 1931-1934
Manchurian Incident Medal.
$20-$25 (£12-£16)
AdvanceGuardMilitaria.**com**

Japanese China Incident
Medal. **$25-$35 (£16-£22)**
AdvanceGuardMilitaria.com

Japanese Women's Patriotic
Association Special Member's
Medal. **$10-$15 (£6-£9)**
AdvanceGuardMilitaria.com

Japanese Order of the Rising
Sun Breast Star: 1st / 2nd
Class. **$1,700-$1,950**
(£1,054-£1,209)
AdvanceGuardMilitaria.com

Supreme Order of the Chrysanthemum, collar. **$11,003 (£6,750)**
Supreme Order of the Chrysanthemum, sash badge.
 $11,003 (£6,750)
Supreme Order of the Chrysanthemum, breast star.
 $6,113 (£3,750)
Order of the Rising Sun, Grand Cordon,. **$7,132 (£4,375)**
Order of the Rising Sun, Grand Cordon, breast star.
 $4,686 (£2,875)
Order of the Rising Sun, I Class . **$2,649 (£1,625)**
Order of the Rising Sun, I Class breast star. **n/a**
Order of the Rising Sun, II Class. **$734 (£450)**
Order of the Rising Sun, II Class breast star. **$2,000 (£1,240)**
Order of the Rising Sun, III Class. **$500 (£310)**
Order of the Rising Sun, IV Class. **$435 (£270)**
Order of the Rising Sun, V Class. **$375 (£233)**
Order of the Rising Sun, VI Class. **$285 (£177)**
Order of the Rising Sun, VII Class. **$75 (£47)**
Order of the Rising Sun, VIII Class. **$45 (£28)**
Order of the Golden Kite, I Class. **n/a**
Order of the Golden Kite, I Class breast star. **n/a**
Order of the Golden Kite, II Class. **$3,491 (£2,625)**
Order of the Golden Kite, II Class, breast star. **n/a**
Order of the Golden Kite, III Class. **$3,491 (£2,625)**
Order of the Golden Kite, IV Class. **$800 (£496)**
Order of the Golden Kite, V Class. **$490 (£304)**
Order of the Golden Kite, VI Class. **$295 (£183)**
Order of the Golden Kite, VII Class. **$245 (£152)**
Order of the Sacred Crown, I Class. **n/a**
Order of the Sacred Crown, II Class. **n/a**
Order of the Sacred Crown, III Class. **n/a**
Order of the Sacred Crown, IV Class. **$445 (£276)**
Order of the Sacred Crown, V Class. **n/a**

Order of the Sacred Crown, VI Class. n/a
Order of the Sacred Crown, VII Class. $1,834 (£1,125)
Order of the Sacred Crown, VIII Class. $1,589 (£975)
Order of the Sacred Treasure, I Class. $1,426 (£875)
Order of the Sacred Treasure, I Class breast star. $1,019 (£625)
Order of the Sacred Treasure, II Class breast star. $815 (£500)
Order of the Sacred Treasure, III Class. $690 (£428)
Order of the Sacred Treasure, IV Class. $345 (£214)
Order of the Sacred Treasure, V Class. $225 (£140)
Order of the Sacred Treasure, VI Class. $125 (£78)
Order of the Sacred Treasure, VII Class. $95 (£59)
Order of the Sacred Treasure, VIII Class. $55 (£34)
Manchurian Incident Medal. $65 (£40)
China Incident Medal. $50 (£31)
Great East Asia War Medal (original). $3,000 (£1,860)
Great East Asia War Medal (restrike). $150 (£93)
Medal of Merit, red ribbon. $326 (£200)
Medal of Merit, blue ribbon. $326 (£200)
Medal of Merit, green ribbon. $326 (£200)
Medal of Merit, gold, yellow ribbon. n/a
Medal of Merit, silver, yellow ribbon. $326 (£200)
Field Marshal's badge. n/a
Wound Badge, combatant. $220 (£135)
Wound Badge, non-combatant. $163 (£100)
Graduate of Staff Academy. $187 (£115)
Army Officer Pilot's Badge. $693 (£425)
Army Enlisted Man Pilot's Badge. $530 (£325)
Time Expired Soldier's Badge. $33 (£20)

LITHUANIA

Order of Gedeminas, Grand Cross, 1st Model. $5,095 (£3,159)
Hermann-Historica.de

Order of Gedeminas, Commander, 2nd Model. $590 (£366)
Hermann-Historica.de

Order of the Cross of Vytis, III Class in silver. $3,885 (£2,409)
Hermann-Historica.de

Order of Vytautus the Great, collar. n/a
Order of Vytautus the Great, breast star. n/a
Order of Vytautus the Great, I Class. $2,649 (£1,625)
Order of Vytautus the Great, I Class breast star. $2,038 (£1,250)
Order of Vytautus the Great, II Class. $1,834 (£1,125)
Order of Vytautus the Great, II Class breast star. $1,630 (£1,000)
Order of Vytautus the Great, III Class. $1,712 (£1,050)
Order of Vytautus the Great, Officer. $978 (£600)
Order of Vytautus the Great, Knight. $815 (£500)
Order of Vytautus the Great Medal, gold. $310 (£190)
Order of Vytautus the Great Medal, silver. $269 (£165)
Order of Vytautus the Great Medal, bronze. $228 (£140)
Order of the Cross of Vytis, I Class. $1,223 (£750)
Order of the Cross of Vytis, I Class breast star. $1,223 (£750)
Order of the Cross of Vytis, II Class. $815 (£500)
Order of the Cross of Vytis, II Class breast star. $815 (£500)
Order of the Cross of Vytis, III Class. $734 (£450)
Order of the Cross of Vytis, IV Class. $571 (£350)
Order of the Cross of Vytis, V Class. $530 (£325)
Vytis Cross, I Class. $448 (£275)

Vytis Cross, II Class. $391 (£240)
Vytis Cross, III Class. $326 (£200)
Order of Gedeminas, Grand Cross. $530 (£325)
Order of Gedeminas, Grand Cross breast star. $489 (£300)
Order of Gedeminas, Grand Officer. $473 (£290)
Order of Gedeminas, Grand Officer breast star. $448 (£275)
Order of Gedeminas, Commander. $408 (£250)
Order of Gedeminas, Officer. $245 (£150)
Order of Gedeminas, Knight. $187 (£115)
Order of Gedeminas, Merit Medal, gold. $147 (£90)
Order of Gedeminas, Merit Medal, silver. $122 (£75)
Order of Gedeminas, Merit Medal, bronze. $106 (£65)
Volunteer Combatants Medal. $163 (£100)
Lifesaving Cross. $326 (£200)
Star for Partisan Service. $350 (£215)
National Guard Merit Cross. $204 (£125)

MANCHUKO (also see JAPAN)

Manchuko Border Incident War Medal. $200-$245 (£124-£152)
AdvanceGuardMilitaria.com

Manchuko Order of the Auspicious Clouds, II/III Class. $650-$725 (£403-£450)
AdvanceGuardMilitaria.com

Manchuko National Census Commemorative Medal. $225-$250 (£140-£155)
Colin R. Bruce II

Order of the Illustrious Dragon, Badge of the Order. $4,483 (£2,750)
Order of the Illustrious Dragon, breast star. $3,464 (£2,125)
Order of the Auspicious Clouds, I Class. $2,445 (£1,500)
Order of the Auspicious Clouds, I Class breast star. $2,160 (£1,325)
Order of the Auspicious Clouds, II Class breast star. $2,038 (£1,250)
Order of the Auspicious Clouds, II Class. $1,100 (£682)
Order of the Auspicious Clouds, III Class. $900 (£558)
Order of the Auspicious Clouds, IV Class. $652 (£400)
Order of the Auspicious Clouds, V Class. $530 (£325)
Order of the Auspicious Clouds, VI Class. $408 (£250)
Order of the Auspicious Clouds, VII Class. $245 (£150)
Order of the Auspicious Clouds, VIII Class. $187 (£115)
Orders of the Pillars of State, I Class badge. n/a
Orders of the Pillars of State, I Class, breast star. $2,038 (£1,250)
Orders of the Pillars of State, II Class. $1,834 (£1,125)
Orders of the Pillars of State, III Class. $1,630 (£1,000)
Orders of the Pillars of State, IV Class. $1,100 (£675)
Orders of the Pillars of State, V Class. $246 (£390)
Orders of the Pillars of State, VI Class. $530 (£325)
Orders of the Pillars of State, VII Class. $473 (£290)
Orders of the Pillars of State, VIII Class. $367 (£225)
National Foundation Merit Medal. $163 (£100)
Enthronement Commemorative Medal. $408 (£250)
Imperial Visit to Japan. $215 (£133)
Border Incident War Medal. $500 (£310)
National Shrine Foundation Medal. $245 (£150)
National Census Commemorative Medal. $235 (£146)

NORWAY

Order of St. Olav, collar. n/a
Order of St. Olav, Grand Cross. $1,019 (£625)
Order of St. Olav, Grand Cross badge with swords. $1,223 (£750)
Order of St. Olav, Grand Cross breast star. $815 (£500)
Order of St. Olav, Grand Cross breast star with swords. $938 (£575)
Order of St. Olav, Commander. $734 (£450)
Order of St. Olav, Commander with swords. $815 (£500)
Order of St. Olav, Commander breast star. $571 (£350)
Order of St. Olav, Commander breast star with swords. $652 (£400)
Order of St. Olav, Knight, I Class. $245 (£150)
Order of St. Olav, Knight, I Class with swords. $285 (£175)
Order of St. Olav, Knight, II Class. $163 (£100)
Order of St. Olav, Knight, II Class with swords. $204 (£125)
Order of St. Olav, Medal of St. Olav. $122 (£75)
War Cross with swords. $65 (£40)
War Cross without swords. $49 (£30)
War Medal. $41 (£25)
King Haakon VII's Liberty Cross. $285 (£175)
King Haakon VII's Liberty Medal. $196 (£120)
War Participation Medal. $73 (£45)
King Haakon VII's 70th Anniversary Medal, 1942. $25 (£40)

PHILIPPINES

Medal of Valor. n/a
Distinguished Conduct Star. $473 (£290)
Bravery Cross for the Air Force. $204 (£125)
Distinguished Aviation Cross. $122 (£75)
Gold Cross for Valor. $73 (£45)
Distinguished Service Star. $228 (£140)
Military Merit Medal. $57 (£35)
Silver Wing Medal. $41 (£25)
Cross for Wounded. $41 (£25)
Exemplary Efficiency and Devotion in Duty. $33 (£20)
Long Service Cross. $41 (£25)
Defense Medal. $65 (£40)
Liberation Medal. $65 (£40)
Independence Medal. $65 (£40)

POLAND

Order of Virtuti Militari, Grand Cross. n/a
Order of Virtuti Militari, Grand Cross breast star. n/a
Order of Virtuti Militari, Commander. $2,852 (£1,750)
Order of Virtuti Militari, Knight. $1,426 (£875)
Order of Virtuti Militari, Merit Cross, gold. $734 (£450)
Order of Virtuti Militari, Merit Cross, silver. $326 (£200)
Order of the White Eagle. $2,649 (£1,625)
Order of the White Eagle, breast star. $2,853 (£1,750)
Order of Polonia Restituta, Grand Cross (London-made).
  $367 (£225)
Order of Polonia Restituta, Grand Cross breast star
  (London-made). $350 (£215)
Order of Polonia Restituta, II Class (London-made). $269 (£165)
Order of Polonia Restituta, II Class breast star (London-made).
  $326 (£200)
Order of Polonia Restituta, Commander (London-made).
  $269 (£165)
Order of Polonia Restituta, Officer (London-made). $122 (£75)
Order of Polonia Restituta, Knight (London-made). $82 (£50)
Cross of Merit, I Class. $163 (£100)
Cross of Merit, I Class with swords. $245 (£150)
Cross of Merit, II Class. $122 (£75)
Cross of Merit, II Class with swords. $163 (£100)
Cross of Merit, III Class. $65 (£40)
Cross of Merit, III Class with swords. $90 (£55)
Valor Cross, 1939. $90 (£55)
Valor Cross, 1940. $90 (£55)

Valor Cross, World War II-issue made in England, Italy or Middle
  East. $65 (£40)
Long Service Medal, 20 years. $73 (£45)
Long Service Medal, 10 years. $41 (£25)
Volunteers at War Cross. $122 (£75)
Volunteers at War Medal. $106 (£65)
Army Active Service Medal. $41 (£25)
Navy Active Service Medal. $245 (£150)
Air Force Active Service Medal. $147 (£90)
Merchant Navy Service Medal. $245 (£150)
Monte Cassino Cross. $122 (£75)
Red Cross Medal. $122 (£75)
Home Army Cross. $122 (£75)
Resistance Medal, France. $41 (£25)
Polish Army in France. $57 (£35)
Oder-Neisse-Baltic Campaign Medal. $41 (£25)
Liberation of Warsaw. $41 (£25)
Conquest of Berlin. $49 (£30)
Victory over Germany. $33 (£20)

RUMANIA

Order of the Star of Rumania, Type II, Grand Cross with swords. $1,020 (£632)
Hermann-Historica.de

Order of the Crown of Rumania, Type II, Grand Cross with swords. $335 (£208)
Hermann-Historica.de

Order of the Crown of Rumania, Type II, Knight. $160-$200 (£99-£124)
Hermann-Historica.de

Order of the Star of Rumania. $350 (£217)
Hermann-Historica.de

Order of King Carol, collar. **n/a**
Order of King Carol, Grand Cross with diamonds. **n/a**
Order of King Carol, Grand Cross. **$2,853 (£1,750)**
Order of King Carol, Grand Cross breast star with diamonds.
  $2,241 (£1,375)
Order of King Carol, Grand Cross breast star. **$1,834 (£1,125)**
Order of King Carol, Grand Officer. **$1,630 (£1,000)**
Order of King Carol, Grand Officer breast star. **$1,630 (£1,000)**
Order of Michael the Brave, Type I, I Class. **$1,426 (£875)**
Order of Michael the Brave, Type I, I Class with swords.
  $1,426 (£875)
Order of Michael the Brave, Type I, II Class. **$1,018 (£625)**
Order of Michael the Brave, Type I, II Class with swords.
  $815 (£500)
Order of Michael the Brave, Type I, III Class. **$530 (£325)**
Order of Michael the Brave, Type I, III Class. **$530 (£325)**
Order of Michael the Brave, Type II, I Class. **$978 (£600)**
Order of Michael the Brave, Type II, II Class. **$774 (£475)**
Order of Michael the Brave, Type II, III Class. **$611. (£375)**
Order of Michael the Brave, Type III, I Class. **$1,018 (£625)**
Order of Michael the Brave, Type III, II Class. **$734 (£450)**
Order of Michael the Brave, Type III, III Class. **$489 (£300)**
Order of King Ferdinand I, collar. **n/a**
Order of King Ferdinand I, Grand Cross. **n/a**
Order of King Ferdinand I, Grand Cross breast star. **n/a**
Order of King Ferdinand I, Grand Officer. **$611 (£375)**
Order of King Ferdinand I, Grand Officer breast star. **$611 (£375)**
Order of King Ferdinand I, Commander. **$571 (£350)**
Order of King Ferdinand I, Officer. **$408 (£250)**
Order of King Ferdinand I, Knight. **$326 (£200)**
Order of St. George, I Class. **$571 (£350)**
Order of St. George, I Class with swords. **$652 (£400)**
Order of St. George, II Class. **$489. (£300)**
Order of St. George, II Class with swords. **$530 (£325)**
Order of St. George, III Class. **$408 (£250)**
Order of St. George, III Class with swords. **$448 (£275)**
Order of St. George, IV Class. **$285 (£175)**
Order of St. George, IV Class with swords. **$326 (£200)**
Order of St. George, V Class. **$245 (£150)**
Order of St. George, V Class with swords. **$269 (£165)**
Order of St. George, VI Class. **$204 (£125)**
Order of St. George, VI Class with swords. **$228 (£140)**
Order of Merit, Grand Cross. **$571 (£350)**
Order of Merit, Grand Cross with swords. **$652 (£400)**
Order of Merit, Commander. **$448 (£275)**
Order of Merit, Commander with swords. **$489 (£300)**
Order of Merit, Officer. **$326 (£200)**
Order of Merit, Officer with swords. **$367 (£225)**
Order of Merit, Knight. **$285 (£175)**
Order of Merit, Knight with swords. **$310 (£190)**
Order of Merit, Merit Cross. **$204 (£125)**
Order of Merit, Merit Cross with swords. **$228 (£140)**
Honor Cross for Merit, I Class. **$285 (£175)**
Honor Cross for Merit, I Class with swords. **$326 (£200)**
Honor Cross for Merit, I Class for females. **$285 (£175)**
Honor Cross for Merit, II Class. **$163 (£100)**
Honor Cross for Merit, II Class with swords. **$204 (£125)**
Faithful Service Order, Collar. **n/a**
Faithful Service Order, Grand Cross. **$367 (£225)**
Faithful Service Order, Grand Cross with swords. **$408 (£250)**
Faithful Service Order, Grand Cross breast star, Type II. **$367 (£225)**
Faithful Service Order, Grand Cross breast star with swords.
  $408 (£250)
Faithful Service Order, Grand Officer. **$285 (£175)**
Faithful Service Order, Grand Officer with swords. **$326 (£200)**
Faithful Service Order, Grand Officer breast star, Type II. **$285 (£175)**
Faithful Service Order, Grand Officer breast star with swords.
  $350 (£215)
Faithful Service Order, Commander. **$285 (£175)**
Faithful Service Order, Commander with swords. **$326 (£200)**
Faithful Service Order, Officer. **$204 (£125)**
Faithful Service Order, Officer with swords. **$245 (£150)**
Order of the Star of Rumania, Type II, Grand Cross. **$571 (£350)**
Order of the Star of Rumania, Type II, Grand Cross with swords.
  $611 (£375)

Order of the Star of Rumania, Type II, Grand Cross with swords
  on ring. **$611 (£375)**
Order of the Star of Rumania, Type II, Grand Cross with swords
  and swords on ring. **$815 (£500)**
Order of the Star of Rumania, Type II, Grand Cross breast star.
  $530 (£325)
Order of the Star of Rumania, Type II, Grand Cross breast star
  with swords. **$571 (£350)**
Order of the Star of Rumania, Type II, I Class badge. **$530 (£325)**
Order of the Star of Rumania, Type II, I Class badge with swords.
  $530 (£325)
Order of the Star of Rumania, Type II, I Class badge with swords
  on ring. **$571 (£350)**
Order of the Star of Rumania, Type II, I Class badge with swords
  and swords on ring. **$611 (£375)**
Order of the Star of Rumania, Type II, I Class breast star.
  $530 (£325)
Order of the Star of Rumania, Type II, I Class breast star with
  swords. **$571 (£350)**
Order of the Star of Rumania, Type II, Grand Officer badge.
  $489 (£300)
Order of the Star of Rumania, Type II, Grand Officer with swords.
  $530 (£325)
Order of the Star of Rumania, Type II, Grand Officer with swords
  on ring. **$571 (£350)**
Order of the Star of Rumania, Type II, Grand Officer with swords
  and swords on ring. **$611 (£375)**
Order of the Star of Rumania, Type II, Grand Officer breast star.
  $489 (£300)
Order of the Star of Rumania, Type II, Grand Officer breast star
  with swords. **$530 (£325)**
Order of the Star of Rumania, Type II, Commander. **$489 (£300)**
Order of the Star of Rumania, Type II, Commander with swords.
  $513 (£315)
Order of the Star of Rumania, Type II, Commander with swords
  on ring. **$554 (£340)**
Order of the Star of Rumania, Type II, Commander with swords
  and swords on ring. **$571 (£350)**
Order of the Star of Rumania, Type II, Officer. **$245 (£150)**
Order of the Star of Rumania, Type II, Officer with swords.
  $285 (£175)
Order of the Star of Rumania, Type II, Officer with swords on r
  ing. **$326 (£200)**
Order of the Star of Rumania, Type II, Officer with swords and
  swords on ring. **$367 (£225)**
Order of the Star of Rumania, Type II, Knight. **$236 (£145)**
Order of the Star of Rumania, Type II, Knight with swords.
  $269 (£165)
Order of the Star of Rumania, Type II, Knight with swords on
  ring. **$285 (£175)**
Order of the Star of Rumania, Type II, Knight with swords and
  swords on ring. **$310 (£190)**
Order of the Crown, Type II, Grand Cross badge. **$350 (£215)**
Order of the Crown, Type II, Grand Cross badge with swords.
  $424 (£260)
Order of the Crown, Type II, Grand Cross breast star. **$408 (£250)**
Order of the Crown, Type II, Grand Cross breast star with swords.
  $375 (£230)
Order of the Crown, Type II, Grand Officer. **$302 (£185)**
Order of the Crown, Type II, Grand Officer with swords.
  $408 (£250)
Order of the Crown, Type II, Grand Officer breast star. **$302 (£185)**
Order of the Crown, Type II, Grand Officer breast star with
  swords. **$342 (£210)**
Order of the Crown, Type II, Commander. **$302 (£185)**
Order of the Crown, Type II, Commander with swords. **$342 (£210)**
Order of the Crown, Type II, Knight. **$179 (£110)**
Order of the Crown, Type II, Knight with swords. **$204 (£125)**
Order of the Crown, Type II, Ladies' Cross of the Order. **$326 (£200)**
Royal Household Order, Honor Cross, I Class. **$571 (£350)**
Royal Household Order, Honor Cross, I Class with swords.
  $611 (£375)
Royal Household Order, Honor Commander Cross badge.
  $489 (£300)
Royal Household Order, Honor Commander Cross badge with
  swords. **$530 (£325)**

Royal Household Order, Honor Commander Cross breast star. **$571 (£350)**

Royal Household Order, Honor Commander Cross breast star with swords. **$611 (£375)**

Royal Household Order, Honor Cross, II Class. **$408 (£250)**

Royal Household Order, Honor Cross, II Class with swords. **$432 (£265)**

Royal Household Order, Honor Cross, III Class. **$350 (£215)**

Royal Household Order, Honor Cross, III Class with swords. **$367 (£225)**

Royal Household Order, Honor Cross, III Class with oak leaves. **$391 (£240)**

Royal Household Order, Honor Cross, III Class with oak leaves and swords. **$432 (£265)**

Royal Household Order, Merit Cross, I Class. **$310 (£190)**

Royal Household Order, Merit Cross, I Class with swords. **$326 (£200)**

Royal Household Order, Merit Cross, II Class. **$245 (£150)**

Royal Household Order, Merit Cross, II Class with swords. **$269 (£165)**

Royal Household Order, Golden Medal. **$114 (£70)**

Royal Household Order, Golden Medal with swords. **$122 (£75)**

Royal Household Order, Golden Medal with crown. **$114 (£70)**

Royal Household Order, Golden Medal with crown and swords. **$139 (£85)**

Royal Household Order, Silver Medal. **$57 (£35)**

Royal Household Order, Silver Medal with swords. **$65 (£40)**

Royal Household Order, Silver Medal with crown. **$65 (£40)**

Royal Household Order, Silver Medal with crown and swords. **$73 (£45)**

Bene Merenti Order of the Royal House, I Class, male. **$408 (£250)**

Bene Merenti Order of the Royal House, I Class, female. **$326 (£200)**

Bene Merenti Order of the Royal House, II Class, male. **$285 (£175)**

Bene Merenti Order of the Royal House, II Class, female. **$245 (£150)**

Bene Merenti Order of the Royal House, III Class, male. **$245 (£150)**

Bene Merenti Order of the Royal House, III Class, female. **$228 (£140)**

Bene Merenti Order of the Royal House, IV Class. **$163 (£100)**

Bene Merenti Order of the Royal House, I Class Medal, gold. **$73 (£45)**

Bene Merenti Order of the Royal House, II Class Medal, silver. **$57 (£35)**

Bene Merenti Order of the Royal House, III Class Medal, bronze. **$41 (£25)**

Air Force Bravery Medal, Commander. **$269 (£165)**

Air Force Bravery Medal, Commander with swords. **$285 (£175)**

Air Force Bravery Medal, Officer. **$228 (£140)**

Air Force Bravery Medal, Officer with swords. **$245 (£150)**

Air Force Bravery Medal, Knight. **$147 (£90)**

Air Force Bravery Medal, Knight with swords. **$163 (£100)**

Air Force Bravery Medal, Merit Cross. **$82 (£50)**

Air Force Bravery Medal, Merit Cross with swords. **$106 (£65)**

Honor Decoration of the Rumanian Eagle, Grand Officer. **$245 (£150)**

Honor Decoration of the Rumanian Eagle, Grand Officer breast star. **$408 (£250)**

Honor Decoration of the Rumanian Eagle, Commander, I Class. **$245 (£150)**

Honor Decoration of the Rumanian Eagle, Commander, II Class. **$228 (£140)**

Honor Decoration of the Rumanian Eagle, Officer. **$187 (£115)**

Honor Decoration of the Rumanian Eagle, Knight. **$82 (£50)**

Military Bravery (Army), I Class, Type I. **$245 (£150)**

Military Bravery (Army), I Class, Type II. **$147 (£90)**

Military Bravery (Army), II Class, Type I. **$82 (£50)**

Military Bravery (Army), II Class, Type II. **$65 (£40)**

Air Force Bravery, I Class. **$204 (£125)**

Air Force Bravery, I Class with swords. **$228 (£140)**

Air Force Bravery, II Class. **$155 (£95)**

Air Force Bravery, II Class with swords. **$163 (£100)**

Air Force Bravery, III Class. **$130 (£80)**

Air Force Bravery, III Class with swords. **$147 (£90)**

Naval Bravery, I Class. **$163 (£100)**

Naval Bravery, I Class with crown. **$187 (£115)**

Naval Bravery, I Class, with crown and swords. **$187 (£115)**

Naval Bravery, II Class. **$147 (£90)**

Naval Bravery, II Class with crown. **$155 (£95)**

Naval Bravery, II Class, with crown and swords. **$163 (£100)**

Naval Bravery, III Class. **$106 (£65)**

Naval Bravery, III Class with crown. **$73 (£45)**

Naval Bravery, III Class with crown and swords. **$49 (£30)**

Civil Guard Order, I Class. **$163 (£100)**

Civil Guard Order, II Class. **$122 (£75)**

Civil Guard Order, III Class. **$82 (£50)**

Civil Guard Order, IV Class. **$65 (£40)**

Civil Guard Merit Decoration, I Class. **$122 (£75)**

Civil Guard Merit Decoration, II Class. **$82 (£50)**

Civil Guard Merit Decoration, III Class. **$41 (£25)**

Pro Virtute Cross of the Civil Guard. **$65 (£40)**

Civil Guard Merit Medal, I Class. **$41 (£25)**

Civil Guard Merit Medal, II Class. **$33 (£20)**

Civil Guard Merit Medal, III Class. **$16 (£10)**

Faithful Service Cross, Type II, I Class. **$41 (£25)**

Faithful Service Cross, Type II, I Class with swords. **$41 (£25)**

Faithful Service Cross, Type II, II Class. **$33 (£20)**

Faithful Service Cross, Type II, II Class with swords. **$33 (£20)**

Faithful Service Cross, Type II, III Class. **$25 (£15)**

Faithful Service Cross, Type II, III Class with swords. **$16 (£10)**

Faithful Service Medal, Type II, I Class. **$25 (£15)**

Faithful Service Medal, Type II, I Class with swords. **$25 (£15)**

Faithful Service Medal, Type II, II Class. **$23 (£14)**

Faithful Service Medal, Type II, II Class with swords. **$25 (£15)**

Faithful Service Medal, Type II, III Class. **$16 (£10)**

Faithful Service Medal, Type II, III Class with swords. **$23 (£14)**

Medal For Steadfastness & Loyalty, I Class. **$33 (£20)**

Medal For Steadfastness & Loyalty, I Class with swords. **$41 (£25)**

Medal For Steadfastness & Loyalty, II Class. **$25 (£15)**

Medal For Steadfastness & Loyalty, II Class with swords. **$33 (£20)**

Medal For Steadfastness & Loyalty, III Class. **$16 (£10)**

Medal For Steadfastness & Loyalty, III Class with swords. **$33 (£20)**

National Recognition Medal for Rumania, I Class. **n/a**

National Recognition Medal for Rumania, II Class. **n/a**

National Recognition Medal for Rumania, III Class. **n/a**

Anti-Communist Campaign Medal. **$25 (£15)**

Anti-Communist Campaign Medal, one bar. **$41 (£25)**

Anti-Communist Campaign Medal, two bars. **$57 (£35)**

Anti-Communist Campaign Medal, three bars. **$73 (£45)**

Anti-Communist Campaign Medal, four bars. **$106 (£65)**

SLOVAKIA (also see CZECHOSLAVAKIA)

Order of Prince Pribina, Grand Cross. **$978 (£600)**

Order of Prince Pribina, Grand Cross with swords. **$1,182 (£725)**

Order of Prince Pribina, Grand Cross breast star. **$897 (£550)**

Order of Prince Pribina, Grand Cross breast star with swords. **$1,043 (£640)**

Order of Prince Pribina, Grand Officer Cross. **$693 (£425)**

Order of Prince Pribina, Grand Officer Cross with swords. **$799 (£490)**

Order of Prince Pribina, Grand Officer breast star. **$652 (£400)**

Order of Prince Pribina, Grand Officer breast star with swords. **$937 (£575)**

Order of Prince Pribina, Commander. **$693 (£425)**

Order of Prince Pribina, Commander with swords. **$774 (£475)**

Order of Prince Pribina, Officer. **$554 (£340)**

Order of Prince Pribina, Officer with swords. **$611 (£375)**

Order of Prince Pribina, Knight. **$448 (£275)**

Order of Prince Pribina,, Knight with swords. **$513 (£315)**

Order of the Slovak Cross, Grand Cross. **$1,508 (£925)**

Order of the Slovak Cross, Grand Cross with swords. **$1,630 (£1,000)**

Order of the Slovak Cross, Grand Cross breast star. **$1,386 (£850)**

Order of the Slovak Cross, Grand Cross breast star with swords. **$1,223 (£750)**

Order of the Slovak Cross, Commander. **$1,035 (£635)**

Order of the Slovak Cross, Commander with swords. **$1,223 (£750)**

Order of the Slovak Cross, Officer. **$734 (£450)**

Order of the Slovak Cross, Officer with swords. **$815 (£500)**
Order of the Slovak Cross, Knight. **$611 (£375)**
Order of the Slovak Cross, Knight with swords. **$652 (£400)**
Order of the War Victory Cross, Type I. **$1,223 (£750)**
Order of the War Victory Cross, Type I, I Class. **$1,223 (£750)**
Order of the War Victory Cross, Type I, I Class breast star. **$652 (£400)**
Order of the War Victory Cross, Type I, II Class. **$611 (£375)**
Order of the War Victory Cross, Type I, III Class. **$530 (£325)**
Order of the War Victory Cross, Type II, Grand Cross. **$1,019 (£625)**
Order of the War Victory Cross, Type II, Grand Cross with swords. **$1,223 (£750)**
Order of the War Victory Cross, Type II, Grand Cross breast star. **$1,060 (£650)**
Order of the War Victory Cross, Type II, Grand Cross breast star with swords. **$1,060 (£650)**
Order of the War Victory Cross, Type II, I Class neck. **$734. (£450)**
Order of the War Victory Cross, Type II, I Class breast star. **$978 (£600)**
Order of the War Victory Cross, Type II, II Class neck. **$652 (£400)**
Order of the War Victory Cross, Type II, III Class. **$489 (£300)**
Order of the War Victory Cross, Type II, IV Class. **$448 (£275)**
Order of the War Victory Cross, Type II, IV Class with swords. **$530 (£325)**
Order of the War Victory Cross, Type II, V Class. **$163 (£100)**
Order of the War Victory Cross, Type II, V Class with swords. **$187 (£115)**
Order of the War Victory Cross, Type II, VI Class. **$122 (£75)**
Order of the War Victory Cross, Type II, VI Class with swords. **$163 (£100)**
Order of the War Victory Cross, Type II, VII Class. **$106 (£65)**
Order of the War Victory Cross, Type II, VII Class with swords. **$147 (£90)**
Bravery Medal, I Class. **$187 (£115)**
Bravery Medal, II Class. **$122 (£75)**
Bravery Medal, III Class. **$82 (£50)**
Defense of Slovakia, Type I. **$147 (£90)**
Defense of Slovakia, Type II. **$122 (£75)**
Suppression of the National Uprising, large, gold. **$448 (£275)**
Suppression of the National Uprising, large, silver. **$285 (£175)**
Suppression of the National Uprising, large, bronze. **$187 (£115)**
Suppression of the National Uprising, small, silver. **$147 (£90)**
Suppression of the National Uprising, small, bronze. **$82 (£50)**
Eastern Front Honor Badge, silver. **$285 (£175)**
Eastern Front Honor Badge, bronze. **$163 (£100)**
Crimean Service Badge. **$285 (£175)**
Tank Service Badge. **$228 (£140)**
Military Sport Badge. **$204 (£125)**
Pilot/Observer Badge. **$530 (£325)**
Flight Engineer Badge. **$310 (£190)**

SOVIET UNION

Note: *Prices are affected by date of manufacture, and in many cases, attribution through numbering. The prices here reflect values with no attribution.*

Hero of the Soviet Union (Gold Star Medal). **$1,850-$2,400 (£1,147-£1,488)**
Hermann-Historica.de

Order of Lenin, Type V. **$1,000-$1,500 (£620-£930)**
Hermann-Historica.de

Order of the Red Banner, Type II. **$1,000-$1,500 (£620-£930)**
Colin R. Bruce II

Order of the Red Banner, Type I. **$4,000-$4,5000 (£2,480-£2,790)**
Colin R. Bruce II

Order of Nakhimov, II Class. **$5,500-$5,800 (£3,410-£3,596)**
Colin R. Bruce II

Order of Suvorov, II Class, Type II. **$8,400-$8,800 (£5,208-5,456)**
Colin R. Bruce II

Order of Glory, II Class. **$750-$875 (£465-£543)**
Colin R. Bruce II

Medal of Valor, Type II, numbered, on standard ribbon. **$150-$175 (£93-£109)**
Colin R. Bruce II

Meritorious Service in Battle, Type I, numbered. **$200-$275 (£124-£171)**
Colin R. Bruce II

Ushakow-Medal. **$1,000-$1,500 (£620-£930)**
Colin R. Bruce II

Nachimvo Medal. **$1,000-$1,200 (£620-£744)**
Colin R. Bruce II

Distinguished Labor Service, II Type. **$20-$35 (£12-£22),**
Colin R. Bruce II

Order of the Red Star with 1945-dated award document. **$245, (£152)**
Hermann-Historica.de

Soviet Union Order of Alexander Nevsky. **$2,200-$2,600 (£1,364-£1,612)**
Hermann-Historica.de

Order of the Patriotic War, I Class, Type II. **$750-$1,250 (£465-£775)**
Colin R. Bruce II

Order of the Red Star, fourth type. **$500-$600 (£310-£372)**
AdvanceGuardMilitaria.com

Defense of Soviet Arctic. **$130-$150 (£81-£93)**
Colin R. Bruce II

Soviet Union Medal for Valor, Type II. **$45-$75 (£28-£47)**
AdvanceGuardMilitaria.com

Hero of the Soviet Union (Gold Star Medal) with 1944-dated booklet. **$6,165 (£3,822)**
Hermann-Historica.de

Hero of the Soviet Union (Gold Star Medal). **$2,200 (£1,364)**
Hero of Socialist Labor. **$1,250 (£775)**
Order of Lenin, Type I . **n/a**
Order of Lenin, Type II. **$3,600 (£2,232)**
Order of Lenin, Type III. **$2,500 (£1,550)**
Order of Lenin, Type IV. **$950-$1,200 (£589-£744)**
Order of Lenin, Type V. **$850-$1,000 (£527-£620)**
Order of the Red Banner, Type I. **$4,500 (£2,790)**
Order of the Red Banner, Type II. **$1,500 (£930)**
Order of the Red Banner, Type II with no. 2. **$1,900 (£1,178)**
Order of the Red Banner, Type II with no. 4. **$2,500 (£1,550)**
Order of the Red Banner, Type III. **$500 (£310)**
Order of Suvorov, I Class. **$10,500 (£6,510)**
Order of Suvorov, II Class. **$8,750 (£5,425)**
Order of Suvorov, III Class. **$6,000 (£3,720)**
Order of Ushakov, I Class. **$10,250 (£6,355)**
Order of Ushakov, II Class. **$5,400 (£3,348)**
Order of Kutuzov, I Class. **$18,500 (£11,470)**
Order of Kutuzov, II Class. **$12,000 (£7,440)**
Order of Kutuzov, III Class. **$10,000 (£6,200)**

There were 433 U.S. Medals of Honor awarded during World War II, 219 of them given after the recipient's death.

Order of Nakhimov, I Class. **$7,000 (£4,340)**
Order of Nakhimov, II Class. **$5,750 (£3,565)**
Order of Bohdan Khmelnitsky, I Class. **$9,600 (£5,952)**
Order of Bohdan Khmelnitsky, II Class. **$5,450 (£3,379)**
Order of Bohdan Khmelnitsky, III Class. **$3,500 (£2,170)**
Order of Alexander Nevsky, Type I. **$2,800 (£1,736)**
Order of Alexander Nevsky, Type II. **$2,200 (£1,364)**
Order of the Patriotic War, I Class. **$750 (£465)**
Order of the Patriotic War, I Class, ribbon-mounted. **$1,500 (£930)**
Order of the Patriotic War, II Class. **$500 (£310)**
Order of the Patriotic War, II Class, ribbon-mounted. **$1,200 (£744)**
Order of the Red Star, first type. **$14,000 (£8,680)**
Order of the Red Star, second type. **$3,000 (£1,860)**
Order of the Red Star, third type. **$1,200 (£744)**
Order of the Red Star, fourth type. **$600 (£372)**
Order of Glory, I Class. **$1,200 (£744)**
Order of Glory, II Class. **$875 (£543)**
Order of Glory, III Class. **$125 (£78)**
Order of the Badge of Honor, Type II. **$1,500 (£930)**
Order of Mother Heroine. **$1,000 (£620)**
Order of Motherhood Glory, I Class (World War II issue). **$500 (£310)**
Order of Motherhood Glory, II Class (World War II issue). **$250 (£155)**
Order of Motherhood Glory, III Class (World War II issue). **$200 (£124)**
Motherhood Medal, I Class. **$30 (£19)**
Motherhood Medal, II Class. **$20 (£12)**
Medal of Valor, Type II, numbered. **$165 (£102)**
Medal of Valor, Type II, not numbered. **$75 (£47)**
Meritorious Service in Battle, first issue. **$550 (£341)**
Meritorious Service in Battle, Type I, numbered. **$250 (£155)**
Meritorious Service in Battle, Type I, not numbered. **$45 (£28)**
Ushakov Medal. **$1,500 (£930)**
Nakhimvo Medal. **$1,200 (£744)**
Partisan Warfare Medal, I Class. **$800 (£496)**
Partisan Warfare Medal, II Class. **$550 (£341)**
Valiant Labor During World War II. **$10 (£6)**
Defense of Soviet Arctic. **$150 (£93)**
Defense of Leningrad. **$45 (£28)**
Defense of Moscow. **$65 (£40)**
Defense of Odessa. **$500 (£310)**
Defense of Sevastopol. **$550 (£341)**
Defense of Stalingrad. **$80 (£50)**
Defense of Caucasus. **$150 (£93)**
Defense of Kiev. **$350 (£217)**
Victory over Germany. **$30 (£19)**
Victory over Japan. **$50 (£31)**
Capture of Budapest. **$100 (£62)**
Capture of Koenigsberg. **$45 (£28)**
Capture of Vienna. **$100 (£62)**
Capture of Berlin. **$35 (£22)**
Liberation of Prague. **$85 (£53)**
Liberation of Belgrade. **$400 (£248)**
Liberation of Warsaw. **$65 (£40)**
Valiant Labor. **$25 (£16)**
Distinguished Labor Service. **$25 (£16)**
Good Conduct Medal, I Class. **$65 (£40)**
Good Conduct Medal, II Class. **$40 (£25)**
Good Conduct Medal, III Class. **$25 (£16)**

SPAIN, Republic

Order of Isabella the Catholic, Type II, Grand Cross. **$530 (£325)**
Order of Isabella the Catholic, Type II, Grand Cross breast star.
 $530 (£325)
Order of Isabella the Catholic, Type II, Grand Officer. **$448 (£275)**
Order of Isabella the Catholic, Type II, Grand Officer breast star.
 $448 (£275)
Order of Isabella the Catholic, Type II, Commander. **$367 (£225)**
Order of Isabella the Catholic, Type II, Knight. **$204 (£125)**
Order of Isabella the Catholic, Type II, Silver Merit Cross.
 $163 (£100)
Order of Isabella the Catholic, Type II, Silver Medal. **$147 (£90)**
Order of Isabella the Catholic, Type II, Bronze Medal. **$122 (£75)**
Republic Merit Order, Grand Cross,. **$571 (£350)**
Republic Merit Order, Grand Cross, breast star. **$571 (£350)**
Republic Merit Order, Grand Officer. **$326 (£200)**
Republic Merit Order, Grand Officer breast star. **$326 (£200)**
Republic Merit Order, Officer. **$245 (£150)**
Republic Merit Order, Knight. **$163 (£100)**

SPAIN, Franco Dictatorship

Spanish Franco-
Era Military Merit
Order, War Merit,
II Class. **$100-$135
(£62-£84)**

AdvanceGuardMilitaria.com

Spanish Order of
the War Cross, III
Class. **$85-$115
(£53-£71)**

AdvanceGuardMilitaria.com

Spanish 1944
Pattern Order of
San Hermenegildo,
Grand Cross.
**$135-$165
(£84-£102)**

AdvanceGuardMilitaria.com

Order of Charles III, collar. **$1,345 (£825)**
Order of Charles III, Grand Cross. **$245 (£150)**
Order of Charles III, Grand Cross breast star. **$245 (£150)**
Order of Charles III, Commander, I Class,. **$163 (£100)**
Order of Charles III, Commander, I Class, breast star. **$163 (£100)**
Order of Charles III, Commander. **$155 (£95)**
Order of Charles III, Knight. **$82 (£50)**
Order of Isabella the Catholic, collar. **$1,549 (£950)**
Order of Isabella the Catholic, Grand Cross. **$245 (£150)**
Order of Isabella the Catholic, Grand Cross breast star. **$245 (£150)**
Order of Isabella the Catholic, Commander, I Class,. **$163 (£100)**
Order of Isabella the Catholic, Commander, I Class, breast star.
 $163 (£100)
Order of Isabella the Catholic, Commander. **$147 (£90)**
Order of Isabella the Catholic, Knight. **$65 (£40)**
Order of Isabella the Catholic, Silver Merit Cross. **$41 (£25)**
Order of Isabella the Catholic, Silver Medal. **$33 (£20)**
Order of Isabella the Catholic, Bronze Medal. **$16 (£10)**
Order of St. Ferdinand, Grand Cross badge. **$285 (£175)**
Order of St. Ferdinand, Grand Cross breast star. **$122 (£75)**
Order of St. Ferdinand, Grand Cross with wreath. **$204 (£125)**
Order of St. Ferdinand, Knight. **$163 (£100)**
Order of St. Hermengildo, Grand Cross. **$204 (£125)**
Order of St. Hermengildo, Grand Cross breast star with crown.
 $204 (£125)
Order of St. Hermengildo, Grand Cross breast star without crown.
 $122 (£75)
Order of St. Hermengildo, Grand Cross, Knight. **$65 (£40)**
Order of the Yoke and Arrows, collar. **$1,630 (£1,000)**
Order of the Yoke and Arrows, Grand Cross. **$204 (£125)**
Order of the Yoke and Arrows, Grand Cross breast star. **$204 (£125)**
Order of the Yoke and Arrows, Grand Officer. **$122 (£75)**
Order of the Yoke and Arrows, Grand Officer breast star. **$122 (£75)**

Order of the Yoke and Arrows, Commander. **$106 (£65)**
Order of the Yoke and Arrows, Golden Medal. **$82 (£50)**
Order of Cisneros, collar. **$1,834 (£1,125)**
Order of Cisneros, Grand Cross. **$432 (£265)**
Order of Cisneros, Grand Cross breast star. **$432 (£265)**
Order of Cisneros, Grand Officer. **$367 (£225)**
Order of Cisneros, Grand Officer breast star. **$367 (£225)**
Order of Cisneros, Commander. **$350 (£215)**
Order of Cisneros, Knight. **$204 (£125)**
Order of Cisneros, Golden Medal. **$114 (£70)**
Military Merit Order, War Merit, IV Class, Grand Cross. **$228 (£140)**
Military Merit Order, War Merit, IV Class. **$55 (£34)**
Military Merit Order, War Merit, IV Class, breast star. **$228 (£140)**
Military Merit Order, War Merit, III Class. **$100 (£62)**
Military Merit Order, War Merit, II Class. **$125 (£78)**
Military Merit Order, War Merit, II Class, breast star. **$228 (£140)**
Military Merit Order, War Merit, I Class. **$33 (£20)**
Military Merit Order, War Merit, I Class, Grand Cross. **$228 (£140)**
Military Merit Order, War Merit, Silver Merit Cross. **$35 (£22)**
Naval Merit Order, War Merit, IV Class, Grand Cross. **$163 (£100)**
Naval Merit Order, War Merit, IV Class, breast star. **$163 (£100)**
Naval Merit Order, War Merit, III Class. **$65 (£40)**
Naval Merit Order, War Merit, II Class. **$41 (£25)**
Naval Merit Order, War Merit, I Class. **$33 (£20)**
Naval Merit Order, War Merit, Silver Merit Cross. **$25 (£15)**
Air Force Merit Order, War Merit, III Class, Grand Cross. **$122 (£75)**
Air Force Merit Order, War Merit, III Class, breast star. **$122 (£75)**
Air Force Merit Order, War Merit, II Class. **$65 (£40)**
Air Force Merit Order, War Merit, I Class. **$33 (£20)**
Air Force Merit Order, War Merit, Silver Merit Cross. **$25 (£15)**
Order of Maria Christina, Military Division, III Class, Grand Cross.
 $122 (£75)
Order of Maria Christina, Military Division, III Class breast star.
 $122 (£75)
Order of Maria Christina, Military Division, II Class. **$82 (£50)**
Order of Maria Christina, Military Division, I Class. **$65 (£40)**
Order of Maria Christina, Military Division, Knight. **$41 (£25)**
Order of Maria Christina, Naval Division, III Class, Grand Cross.
 $187 (£115)
Order of Maria Christina, Naval Division, III Class breast star.
 $187 (£115)
Order of Maria Christina, Naval Division, II Class. **$147 (£90)**
Order of Maria Christina, Naval Division, I Class. **$122 (£75)**
Order of Maria Christina, Naval Division, Knight. **$82 (£50)**
Civil Merit Order, collar. **$1,630 (£1,000)**
Civil Merit Order, Grand Cross. **$204 (£125)**
Civil Merit Order, Grand Cross breast star. **$204 (£125)**
Civil Merit Order, Grand Officer badge. **$122 (£75)**
Civil Merit Order, Grand Officer breast star. **$122 (£75)**
Civil Merit Order, Commander. **$106 (£65)**
Civil Merit Order, Officer. **$65 (£40)**
Civil Merit Order, Knight. **$41 (£25)**
Civil Merit Order, Silver Merit Cross. **$33 (£20)**
Order of St. Raymond of Penafort, Collar of the Grand Cross.
 $1,834 (£1,125)
Order of St. Raymond of Penafort, Collar of the Honor Cross.
 $774 (£475)
Order of St. Raymond of Penafort, Grand Cross. **$204 (£125)**
Order of St. Raymond of Penafort, Grand Cross breast star.
 $204 (£125)
Order of St. Raymond of Penafort, Honor Cross. **$147 (£90)**
Order of St. Raymond of Penafort, Honor Cross breast star.
 $147 (£90)
Order of St. Raymond of Penafort, Commander. **$122 (£75)**
Order of St. Raymond of Penafort, Commander breast star.
 $122 (£75)
Order of St. Raymond of Penafort, Officer. **$106 (£65)**
Order of St. Raymond of Penafort, Knight. **$41 (£25)**
Order of St. Raymond of Penafort, Gold Medal. **$33 (£20)**
Order of St. Raymond of Penafort, Silver Medal. **$25 (£15)**
Order of St. Raymond of Penafort, Bronze Medal with silver.
 $25 (£15)
Order of St. Raymond of Penafort, Bronze Medal. **$16 (£10)**
Order of Africa, Grand Cross. **$204 (£125)**
Order of Africa, Grand Cross breast star. **$204 (£125)**

Order of Africa, Grand Officer. **$106 (£65)**
Order of Africa, Grand Officer breast star. **$106 (£65)**
Order of Africa, Commander. **$82 (£50)**
Order of Africa, Officer. **$65 (£40)**
Order of Africa, Silver Honor. **$41 (£25)**
Order of the War Cross, Grand Cross. **$228 (£140)**
Order of the War Cross, Grand Cross breast star. **$228 (£140)**
Order of the War Cross, II Class. **$187 (£115)**
Order of the War Cross, III Class. **$122 (£75)**
Order of the War Cross, IV Class. **$82 (£50)**
War Cross. **$49 (£30)**
Victory in the Civil War. **$11 (£7)**
Volunteers Medal for the Spanish Blue Division. **$187 (£115)**
German Medal for Spanish Volunteers. **$106 (£65)**

UNITED STATES

U.S. Marine Corps
Good Conduct Medal.
$65-$95 (£40-£59)
AdvanceGuardMilitaria.com

U.S. Coast Guard
Good Conduct
Medal, Type I.
$75-$100 (£47-£62)
AdvanceGuardMilitaria.com

U.S. Soldier's
Medal. **$20-$25
(£12-£16)**
AdvanceGuardMilitaria.com

U.S. Distinguished
Service Cross.
$125-$165 (£78-£102)
AdvanceGuardMilitaria.com

U.S. Army
Distinguished
Service Medal.
$135-$175 (£84-£109)
AdvanceGuardMilitaria.com

U.S. Legion of Merit
Medal, wrap brooch.
$65-$85 (£40-£53)
AdvanceGuardMilitaria.com

U.S. Medal
of Freedom
Legionnaire.
$55-$85 (£34-£53)
AdvanceGuardMilitaria.com

U.S. Air Medal.
$35-$50 (£22-£31)
AdvanceGuardMilitaria.com

U.S. WAC Service
Medal. **$50-$75
(£31-£47)**
AdvanceGuardMilitaria.com

U.S. Navy Cross
and issue carton.
$325-365 (£202-£226)
AdvanceGuardMilitaria.com

U.S. Merchant Marine
Distinguished Service
Medal. **$200-$265
(£124-£164)**
AdvanceGuardMilitaria.com

U.S. Distinguished
Flying Cross.
$100-$145 (£62-£90)
AdvanceGuardMilitaria.com

U.S. Presidential
Medal For Merit.
$200-$265 (£124-£164)
AdvanceGuardMilitaria.com

U.S. Purple Heart
Medal, ribbon bar
and lapel button.
$65-$95 (£40-£59)
AdvanceGuardMilitaria.com

Distinguished
Service Medal,
U.S. Navy.
**$375-$425
(£233-£264)**
Colin R. Bruce II

Selected Marine
Corps Reserve Medal,
Third style. **$45-$65
(£28-£40)**
AdvanceGuardMilitaria.com

U.S. Navy and
Marine Corps
Medal. **$225-$270
(£140-£167)**
AdvanceGuardMilitaria.com

U.S. Silver Star.
$65-$115 (£40-£71)
AdvanceGuardMilitaria.com

U.S. Army Good Conduct Medal, knob
suspension, named. **$25-$50 (£16-£31)**
Author's collection

Medal of Honor
Note: *Under current U.S. law, it is illegal to sell, buy or transfer a Medal of Honor. Therefore, no pricing information is provided here.*

Distinguished Service Cross, numbered. **$325 (£202)**
Distinguished Service Cross, unnumbered. **$175 (£109)**
Navy Cross. **$400 (£248)**
Distinguished Service Medal, Army, numbered. **$300 (£186)**
Distinguished Service Medal, Army, unnumbered. **$150 (£93)**
Distinguished Service Medal, Navy. **$400 (£248)**
Silver Star, Army, numbered, wrap brooch. **$145 (£90)**
Silver Star, Army, numbered, slot brooch. **$100 (£62)**
Silver Star, Army, unnumbered, slot brooch. **$75 (£47)**
Silver Star, Navy, unnumbered. **$250 (£155)**
Legion of Merit, Chief Commander breast star, numbered.
 $2,500 (£1,550)
Legion of Merit, Chief Commander breast star, unnumbered.
 $1,000 (£620)
Legion of Merit, Commander, numbered. **$950 (£589)**
Legion of Merit, Commander, unnumbered. **$450 (£279)**
Legion of Merit, Officer, numbered. **$375 (£233)**
Legion of Merit, Officer, unnumbered. **$150 (£93)**
Legion of Merit, Legionnaire, numbered. **$200 (£124)**
Legion of Merit, Legionnaire, unnumbered. **$150 (£93)**
Presidential Medal for Merit. **$250 (£155)**
Distinguished Flying Cross, Army, numbered. **$220 (£136)**
Distinguished Flying Cross, Army, unnumbered. **$120 (£74)**
Distinguished Flying Cross, Army, frosted. **$145 (£90)**
Distinguished Flying Cross, Navy. **$175 (£109)**
Soldier's Medal, numbered. **$125 (£78)**
Soldier's Medal, unnumbered. **$35 (£22)**
Navy and Marine Corps Medal. **$225 (£140)**
Bronze Star, Army. **$35 (£22)**
Bronze Star, Navy. **$150 (£93)**
Air Medal, Army, wrap brooch, numbered. **$85 (£53)**
Air Medal, Army, wrap brooch, unnumbered. **$55 (£34)**
Air Medal, Army, slot brooch. **$40 (£25)**
Air Medal, Navy. **$125 (£78)**
Purple Heart, Army, Type I . **$155 (£96)**
Purple Heart, Army, Type II. **$95 (£59)**
Purple Heart, Army, Type II. **$65 (£40)**
Purple Heart, Navy, Type I . **$165 (£102)**
Purple Heart, Navy, Type II. **$95 (£59)**
Good Conduct Medal, Army, knob suspension, numbered. **$75 (£47)**
Good Conduct Medal, Army, knob suspension, unnumbered. **$15 (£9)**
Good Conduct Medal, Navy, Type II, engraved. **$75 (£47)**
Good Conduct Medal, Navy, Type II, impressed. **$60 (£37)**
Good Conduct Medal, Navy, Type II unnamed. **$30 (£19)**
Good Conduct Medal, Marine, impressed. **$95 (£59)**
Good Conduct Medal, Marine, unnamed. **$45 (£28)**
Good Conduct Medal, Coast Guard, Type I, named. **$185 (£115)**
Good Conduct Medal, Coast Guard, Type I, unnamed. **$100 (£62)**
Good Conduct Medal, Coast Guard, Type II. **$20 (£12)**
Naval Reserve Medal, Type I. **$75 (£47)**
Naval Reserve Medal, Type II. **$20 (£12)**
Fleet Marine Corps Reserve. **$950 (£589)**
Selected Marine Corps Reserve Medal. **$165 (£102)**
American Defense Service Medal, Type I. **$35 (£22)**
American Defense Service Medal, Type II. **$15 (£9)**
American Defense Service Medal, bar, Foreign Service. **$25 (£16)**
American Defense Service Medal, bar, Fleet. **$20 (£12)**
American Defense Service Medal, bar, Base. **$30 (£19)**
American Defense Service Medal, bar, Sea. **$75 (£40)**
American Campaign Medal. **$15 (£9)**
European-African-Middle Eastern Campaign Medal. **$15 (£9)**
5th Army Liberation of Naples Medal. **$20 (£12)**
Asiatic Pacific Campaign Medal. **$15 (£9)**
World War II Victory Medal. **$10 (£6)**
Women's Army Corps Medal, 1st issue. **$85 (£53)**
Women's Army Corps Medal, 2nd issue. **$55 (£34)**
Army of Occupation. **$15 (£9)**
Army of Occupation, bar, Germany. **$20 (£12)**
Army of Occupation, bar, Japan. **$20 (£12)**

Navy Occupation. **$20 (£12)**
Navy Occupation, bar, Asia. **$25 (£16)**
Navy Occupation, bar Europe. **$30 (£19)**
USMC Occupation. **$25 (£16)**
USMC Occupation, bar, Asia. **$30 (£19)**
USMC Occupation, bar, Europe. **$40 (£25)**
China Service, USN. **$40 (£25)**
China Service, USMC. **$40 (£25)**
Merchant Marine, Distinguished Service Medal. **$1,750 (£1,085)**
Merchant Marine, Meritorious Service, numbered. **$300 (£186)**
Merchant Marine, Meritorious Service, named and numbered.
 $400 (£248)
Merchant Marine, Mariner's Medal. **$200 (£124)**
Merchant Marine, Defense Medal. **$25 (£16)**
Merchant Marine, Atlantic War Zone Medal. **$30 (£19)**
Merchant Marine, Mediterranean Middle East War Zone Medal.
 $25 (£16)
Merchant Marine, Pacific War Zone Medal. **$25 (£16)**
Merchant Marine, World War II Victory. **$95 (£59)**
Selective Service System Medal. **$10 (£6)**
Medal of Freedom. **$60 (£37)**

YUGOSLAVIA (also see CROATIA)

Order of the Crown, Knight.
$90-$150 (£56-£93)
Hermann-Historica.de

Order of the Crown,
Commander. **$200-$400
(£124-£248)**
Hermann-Historica.de

Order of the Crown ,
Grand Cross.
$500-$675 (£310-£419)
Hermann-Historica.de

Order of the Crown, Grand Cross. **$367 (£225)**
Order of the Crown, Grand Cross breast star. **$367 (£225)**
Order of the Crown, Commander, I Class. **$269 (£165)**
Order of the Crown, Commander, I Class breast star. **$285 (£175)**
Order of the Crown, Commander, II Class . **$269 (£165)**
Order of the Crown, Officer. **$163 (£100)**
Order of the Crown, Knight. **$147 (£90)**
Commemorative Medal of the Liberation of the Northern
Territories. **$41 (£25)**
Commemorative Medal of the Liberation of Southern Serbia.
 $41 (£25)
World War II Commemorative Cross. **$122 (£75)**

Chapter 5

Firearms

Weapons have long been considered to be the "perfect" trophy of someone who served in combat. Soldiers returning from the war selected examples of captured weapons or even one of their own favorites to remind them of their days in service. Apart from the occasional presentation piece or rare sniper weapon that might have returned as a trophy, the bulk of the weapons available to collectors entered the market through surplus sources.

The millions of rifles, handguns, and submachine guns that were collected after the war could not be absorbed by the current military structure. Furthermore, many of the weapons were simply out of date and no longer of interest to a nation rearming itself. Therefore, stacks of weapons became available to the secondary, civilian market.

Like all areas of World War II collecting, if you intend to collect long arms, decide how you are going to collect before making your initial purchase. For example: Do you simply desire a representative weapon from both sides? If so, an M1 Garand or a British SMLE and a German 98k or Japanese Arisaka Type 99 might suffice. Perhaps you want to collect weapons used by a particular nation. For example, if you decided to assemble a collection of rifles used by the United States, you would be able to limit yourself to about a dozen weapons (albeit, a few will cost you several thousand dollars). This sort of approach will provide for a limited variety and also help develop a feel for the arming of one nation.

Collecting long arms can be addictive. Perhaps you will begin by buying a nice Inland M1 carbine at a show. Pretty soon you might think, "Hmm, it might be fun to collect one of each of the M1 carbine manufacturers." After several thousand dollars spent, your habit might blossom into, "Now that I have those, I will need to have a representative M1 rifle." Before you know it, you have branched out into full-auto machine guns and you are mortgaging your house to buy an M2 Browning! As pointed out earlier, formulate a plan before you begin to buy. There are too many weapons out there, and you simply can't buy them all. Choices will have to be made to form a meaningful and valuable collection.

Know the Law

Before you buy, become familiar with any local or national laws that regulate the private ownership of firearms. In the United States, these vary from state to state. In many locations in the United States and Europe, one may not own a weapon capable of firing. For these people and those who simply do not want the liability of live weapons, a market of "demilitarized" weapons has emerged. These weapons, though usually built with original parts, are totally non-firing and cannot be made to fire. Values of these weapons are proportional to their live-firing counterparts.

AUSTRALIA

Australian Owens Mk I submachine gun.
$10,000-$30,000 (£62,000-£18,600)
Rock Island Auction Co.

Australian Austen Mark I. **$12,000-$17,500 (£7,440-£10,850)**
Rock Island Auction Co.

Submachine Guns

Austen Mark I. **$12,000-$17,500 (£7,440-£10,850)**
Owens Mk I. **$10,000-$30,000 (£6,200-£18,600)**

AUSTRIA

Submachine Guns

Steyr-Solothurn MP 30.
  $10,000-$17,500 (£6,200-£10,850)
Steyr-Solothurn S1-100 (MP34(o)).
  $10,000-$17,500 (£6,200-£10,850)

Values at a Glance

Commonly encountered firearms:

- British No. 1 SMLE Mark III rifle
  $150-$650 (£93-£403)
- German Luger dated 1942
  $400-$2,000 (£248-£1,240)
- German Model 98 rifle
  $200-$600 (£124-£372)
- Japanese Nambu "Type 14" pistol
  $250-$650 (£155-£403)
- Japanese Arisaka Type 99 rifle
  $125-$350 (£78-£217)
- Soviet Union Mosin-Nagant Model 1891/30 rifle
  $100-$300 (£62-£186)
- U.S. Remington Rand M1911A1 pistol, 1943-45 production
  $650-$1,800 (£403-£1,116)
- U.S. Model 1903A3 rifle
  $350-$1,000 (£217-£620)
- U.S. Inland M1 carbine
  $525-$1,900 (£326-£1,178)
- U.S. Springfield M1 rifle, serial number 410000-3880000
  $700-$3,500 (£434-£2,170)

Rifles

Austrian Steyr Model 29/40 (600) rifle.
$300-$1,000 (£186-£620)
Rock Island Auction Co.

Steyr Model 1888/1890 Mannlicher rifle.
$175-$750 (£109-£465)
Steyr Model 1890 Mannlicher carbine.
$200-$750 (£124-£465)
Steyr Model 1895 Mannlicher rifle.
$175-$550 (£109-£341)
Steyr Model 1895 Mannlicher sharpshooter's rifle.
$350-$1,500 (£217-£930)
Steyr Model 1895 Mannlicher sniper rifle.
$2,000-$5,000 (£1,240-£3,100)

Machine Guns

Model 07/12 Schwarzlose.
$25,000-$30,000 (£15,500-£18,600)

BELGIUM

Handguns

Armand Gavage 7.65mm pistol.
$175-$650 (£109-£403)
Model 1903 FN pistol. **$250-$850 (£155-£527)**
Model 1922 FN pistol. **$125-$500 (£78-£310)**
Model 1935 FN pistol. **$300-$1,750 (£186-£1,085)**

Belgian Model 1922 FN pistol.
$125-$500 (£78-£310)
Chris William

German Military Pistole
Model 640(b) pistol
produced by Belgian FN
plant. **$300-$950 (£186-£589)**
HA.com

German Military Pistole Model 640(b) pistol.
$300-$950 (£186-£589)
Captured Pre War Commercial Model 1935 pistol.
$750-$1,800 (£465-£1,116)

Rifles

Belgian M1889/36 rifle. **$240 (£149)**
HA.com

Belgian De L'Etat-produced M1935
short rifle. **$250-$750 (£155-£465)**
Rock Island Auction Co.

M1935 Mauser short rifle. **$250-$750 (£155-£465)**
M1889/36 Mauser short rifle. **$150-575 (£93-£350)**
M24/30 Mauser Training rifle, Army.
$275-$850 (£171-£527)
M24/30 Mauser Training rifle, Navy.
$300-$850 (£186-£527)
FN BAR Model D. **$27,500-$37,500 (£17,050-£23,250)**

BRAZIL

Rifles

M1922 Mauser carbine. **$150-$850 (£93-£527)**
VZ24 short rifle. **$200-$850 (£124-£527)**
M1935 Mauser Banner rifle. **$175-$850 (£109-£527)**
M1935 Mauser Banner carbine.
$200-$850 (£124-£527)
M1908/34 short rifle. **$150-$550 (£93-£341)**

CANADA

Handguns

Canadian No. 2 Mk. 1*
John Inglis & Co. pistol.
$450-$1,500 (£279-£930)
Rock Island Auction Co.

No. 1 Mk. 1 John Inglis & Co. pistol,
Chinese-marked. **$400-$2,500 (£248-£1,550)**
No. 1 Mk. 1 John Inglis & Co. pistol.
$350-$1,000 (£217-£620)

No. 2 Mk. 1 John Inglis & Co. pistol.
$350-$1,000 (£217-£620)
No. 2 Mk. 1* John Inglis & Co. pistol.
$450-$1,500 (£279-£930)

Submachine Guns

Canadian Sten Mk II. $4,000-$6,500 (£2,480-£4,030)

Rifles

Canadian Long Branch No. 4 Mark I rifle.
$150-$600 (£93-£372)
Rock Island Auction Co.

Lee Enfield Rifle No. 4, Mark I (T).
$150-$600 (£93-£372)

Machine Guns

Canadian Bren Mk I.
$40,000-$45,000 (£24,800-£27,900)
Canadian Bren Mk II.
$40,000-$45,000 (£24,800-£27,900)
Canadian Chinese Bren Mk II.
$40,000-$45,000 (£24,800-£27,900)

CHINA

Chinese Shansei
Arsenal Type 18
(Mauser 96) .45 caliber
"broom handle" pistol.
$800-$2,500
(£496-£1,550)
Rock Island Auction Co.

Handguns

Chinese-marked handmade Mauser 96 pistol.
$250-$500 (£155-£310)
Taku-Naval Dockyard Mauser 96 pistol.
$300-$1,700 (£186-£1,054)
Shansei Arsenal Mauser 96 pistol.
$800-$2,500 (£496-£1,550)

Rifles

M98/22 Mauser rifle. $200-$650 (124£-£403)
FN M24 Mauser short rifle. $150-$600 (£93-£372)
FN M30 Mauser short rifle. $150-$600 (£93-£372)

Chiang Kai-shek Mauser short rifle.
$100-$500 (£62-£310)
VZ24 Mauser short rifle. $150-$600 (£92-£372)
VZ24 Mauser short rifle with Japanese folding
bayonet. $250-$1,000 (£155-£620)
M1933 Standard Model Mauser short rifle.
$175-$900 (£109-£558)

Machine Guns

Type 24. $15,000-$25,000 (£9,300-£15,550)
Type 26. $24,000-$28,000 (£14,880-£17,360)

Collecting Hints

Pros:

- Firearm are great visual aids for learning or teaching about World War II. A soldier's existence came down to the weapon he carried. Collecting weapons places your hands on the very tools that made history.

- Firearms tend to hold their value, making them a tangible hedge against inflation.

- World War II firearms are in plentiful supply, so it is fairly easy to enter the hobby and find a niche that will provide variety and collecting satisfaction.

Cons:

- It is easy for those who don't understand your hobby to label you as a "gun nut."

- There are a lot of laws governing the private ownership of firearms. It is your responsibility to know what they are.

- Guns draw attention, both welcome and unwelcome. They are prime targets of thieves.

- Long arms are cumbersome to display and collect. As your collection grows, you will find that wall space fills quickly.

- You must answer the question, "Do I restore a weapon to the way it appeared when issued, or keep it in the condition as I found it?"

- Because of the quantity and variety of weapons available, unless you are independently wealthy, you will be faced with a limited collection.

Availability: ✪ ✪ ✪ ✪
Price: ✪ ✪ ✪
Reproduction Alert: ✪ ✪

CZECHOSLOVAKIA

Handguns

German Nazi-proofed
Czechoslovakian CZ 1927
pistol. **$250-$650 (£155-£403)**
HA.com

Czechoslovakian CZ 1938
pistol. **$250-$800 (£155-£496)**
Chris William

Army Pistole 1922. **$200-$700 (£124-£434)**
CZ 1927 pistol. **$200-$500 (£124-£310)**
CZ 1927 pistol, Nazi-proofed. **$250-$650 (£155-£403)**
CZ 1938. **$250-$800 (£155-£496)**

Submachine Guns

CZ 23/25. **$10,000-$12,500 (£6,200-£7,750)**
ZK 383. **$12,000-$14,000 (£7,440-£8,680)**

Rifles

Czechoslovakian VZ24 bolt-action
rifle. **$70 (£43)**
HA.com

Czechoslovakia G24(t) rifle.
$2,000-$3,000 (£1,240-£1,860)
Rock Island Auction Co.

M1898/22 Mauser rifle. **$150-$600 (£93-£372)**
VZ23 Mauser rifle. **$175-$800 (£109-£496)**

VZ16/33 Mauser carbine. **$200-$500 (£124-£310)**
M1895 Mannlicher rifle. **$150-$600 (£93-£372)**
Model 24 (VZ24) rifle. **$85-$550 (£53-£341)**
Model G24(t), Nazi-proofed.
  $2,000-$3,000 (£1,240-£1,860)
Model ZH29. **$5,000-$13,500 (£3,100-£8,370)**

Machine Guns

ZB VZ26. **$30,000-$35,000 (£18,600-£21,700)**
ZB VZ30. **$17,000-$20,000 (£10,540-£12,400)**
ZGB VZ30. **$18,000-$25,000 (£11,160-£15,550)**
ZB VZ37. **$22,000-$30,000 (£13,640-£18,600)**

ENGLAND

Handguns

Enfield No. 2, Mark
I revolver. **$150-$450
(£93-£279)**
Chris William

Webley & Scott Mark IV,
.380 caliber revolver.
$175-$450 (£109-£279)
Chris William

Smith & Wesson
Model 10 M&P
revolver. **$275-$750
(£171-£465)**
Rock Island Auction Co.

British Molins No. 1 Mk
V flare pistol. **$65 (£40)**
HA.com

How Much For That Tank?

There is hardly a World War II buff alive who hasn't at one time thought, "Gee, I would like to own a tank…I wonder how much one would cost?" It isn't as crazy as what one's neighbors might think!

In the United States, nearly 30,000 people call themselves "MV (military vehicle) enthusiasts." The most common World War II vehicle to be restored is the most numerous to have been built during the war—the jeep. But many also like to restore and drive larger vehicles ranging from 2-1/2-ton GMC trucks to Sherman tanks.

The largest club for MV enthusiasts is the Military Vehicle Preservation Organization (www.mvpa. org). With 9,000 members worldwide, it serves as a connecting point for people who yearn to drive something in olive drab. The most popular magazine for folks in the hobby is *Military Vehicles Magazine*. Filled with technical and historical articles about military jeeps, trucks and tracked vehicles, it also is a place to find dealers in vehicles and parts. Check it out online at www.militaryvehiclesmagazine.com.

This brief guide will give you an idea of the prices of some of the most popular vehicles:

Willys or Ford Jeep
$10,000-$18,000 (£6,200-£11,600)
WC 3/4-ton weapons carrier
$12,000-$17,000 (£7,440-£10,540)
CCKW 2-1/2-ton truck
$11,000-$17,000 (£6,820-£10,540)
M3/M3A1 half-track
$25,000-$40,000 (£15,500-£24,800)
M29 Weasel
$10,000-$16,000 (£6,200-£9,920)
US 37mm anti-tank gun (non-firing)
$12,000-$15,000 (£7,440-£9,300)
M4A3 Sherman medium tank
$120,000-$340,000 (£74,400-£210,800)
M5A1 Stuart light tank
$95,000-$165,000 (£58,900-£102,300)
German Kübelwagen
$25,000-$40,000 (£15,500-£24,800)
German Schwimmwagen
$90,000-$150,000 (£55,800-£93,000)
German "Hetzer" tank destroyer
$250,000-$350,000 (£155,000-£217,000)
Soviet T34 tank
$85,000-$115,000 (£52,700-£71,300)
British Bren Carrier
$30,000-$45,000 (£18,600-£27,900)

Who hasn't fantasized about owning his own Sherman tank? It is possible, but it will cost more than **$120,000 (£74,400)** before your restoration begins!

Wehrmacht BMW R75 motorcycle with sidecar. **$50,920 (£31,570)**
Hermann-Historica.de

1944 VW Kübelwagen Type 82. **$57,620 (£35,725)**
Hermann-Historica.de

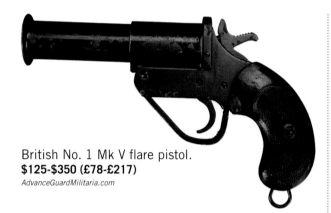

British No. 1 Mk V flare pistol.
$125-$350 (£78-£217)
AdvanceGuardMilitaria.com

Webley & Scott Mark IV, .380 caliber revolver.
  $175-$450 (£109-£279)
Enfield No. 2, Mark I revolver. **$150-$450 (£93-£279)**
Enfield No. 2, Mark I* revolver. **$125-$350 (£78-£217)**
Model 1935 FN pistol. **$550-1,200 (£341-£744)**
Smith & Wesson Model 10 M&P revolver.
  $275-$750 (£171-£465)

Flare Pistols

No. 1 Mk III flare pistol. **$300-$350 (£186-£217)**
No. 1 Mk V flare pistol. **$60-$150 (£37-£93)**
No. 2 Mk V flare pistol. **$75-$150 (£47-£93)**
Webley Mk III*. **$350-$500 (£217-£310)**
Webley & Scott flare pistol. **$250-$300 (£155-£186)**
Model M Royal Air Force flare pistol.
  $200-$250 (£124-£155)

Submachine Guns

British Sten Mark II submachine
gun. **$4,000-$10,000 (£2,480-£6,200)**
Rock Island Auction Co.

British Sten Mark V submachine gun.
$4,000-$10,000 (£2,480-£6,200)
JamesDJulia.com

Lancaster Mk1. **$6,000-$7,000 (£3,720-£4,340)**
Sten Mark II. **$4,000-$10,000 (£2,480-£6,200)**
Sten Mark III. **$4,000-$10,000 (£2,480-£6,200)**
Sten Mark V. **$4,000-$10,000 (£2,480-£6,200)**

Rifles

British Enfield No. 1 SMLE, Mark V rifle.
$335 (£208)
HA.com

British Enfield No. 1 SMLE Mark III*.
$290 (£180)
HA.com

British No. 5, Mark I jungle carbine.
$450 (£279)
HA.com

British rifle No. 4, Mark 1*. **$150-$500
(£93-£310)**
PoulinAntiques.com

British Boys Anti-Tank
rifle. **$3,000-$8,000
(£1,860-£4,960)**
JamesDJulia.com

Rifle No. 4, Mark 1 sniper rifle with No.
32 telescopic sight. **$9,068 (£5,622)**
PoulinAntiques.com

British No.4 Mark 1(T) sniper rifle with transit case
and accessories. **$9,500 (£5,890)**
Rock Island Auction Co.

No. 1 SMLE Mark III. **$150-$650 (£93-£403)**
No. 1 SMLE Mark III Drill rifle. **$60-$100 (£37-£62)**
Mo. 1 Mark III single shot rifle. **$100-$500 (£62-£310)**
No. 1 Mark III grenade launching rifle.
  $150-$600 (£93-£372)
Lee-Enfield .410 musket (shotgun).
  $100-$300 (£62-£186)
No. 1 SMLE Mark IV. **$200-$600 (£124-£372)**
No. 1 SMLE Mark III*. **$150-$550 (£93-£341)**

No. 1 SMLE Mark V. **$350-$1,700 (£217-£1,054)**
No. 1 SMLE Mark VI. **$1,000-$4,000 (£620-£2,480)**
Rifle No. 4, Mark I trials model.
  $500-$2,500 (£310-£1,550)
Rifle No. 4, Mark 1. **$150-$650 (£93-£403)**
Rifle No. 4, Mark 1*. **$150-$500 (£93-£310)**
Rifle No. 4, Mark 1 / 2. **$175-$450 (£109-£279)**
Rifle No. 5, Mark 1. **$175-$650 (£109-£403)**
SMLE Sniper rifle (optical sights).
  $1,500-$7,500 (£930-£4,650)
SMLE Sniper rifle (telescopic sights).
  $1,500-$7,500 (£930-£4,650)
Rifle No. 4, Mark I(T) sniper rifle.
  $1,250-$4,500 (£775-£2,790)
De Lisle Carbine. **$5,000-$7,500 (£3,100-£4,650)**
Boys Anti-Tank Rifle. **$3,000-$8,000 (£1,860-£4,960)**

Machine Guns

British Bren Mk2 machine gun.
$38,000-$42,000 (£23,560-£26,040)
JamesDJulia.com

Australian Bren. **$30,000-$40,000 (£18,600-£24,800)**
Bren Mk1. **$35,000-$50,000 (£21,700-£31,000)**
Bren Mk2. **$38,000-$42,000 (£23,560-£26,040)**
Vickers Mark I. **$18,000-$35,000 (£11,160-£21,700)**
Hotchkiss Mark I. **$10,000-$18,000 (£6,200-£11,160)**

FINLAND

Handguns

L-35 Lahti pistol, Type I
(serial nos. 1105-3700).
$1,250-$2,500 (£775-£1,550)
Hermann-Historica.de

L-35 Lahti pistol, Type II
(serial nos. 3701-4700).
$1,850-$3,500 (£1,147-£2,170)
Hermann-Historica.de

L-35 Lahti pistol, Type I (serial nos. 1105-3700).
  $1,250-$2,500 (£775-£1,550)
L-35 Lahti pistol, Type II (serial nos. 3701-4700).
  $1,850-$3,500 (£1,147-£2,170)
L-35 Lahti pistol, Type II (serial nos. 4701-6800).
  $1,850-$3,500 (£1,147-£2,170)

Submachine Guns

Suomi Model 1931. **$13,000-$16,000 (£8,060-£9,920)**
Suomi Model 1944. **$13,000-$16,000 (£8,060-£9,920)**

Rifles

Model 91/24 Civil Guard infantry rifle.
  $150-$500 (£93-£310)
Model 1927 Army short rifle. **$150-$375 (£93-£233)**
Model 1927 Cavalry carbine.
  $500-$2,000 (£310-£1,240)
Model 1928.30 Civil Guard short rifle.
  $250-$575 (£155-£357)
Finnish Model 91/30 rifle. **$150-$350 (£93-£217)**
Model 1939 short rifle. **$150-$375 (£93-£233)**
Swedish Model 1896 rifle. **$200-$600 (£124-£372)**
Italian Carcano. **$125-$300 (£78-£186)**

FRANCE

Handguns

French Model 1892 Revolver,
Army. **$200-$450 (£124-£279)**
Chris William

French Model 1935A
pistol. **$240 (£149)**
HA.com

French Model 1935A pistol.
$125-$350 (£78-£217)
PoulinAntiques.com

Model 1892 Revolver, Navy. **$275-$600 (£171-£372)**
Model 1892 Revolver, Army. **$200-$450 (£124-£279)**
Le Francais Model 28 Type Armee pistol.
 $500-$1,250 (£310-£775)
Model 1935A pistol. **$125-$300 (£78-£186)**
Model 1935A pistol, Nazi-proofed.
 $200-$475 (£124-£295)
Model 1935S. **$125-$300 (£78-£186)**
MAB Model D pistol. **$200-$500 (£124-£310)**
Unique Model 16 pistol, Nazi-proofed.
 $150-$550 (£93-£341)
Unique Model 17 pistol, Nazi-proofed.
 $150-$500 (£93-£310)
Unique Kriegsmodell pistol, Nazi-proofed.
 $150-$600 (£93-£372)

Submachine Guns

French MAS 38 submachine
gun. **$5,500-$7,000
(£3,410-£4,340)**
Rock Island Auction Co.

MAS 35 SE. **$5,500-$7,500 (£3,410-£4,650)**
MAS 38. **$5,500-$7,000 (£3,410-£4,650)**

Rifles

French World War II Lebel Model 1886/
M93/R35 carbine and bayonet. **$245 (£152)**
AdvanceGuardMilitaria.com

French MAS 36 rifle. **$150-$550 (£93-£341)**
PoulinAntiques.com

Lebel Model 1886/M93/R35 rifle.
 $250-$550 (£155-£341)
Lebel Model 1886/M93/R35 rifle, Nazi-proofed.
 $425-$825 (£264-£512)
Berthier-Mannlicher Model 1907/15-M34.
 $250-$650 (£155-£403)
MAS 36 rifle. **$150-$550 (£93-£341)**
MAS 44 rifle. **$300-$800 (£186-£496)**
MAS 45 rifle. **$150-$500 (£93-£310)**

Machine Guns

French Chatellerault M1924/M29
machine gun. **$10,000-$17,500
(£6,200-£10,850)**
JamesDJulia.com

French Darne Model 1934 aviation machine gun.
$8,000-$15,500 (£4,960-£9,610)
JamesDJulia.com

Hotchkiss Model 1914.
 $9,000-$12,000 (£5,580-£7,440)
Chatellerault M1924/M29.
 $10,000-$17,500 (£6,200-£10,850)
Darne Model 1934 aviation machine gun.
$8,000-$15,500 (£4,960-£9,610)

GERMANY

Handguns

German Luger S/42,
1937-dated. **$2,500 (£1,550)**
HistoryHunter.com

German Walther P.38,
ac44 code semi-automatic
pistol. **$1,135**
HA.com

German Luger S/42 1937 pistol with 1937-dated holster, extra magazine, and loading tool. **$1,675 (£1,039)**
HA.com

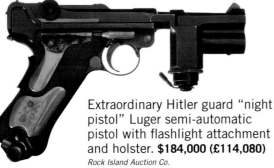

German Walther P.38 Third issue, zero series, circa 1940, 5" barrel. **$1,495 (£927)**
HA.com

Extraordinary Hitler guard "night pistol" Luger semi-automatic pistol with flashlight attachment and holster. **$184,000 (£114,080)**
Rock Island Auction Co.

German factory-cased, gold-plated and relief-engraved Walther Model PP pistol as presented to SA officer, Viktor Lutze. **$241,500 (£149,730)**
Rock Island Auction Co.

German Mauser P.38, byf43 pistol. **$660 (£409)**
HA.com

Walther P.38 automatic pistol, factory scroll-engraved with factory white plastic grips. **$1,135 (£704)**
HA.com

German police-marked Sauer Model 38-H semi-automatic pistol. **$180 (£111)**
HA.com

German Walther Model PP, .32 cal., RJ-marked.
$400-$850 (£248-£527)
PoulinAntiques.com

German Walther PP pistol presented to Ernst Bauer of the NSDAP Regional Group Obergiesing. **$5,750 (£3,565)**
JamesDJulia.com

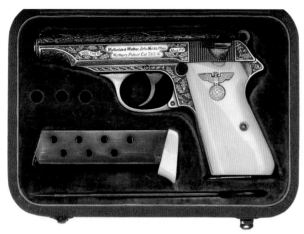

German Walter PP 7.65mm pistol with SS engraving. **$15,525 (£9,626)**
JamesDJulia.com

German Walther Model PPK, .32 caliber, Duraluminum frame. **$650-$1,575 (£403-£977)**
Rock Island Auction Co.

German Walther PPK party leader pistol with matching party leader leather holster. **$10,925 (£6,774)**
Rock Island Auction Co.

Steyr Hahn Model 1911 (World War II issue marked "P.08"). **$250-$1,000 (£155-£620)**
Mauser Snellfeuer Model 712 (also know as "Model 32"). **$12,500-$20,000 (£7,750-£12,400)**
Luger, Death's Head rework.
  $600-$2,800 (£372-£1,736)
Luger, Kadetten Institute rework.
  $800-$3,200 (£496-£1,984)
Luger, Mauser unmarked rework.
  $600-$1,450 (£372-£899)

Luger, Mauser Oberndorf.
  $1,500-$5,000 (£930-£3,100)
Luger, 1935/06 Portuguese "GNR".
  $750-$3,500 (£465-£2,170)
Luger S/42 K Date. **$1,200-$6,000 (£744-£3,720)**
Luger S/42 G Date. **$650-$2,800 (£403-£1,736)**
Luger, dated chamber S/42.
  $500-$2,000 (£310-£1,240)
Luger, code 42 dated chamber.
  $400-$1,850 (£248-£1,147)
Luger, 41/42 code. **$700-$3,500 (£434-£2,170)**
Luger, byf code. **$450-$2,000 (£279-£1,240)**
Luger, 1934 Mauser Dutch contract.
  $1,100-$3,500 (£682-£2,170)
Luger, 1934 Mauser Swedish contract.
  $1,250-$3,750 (£775-£2,325)
Luger, 1934 Mauser German contract.
  $800-$3,000 (£496-£1,860)
Luger, Austrian Bundes Heer.
  $700-$2,800 (£434-£1,736)
Luger, Mauser two-digit date.
  $900-$3,000 (£558-£1,860)
Luger, S code Krieghoff. **$1,000-$5,000 (£620-£3,100)**
Luger, grip safety Krieghoff.
  $1,500-$7,500 (£930-£4,650)
Luger, 36 date Krieghoff. **$1,500-$4,500 (£930-£2,790)**
Luger, 4-digit date Krieghoff.
  $1,500-$4,500 (£930-£2,790)
P.38, Model HP, early with high gloss bluing.
  $600-$3,000 (£372-£1,860)
P.38, Model HP, early with high gloss bluing and alloy frame. **$2,000-$8,000 (£1,240-£4,960)**
P.38, Model HP, late with military blue finish.
  $550-$2,000 (£341-£1,240)
P.38, First issue, zero series.
  $2,500-$9,000 (£1,550-£5,580)
P.38, Second issue, zero series.
  $2,000-$7,500 (£1,240-£4,650)
P.38, Third issue, zero series.
  $800-$3,500 (£496-£2,170)
P.38, 480 code. **$1,750-$6,500 (£1,085-£4,030)**
P.38, ac code. **$2,800-$8,000 (£1,736-£4,960)**
P.38, ac40 code ("40" added).
  $1,000-$3,750 (£620-£2,325)
P.38, ac40 code. **$700-$2,500 (£434-£1,550)**
P.38, ac41 code. **$500-$2,000 (£310-£1,240)**
P.38, ac42 code. **$300-$1,000 (£186-£620)**
P.38, ac43 code. **$250-$900 (£155-£558)**
P.38, ac44 code. **$250-$1,150 (£155-£713)**
P.38, ac45 code. **$250-$950 (£155-£589)**
P.38, ac45 zero series code.
  $500-$2,800 (£310-£1,736)
P.38, byf42 code. **$500-$1,900 (£310-£1,178)**
P.38, byf43 code. **$250-$850 (£155-£527)**
P.38, byf44 code. **$250-$850 (£155-£527)**
P.38, cyq code (first variation).
  $500-$1,400 (£310-£868)
P.38, cyq code (standard variation).
  $350-$650 (£217-£403)
P.38, cyq zero series. **$350-$1,250 (£217-£775)**
P.38, AC43/44-FN slide. **$600-$2,000 (£372-£1,240)**

P.38, police, byf/43 code. **$800-$2,500 (£496-£1,550)**
P.38, police, byf/44 code. **$800-$2,500 (£496-£1,550)**
P.38, police, ac/43 code.
  $1,250-$5,000 (£775-£3,100)
P.38, police, ac/44 code.
  $1,250-$5,000 (£557-£3,100)
P.38, police, svw/45 code.
  $1,600-$6,000 (£992-£3,720)
Mauser Model 1934 pistol. **$150-$550 (£93-£341)**
Mauser Model HSC early Army model.
  $250-$650 (£155-£403)
Mauser Model HSC late Army model.
  $225-$550 (£140-£341)
Mauser Model HSC Navy model.
  $400-$1,000 (£248-£620)
Mauser Model HSC early police model.
  $250-$650 (£155-£402)
Mauser Model HSC wartime police model.
  $250-$600 (£155-£372)
Mauser Model HSC wartime commercial model.
  $200-$500 (£124-£310)
Sauer Model 1913, second series, paramilitary-
  marked. **$200-$500 (£124-£310)**
Sauer Model 38, one-line legend.
  $600-$2,500 (£372-£1,550)
Sauer Model 38, two-line legend.
  $500-$1,850 (£310-£1,147)
Sauer Model 38 paramilitary-marked.
  $500-$3,000 (£310-£1,860)
Sauer Model 38-H. **$300-$850 (£186-£527)**
Sauer Model 38-H paramilitary-marked.
  $350-$2,500 (£217-£1,550)
Sauer Model 38-H L.M. Model.
  $1,000-$3,500 (£620-£2,170)
Sauer Model 38-H Type II, police.
  $300-$850 (£186-£527)
Sauer Model 38-H Type II, military variation.
  $400-$1,200 (£248-£744)
Sauer Model 38-H Type III, military-accepted.
  $275-$550 (£171-£341)
Sauer Model 38-H Type III, commercial.
  $250-$475 (£155-£295)
Sauer Model 38-H Type III, police.
  $250-$600 (£155-£372)
Sauer Model 38-H Type IV, military-accepted.
  $275-$575 (£171-£357)
Sauer Model 38-H Type IV, commercial.
  $250-$450 (£155-£279)
Sauer Model 38-H Type IV, police.
  $250-$600 (£155-£372)
Sauer Model 38-H Type IV, SA-marked.
  $450-$3,000 (£279-£1,860)
Sauer Model 38 Type IV, military-accepted.
  $250-$500 (£155-£310)
Sauer Model 38 Type IV, police.
  $300-$575 (£186-£357)
Sauer Model 38-H Type V. **$200-$750 (£124-£465)**
Walther Model PP, .22 caliber.
  $250-$900 (£155-£558)
Walther Model PP, .25 caliber.
  $1,500-$4,800 (£930-£2,976)

Walther Model PP, .32 caliber, high-polished finish.
  $225-$650 (£140-£403)
Walther Model PP, .32 caliber, milled finish.
  $200-$550 (£124-£341)
Walther Model PP, **.380 caliber. $475-$950 (£295-£589)**
Walther Model PP, .32 caliber, Duraluminum frame.
  $400-$900 (£248-£558)
Walther Model PP, .32 with bottom magazine.
  $400-$1,100 (£248-£682)
Walther Model PP, .32 caliber with Verchromt finish.
  $700-$2,000 (£434-£1,240)
Walther Model PP, .32 caliber, blue, silver, or gold
  finish and full engraving.
  $1,200-$6,500 (£744-£4,030)
Walther Model PP, .32 cal., with Waffenamt stamp,
  high finish. **$275-$1,500 (£171-£930)**
Walther Model PP, .32 cal., with Waffenamt stamp,
  milled finish. **$250-$650 (£155-£403)**
Walther Model PP, .32 cal., police, high-polished
  finish. **$300-$1,200 (£186-£744)**
Walther Model PP, .32 cal., police, milled finish.
  $300-$900 (£186-£558)
Walther Model PP, .32 cal., NSKK-marked.
  $550-$2,000 (£341-£1,240)
Walther Model PP, .32 cal., NSDAP group-marked.
  $500-$2,000 (£310-£1,240)
Walther Model PP, .32 cal., PDM-marked.
  $475-$850 (£295-£527)
Walther Model PP, .32 cal., RJ-marked.
  $400-$850 (£248-£527)
Walther Model PP, .32 cal., RFV mark, high-polished
  finish. **$400-$850 (£248-£527)**
Walther Model PP, .32 cal., RBD-marked.
  $650-$2,200 (£403-£1,364)
Walther Model PP, .32 cal., RpLt-marked.
  $275-$850 (£171-£527)
Walther Model PP, .32 cal., RZM-marked.
  $600-$2,500 (£375-£1,550)
Walther Model PP, .32 cal., Statens Vattenfallsverk-
  marked. **$375-$1,000 (£233-£620)**
Walther Model PP, .32 cal., AC-marked.
  $250-$675 (£155-£419)
Walther Model PP, .32 cal., Duraluminum frame.
  $300-$750 (£186-£465)
Walther Model PP, .380 cal., bottom release,
Waffenamt-marked. **$500-$2,000 (£310-£1,240)**
Walther Model PPK, .22 caliber.
  $500-$1,750 (£310-£1,085)
Walther Model PPK, .25 caliber.
  $1,200-$7,000 (£744-£4,340)
Walther Model PPK, .32 caliber, high-polished
  finish. **$250-$650 (£155-£403)**
Walther Model PPK, .32 caliber milled finish.
  $250-$575 (£155-£357)
Walther Model PPK, .380 caliber. **$750-$2,200 (£465-£1,364)**
Walther Model PPK, .32 caliber, Duraluminum
  frame. **$650-$1,575 (£403-£977)**
Walther Model PPK, .32 caliber, Verchromt finish.
  $700-$2,500 (£434-£1,550)

Walther Model PPK, .32 cal., blue, silver, or gold
  finish and full engraving. **$1,200-$6,500 (£744-£4,030)**
Walther Model PPK, .32 cal., marked "Mod. PP".
  $1,000-$3,000 (£620-£1,860)
Walther Model PPK, .32 cal., panagraphed slide.
  $300-$1,800 (£186-£1,116)
Walther Model PPK, .32 cal., Czechoslovakia
  contract. **$450-$1,550 (£279-£961)**
Walther Model PPK, .32 cal., Allemagne-marked.
  $400-$1,250 (£248-£775)
Walther Model PPK, .32 cal., Waffenamt proofed,
  high-polished finish. **$400-$1,800 (£248-£1,116)**
Walther Model PPK, .32 cal., Waffenamt proofed,
  milled finish. **$400-$1,200 (£248-£744)**
Walther Model PPK, .32 cal., police, high-polished
  finish. **$425-$1,800 (£263-£1,116)**
Walther Model PPK, .32 cal., police, milled finish.
  $400-$1,500 (£248-£930)
Walther Model PPK, .32 cal., police, Duraluminum
  frame. **$575-$2,000 (£357-£1,240)**
Walther Model PPK, .22 cal., late war, black grips.
  $450-$1,200 (£279-£744)
Walther Model PPK, .32 cal., party leader grips,
  brown. **$1,800-$7,500 (£1,116-£4,650)**
Walther Model PPK, .32 cal., party leader grips,
  black. **$1,200-$5,000 (£744-£3,100)**
Walther Model PPK, .32 cal., RZM-marked.
  $500-$2,800 (310£-£1,736)
Walther Model PPK, .32 cal., PDM-marked,
  Duraluminum frame. **$750-$2,800 (£465-£1,736)**
Walther Model PPK, .32 cal., RFV-marked.
  $650-$2,000 (£403-£1,240)
Walther Model PPK, .32 cal., DRP-marked.
  $600-$2,500 (£372-£1,550)
Walther Model PPK, .32 cal., Statens
Vattenfallsverk. **$450-$1,400 (£282-£868)**

Flare Pistols

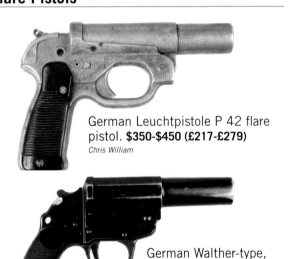

German Leuchtpistole P 42 flare
pistol. **$350-$450 (£217-£279)**
Chris William

German Walther-type,
aluminum flare pistol.
$325-$365 (£202-£226)
Chris William

German Walther Model SLD
double-barrel flare pistol.
$1,200-$5,500 (£744-£3,410)
JamesDJulia.com

Fliegerleuchtpistole Model L double-barrel flare
  pistol. **$350-$700 (£217-£434)**
Hebel flare pistol. **$200-$300 (£124-£186)**
Leuchtpistole P 42 flare pistol.
  $350-$450 (£217-£279)
Walther Model 1934 flare pistol.
  $125-$250 (£78-£155)
Walther-type, aluminum flare pistol.
  $325-$365 (£202-£226)
Walther-type, steel flare pistol.
  $375-$450 (£233-£279)
Walther-type, zinc flare pistol. **$500-$550 (£310-£341)**
Walther Model SLD double-barrel flare pistol.
  $1,200-$5,500 (£744-£3,410)

Submachine Guns

German MP34 submachine gun.
$12,500-$18,000 (£7,750-£11,160)
JamesDJulia.com

German MP38 submachine
gun. **$17,500-$25,000
(£10,850-£15,500)**
Hermann-Historica.de

German MP40 submachine
gun. **$19,305 (£11,969)**
PoulinAntiques.com

Bergman MP28. **$10,000-$18,500 (£6,200-£11,470)**
Erma EMP. **$12,000-$18,000 (£7,440-£11,160)**
MP34/I. **$12,500-$18,000 (£7,750-£11,160)**
MP35/I. **$12,500-$18,000 (£7,500-£11,160)**
MP38. **$17,500-$25,000 (£10,850-£15,500)**
MP40. **$10,000-$20,500 (£6,200-£12,710)**
MP41. **$12,000-$22,500 (£7,440-£13,950)**

Rifles

German Model G43 rifle. **$800-$2,500 (£496-£1,550)**
PoulinAntiques.com

German 98K (1944) Mauser bolt-action rifle. **$205 (£127)**
HA.com

German Mauser Model 98k rifle, byf 44, Russian capture. **$185 (£115)**
HA.com

German Model 33/40 carbine. **$400-$1,800 (£248-£1,116)**
JamesDJulia.com

German Model 98 rifle (1937) with S/27 bolt. **$1,990 (£1,234)**
PoulinAntiques.com

German Model KAR 98k sniper rifle (long rail). **$3,000-$14,500 (£1,860-£8,990)**
JamesDJulia.com

German Model KAR 98k sniper rifle (claw mount). **$3,000-$17,500 (£1,860-£10,850)**
JamesDJulia.com

German Model G41 (M) rifle. **$4,000-$12,500 (£2,480-£7,750)**
JamesDJulia.com

German Model G41 (W) rifle with ZF 40 scope (side rail mount). **$8,850 (£5,487)**
JamesDJulia.com

German Model VG-1. **$4,000-$13,000 (£2,480-£8,060)**
JamesDJulia.com

German Model VG-2. **$6,000-$23,000 (£3,720-£14,260)**
JamesDJulia.com

German Model 98k sniper rifle (high turret). **$2,000-$12,500 (£1,240-£7,750)**
Rock Island Auction Co.

German Sturmgewehr 44 (MP 44). **$13,000-$18,500 (£8,060-£11,470)**
Hermann-Historica.de

German Model VG-1. **$43,125 (£26,738)**
Rock Island Auction Co.

Model 98 transitional rifle. **$150-$600 (£93-£372)**
Model 98K rifle. **$200-$600 (£124-£372)**
Model 98k carbine. **$350-$1,500 (£217-£930)**
Model 98k carbine with extended magazine. **$1,800-$5,000 (£1,116-£3,100)**
Model 98k sniper rifle (high turret). **$2,000-$12,500 (£1,240-£7,750)**
Model 98k sniper rifle (low turret). **$2,000-$12,500 (£1,240-£7,750)**
Model KAR 98k sniper rifle (short rail). **$2,000-$8,000 (£1,240-£4,960)**
Model KAR 98k sniper rifle (long rail). **$3,000-$14,500 (£1,860-£8,990)**
Model KAR 98k sniper rifle (claw mount). **$3,000-$17,500 (£1,860-£10,850)**
Model KAR 98k sniper rifle (zf41 scope). **$750-$4,500 (£465-£2,790)**
Model 1933 standard model short rifle. **$350-$1,200 (£217-£744)**
Model 1933 standard model carbine. **$400-$1,500 (£248-£930)**

Model 33/40 carbine. **$400-$1,800 (£248-£1,116)**
Model 29/40 rifle (G29o). **$300-$1,000 (£186-£620)**
Model 24 (t) rifle. **$250-$950 (£155-£589)**
Model VG-98. **$1,800-$9,000 (£1,116-£5,580)**
Model VG-1. **$4,000-$13,000 (£2,480-£8,060)**
Model VG-2. **$6,000-$23,000 (£3,720-£14,260)**
Model VG-5. **$5,000-$20,000 (£3,100-£12,400)**
Model G41 (M) rifle. **$4,000-$12,500 (£2,480-£7,750)**
Model G41 (W) rifle. **$3,000-$7,500 (£1,860-£4,650)**
Model G43(W) (K43). **$800-$2,500 (£496-£1,550)**
Model FG42. **$25,000-$45,000 (£15,500-£27,900)**
MKb42(W). **$15,000-$25,000 (£9,300-£15,500)**
MKb42(H). **$12,500-$25,000 (£7,750-£15,500)**
MP43. **$9,500-$18,500 (£5,890-£11,470)**
MP44. **$13,000-$18,500 (£8,060-£11,470)**
StG44. **$12,500-$18,500 (£7,750-£11,470)**

Machine Guns

German MG34 light machine gun.
$30,000-$38,000 (£18,600-£23,560)
PoulinAntiques.com

Krieghoff Waffenfabrik Model FG42
paratrooper's machine gun. **$143,750 (£89,125)**
Cowan's Auctions, Inc.

MG13. **$15,000-$22,500 (£9,300-£13,950)**
MG15. **$16,500-$20,000 (£10,230-£12,400)**
MG15 water-cooled, ground gun.
 $15,000-$22,500 (£9,300-£13,950)
MG15 air-cooled, ground gun.
 $21,500-$25,000 (£13,330-£15,500)
MG34. **$30,000-$38,000 (£18,600-£23,560)**
MG42. **$32,500-$40,000 (£20,150-£24,800)**

HOLLAND

Handguns

Model 1873/1919 revolver. **$300-$1,200 (£186-£744)**
Model 94 revolver. **$200-$600 (£124-£372)**

Rifles

Beaumont Model 1871/88. **$150-$400 (£93-£248)**
Mannlicher Model 1895. **$175-$600 (£109-£372)**
Mannlicher Model 1895 No. 1 cavalry carbine.
 $175-$500 (£109-£310)
Mannlicher Model 1895 N. 2 gendarmerie carbine.
 $200-$550 (£124-£341)
Mannlicher Model 1895 No. 3 engineer and artillery
 carbine. **$200-$550 (£124-£341)**
Mannlicher Model 1895 No. 5 carbine A5.
 $200-$600 (£124-£372)
Mannlicher Model 1917. **$200-$750 (£124-£465)**

HUNGARY

Handguns

Hungarian Model 37
pistol, Nazi-proofed.
$150-$650 (£93-£403)
Chris William

Fegyvergyar Model 1929 pistol.
 $175-$500 (£109-£310)
Fegyvergyar Model 37 pistol, Nazi-proofed.
 $150-$650 (£93-£403)

Submachine Guns

Model 39. **$6,000-$15,000 (£3,720-£9,300)**
Model 43. **$9,500-$12,500 (£5,890-£7,750)**

Rifles

Hungarian Fegyvergyar Model Gewehr 98/40.
 $300-$1,800 (£186-£1,116)
PoulinAntiques.com

Mannlicher Model 1935. **$300-$1,250 (£186-£)**
Fegyvergyar Model Gewehr 98/40.
 $300-$1,800 (£186-£)
Fegyvergyar Model 43. **$300-$900 (£186-£558)**
Fegyvergyar 44.M. **$100-$300 (£62-£186)**
Steyr Model 95. **$100-$500 (£62-£310)**

ITALY

Handguns

Italian Bodeo Modello 1889 revolver (enlisted). **$100-$850 (£62-£527)**
Chris William

Italian Bodeo Modello 1889 revolver (officer). **$100-$850 (£62-£527)**
Chris William

Italian Glisenti Model 1910 pistol. **$250-$750 (£155-£465)**
Chris William

Beretta Model 1934 pistol, Army, RE-marked. **$225-$600 (£140-£372)**
PoulinAntiques.com

Italian Beretta Model 1934 pistol, Air Force, RA-marked. **$250-$700 (£155-£434)**
HistoryHunter.com

Modello 1874 revolver. **$200-$900 (£124-£558)**
System Bodeo Modello 1889 revolver (enlisted). **$150-$500 (£93-£310)**
System Bodeo Modello 1889 revolver (officer). **$150-$500 (£93-£310)**
Glisenti Model 1910 pistol. **$250-$750 (£155-£465)**
Beretta Model 1915 pistol. **$200-$800 (£124-£496)**
Beretta Model 1915 pistol, 2nd variation. **$250-$1,000 (£155-£620)**
Beretta Model 1915/1919 pistol. **$150-$600 (£93-£372)**
Beretta Model 1923 pistol. **$400-$1,500 (£248-£930)**
Beretta Model 1931 pistol. **$200-$800 (£124-£496)**
Beretta Model 1934 pistol, Army, RE-marked. **$225-$600 (£140-£372)**
Beretta Model 1934 pistol, Air Force, RA-marked. **$225-$675 (£140-£419)**
Beretta Model 1934 pistol, Navy, RM-marked. **$250-$750 (£155-£465)**
Beretta Model 1935 pistol. **$150-$550 (£93-£341)**

Flare Pistols

Italian Modello 1900 flare pistol. **$175-$275 (£109-£171)**
Chris William

Modello 1900 flare pistol. **$175-$275 (£109-£171)**

"We feared that German '88' because it fired like a large rifle and was extremely accurate."

— Allen A. Johnson, 409th Infantry Regiment

Submachine Guns

Italian Beretta Model 1938A submachine gun.
$7,500-$12,500 (£4,650-£7,750)
JamesDJulia.com

Villar Perosa Model 1918. **$8,000-$9,500 (£4,960-£5,890)**
Beretta Model 1938A. **$7,500-$12,500 (£4,650-£7,750)**
Beretta Model 38/42. **$7,000-$10,500 (£4,340-£6,510)**
F.N.A.-B Model 1943. **$10,000-$12,500 (£6,200-£7,750)**

Rifles

Italian Carcano Model 1938 cavalry carbine. **$125-$350 (£78-£217)**
AdvanceGuardMilitaria.com

Carcano Fucile Modello 1891 rifle.
$175-$450 (£109-£279)
Carcano Model 1891 carbine. **$150-$400 (£93-£248)**
Carcano Model 1891 Truppe Speciali.
$150-$400 (£93-£248)
Carcano Model 1891/24 carbine.
$150-$350 (£93-£217)
Carcano Model 1891/28 carbine.
$150-$350 (£93-£217)
Carcano Model 1938 short rifle.
$125-$350 (£78-£217)
Carcano Model 1938 T.S. carbine.
$125-$350 (£78-£217)
Carcano Model 1938/43 cavalry and T.S. carbine.
$400-$800 (£248-£496)
Carcano Model 1941. **$125-$300 (£78-£186)**
Carcano Italian Youth rifle. **$250-$500 (£155-£310)**
Breda Model PG. **$1,000-$2,500 (£620-£1,550)**

Machine Guns

Italian Breda Model 30 light machine gun.
$10,000-$15,000 (£6,200-£9,300)
JamesDJulia.com

Revelli Model 1914.
$10,000-$18,000 (£6,200-£11,160)
Revelli/Fiat Model 35.
$14,500-$16,000 (£8,990-£9,920)
Breda Model 30. **$10,000-$15,000 (£6,200-£9,300)**
Breda Model 37. **$18,000-$28,000 (£11,160-£17,360)**

JAPAN

Handguns

Japanese Type 26 revolver. **$300-$950 (£186-£589)**
Chris William

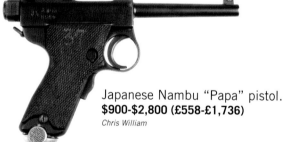

Japanese Nambu "Papa" pistol.
$900-$2,800 (£558-£1,736)
Chris William

Japanese Nambu "Type 14" pistol.
$250-$650 (£155-£403)
Chris William

Japanese Type 94 pistol.
$175-$500 (£109-£310)
Chris William

Type 26 revolver. **$300-$950 (£186-£589)**
4th Year Nambu "Grandpa" pistol.
$2,200-$9,000 (£1,364-£5,580)
4th Year Nambu "Papa" pistol.
$900-$2,800 (£558-£1,736)
4th Year Nambu "Baby" pistol.
$1,000-$4,800 (£620-£2,976)
14th Year Nambu "Type 14" pistol.
$250-$650 (£155-£403)
Type 94 pistol. **$175-$500 (£109-£310)**
Hamada Skiki Type 2. **$2,000-$5,000 (£1,240-£3,100)**

Flare Pistols

Japanese Type 10 flare pistol.
$500-$800 (£310-£496)
Chris William

Type 10 flare pistol 37mm. **$500-$800 (£310-£496)**

Submachine Guns

Japanese Type 100 submachine gun.
$10,000-$18,000 (£6,200-£11,160)
JamesDJulia.com

Type 100. **$10,000-$18,000 (£6,200-£11,160)**

Rifles

Japanese Arisaka Type 30 rifle. **$300-$900 (£186-£558)**
Rock Island Auction Co.

Japanese Arisaka Type 38 bolt-action rifle. **$110 (£68)**
HA.com

Japanese Arisaka Type 38 carbine.
$175-$650 (£109-£403)
PoulinAntiques.com

Japanese Arisaka Type 99 short rifle.
$180 (£111)
HA.com

Japanese Type 2 paratrooper rifle.
$1,500-$4,500 (£930-£2,790)
Rock Island Auction Co.

Japanese Imperial Navy Arisaka Type 38 naval training rifle. **$155 (£96)**
HA.com

Arisaka Type 99 rifle. **$125-$350 (£78-£217)**
AdvanceGuardMilitaria.com

Japanese Type 44 cavalry carbine.
$300-$1,200 (£186-£744)
Rock Island Auction Co.

Arisaka Type 30 rifle (M.**1897**). **$300-$900 (£186-£558)**
Arisaka Type 30 carbine. **$300-$900 (£186-£558)**
Arisaka Type 35 Navy rifle (M.1902).
$250-$800 (£155-£496)
Arisaka Type 38 rifle (M.1905). **$150-$300 (£93-£186)**
Arisaka Type 38 carbine. **$175-$650 (£109-£403)**
Manchurian Mauser Rifle. **$250-$700 (£155-£434)**
Arisaka Type 44 carbine. **$300-$1,000 (£186-£620)**
Arisaka Type 97 sniper rifle. **$600-$4,000 (£372-£2,480)**
Arisaka Type 99 short rifle. **$125-$500 (£78-£310)**
Arisaka Type 99 "last ditch" rifle. **$125-$350 (£78-£217)**
Type 100 paratrooper rifle. **$1,500-$4,500 (£930-£2,790)**
Type 2 paratrooper rifle. **$500-$2,500 (£310-£1,550)**
Type 99 sniper rifle. **$1,200-$3,000 (£744-£1,860)**
Type 5 rifle. **$7,500-$22,000 (£4,650-£13,640)**

Machine Guns

Japanese Type 92 heavy machine gun with tripod and accessories. $20,700 (£12,834)
JamesDJulia.com

Type 1. **$11,000-$14,000 (£6,820-£8,680)**
Type 3. **$9,000-$12,000 (£5,580-£7,440)**
Type 11. **$7,000-$9,500 (£4,340-£5,890)**
Type 89. **$13,000-$16,500 (£8,060-£10,230)**
Type 92. **$14,000-$19,000 (£8,680-£11,780)**
Type 92 Lewis. **$9,000-$11,000 (£5,580-£6,820)**
Type 96. **$4,500-$9,500 (£2,790-£5,890)**
Type 97. **$5,000-$9,000 (£3,100-£5,580)**
Type 98. **$5,000-$12,000 (£3,100-£7,440)**
Type 99. **$5,000-$12,000 (£3,100-£7,440)**
  Machine gun trainer. **$2,500-$5,000 (£1,550-£3,100)**

MEXICO

Rifles

FN M24 short rifle. **$250-$800 (£155-£496)**
FN M24 carbine. **$250-$950 (£155-£589)**
VZ12/33 carbine. **$200-$850 (£124-£527)**
Fabrica Nacional de Armas Model 1936.
  $275-$800 (£171-£496)

NORWAY

Handguns

Norwegian Kongsberg Vappenfabrikk M1914 pistol.
$850-$3,500 (£527-£2,170)
PoulinAntiques.com

Model 1883 revolver. **$275-$1,250 (£171-£775)**
Model 1887/93 revolver. **$275-$1,250 (£171-£775)**
Kongsberg Vappenfabrikk M1914 pistol.
  $850-$3,500 (£527-£2,170)
Kongsberg Vappenfabrikk M1914 pistol with Nazi
  proofs. **$3,000-$5,500 (£1,860-£3,410)**

Rifles

Krag Jorgenson Model 1894 rifle.
  $400-$1,000 (£248-£620)
Krag Jorgenson Model 1895 carbine.
  $400-$1,500 (£248-£930)
Krag Jorgenson Model 1904 carbine.
  $400-$1,600 (£248-£992)
Krag Jorgenson Model 1907 carbine.
  $400-$1,500 (£248-£930)
Krag Jorgenson Model 1912 carbine.
  $300-$1,200 (£186-£744)
Krag Jorgenson Model 1923 sniper rifle.
  $2,000-$4,500 (£1,240-£2,790)
Krag Jorgenson Model 1925 sniper rifle.
  $2,000-$4,500 (£1,240-£2,790)
Krag Jorgenson Model 1930 sniper rifle.
  $2,000-$4,500 (£1,240-£2,790)

POLAND

Handguns

Radom VIS-35 pistol, Nazi-captured, Waffenamt-marked.
$650-$4,000 (£403-£2,480)
Chris William

Radom Ng 30 revolver. **$500-$3,000 (£310-£1,860)**
Radom VIS-35 pistol. **$750-$3,500 (£465-£2,170)**
Radom VIS-35 pistol, Nazi captured,
  Waffenamt-marked. **$650-$4,000 (£403-£2,480)**
Radom VIS-35, Nazi produced (Model 35[p]).
  $200-$1,200 (£124-£744)
Radom VIS-35, Nazi produce, bnz code.
  $650-$3,500 (£403-£2,170)

Rifles

Polish Wz 29 rifle with bayonet.
  $400-$1,000 (£248-£620)
Rock Island Auction Co.

Mauser M98 rifle. **$250-$850 (£155-£527)**
Mauser M98AZ rifle. **$300-$950 (£186-£589)**
Wz 29 short rifle. **$400-$1,000 (£248-£)**
Wz 98a rifle. **$400-$1,000 (£248-£)**
Wz 29 .22 caliber training rifle.
  $750-$2,000 (£465-£1,240)

Kbk 8 Wz 31 .22 caliber training rifle.
  $750-$2,000 (£465-£1,240)
Model 1891/30 sniper rifle. **$400-$1,200 (£248-£744)**
Model 1891/98/25 Nagant. **$400-$1,100 (£248-£682)**
Model 1944 Nagant. **$125-$450 (£78-£279)**

Machine Guns

Wz 28 BAR. **$20,000-$25,000 (£12,400-£15,500)**

PORTUGAL

Rifles

Mauser M1904/M39 rifle. **$125-$350 (£78-£217)**
Mauser M1933 Standard model rifle.
  $250-$850 (£155-£527)
Mauser M1933 Standard model carbine.
  $250-$850 (£155-£527)
Mauser M1937-A short rifle. **$250-$900 (£155-£558)**
Mauser M1941 short rifle. **$450-$1,000 (£279-£620)**

RUMANIA

Handguns

Steyr Hahn Model 1911 pistol.
  $250-$750 (£155-£465)
Beretta Model 1934 Rumanian contract.
  $225-$550 (£140-£341)

Rifles

Mauser VZ24 short rifle. **$200-$850 (£124-£527)**
Rumanian Mosin-Nagant. **$75-$350 (£47-£217)**

SOVIET UNION

Handguns

Soviet Union Tokarev TT-33
pistol. **$300-$950 (£186-£589)**
Hermann-Historica.de

Nagant Model 1895 "gas seal" revolver.
  $250-$750 (£155-£465)
Nagant Model 1895 .22 caliber revolver.
  $200-$850 (£124-£527)

Nagant Model 1895 KGB revolver.
  $500-$2,000 (£310-£1,240)
FN 1900 Russian contract pistol.
  $300-$1,000 (£186-£620)
Tokarev TT-30 pistol. **$300-$950 (£186-£589)**
Tokarev TT-33 pistol. **$300-$950 (£186-£589)**
Tokarev TT-30 or TT-33 pistol, Nazi-captured.
  $450-$1,400 (£279-£868)
Tokarev Model R-3 pistol. **$300-$1,000 (£186-£620)**
Tokarev Model R-4 pistol. **$300-$1,000 (£186-£620)**
TK TOZ pistol. **$250-$950 (£155-£589)**

Flare Pistols

Soviet Model 30 26mm flare
pistol. **$200-$325 (£124-£202)**
Chris William

Model 30 flare pistol. **$200-$325 (£124-£202)**

Submachine Guns

Soviet Union PPD-1940 submachine gun.
$13,000-$17,000 (£8,060-£10,540)
JamesDJulia.com

Soviet Union PPsh-41 submachine gun.
$17,500-$25,000 (£10,850-£15,500)
PoulinAntiques.com

PPD-1934/38. **$13,000-$17,000 (£8,060-£10,540)**
PPD-1940. **$13,000-$17,000 (£8,060-£10,540)**
PPsh-41. **$17,500-$25,000 (£10,850-£15,500)**
PPS 1943. **$12,500-$18,500 (£7,750-£11,470)**

Rifles

Soviet Mosin-Nagant Model 1944 carbine.
$145 (£90)
HA.com

Soviet Tokarev M1940 rifle (SVT). **$500-$1,500
(£310-£930)**
PoulinAntiques.com

Soviet Mosin-Nagant Model 1891/30 sniper rifle
with 3.5x scope. **$400-$1,250 (£248-£775)**
Hermann-Historica.de

Soviet PTRD-41
anti-tank rifle.
**$2,500-$6,000
(£1,550-£3,720)**
Hermann-Historica.de

Mosin-Nagant Model 1891/30. **$100-$300 (£62-£186)**
Mosin-Nagant Model 1891/30 sniper rifle with
  3.5x scope. **$400-$1,250 (£248-£775)**
Mosin-Nagant Model 1891/30 sniper rifle with
  4x scope. **$850-$2,250 (£527-£1,395)**
Model 1907/1910 carbine.
  $500-$1,800 (£310-£1,116)
Model 1938 carbine. **$75-$450 (£47-£279)**
Model 1944 carbine. **$100-$350 (£62-£217)**
Tokarev M1938 rifle (SVT).
  $750-$2,000 (£465-£1,240)
Tokarev M1940 rifle (SVT). **$500-$1,500 (£310-£930)**
Simonov AVS-36 rifle. **$8,000-$10,000 (£4,960-£6,200)**
PTRD-41 anti-tank rifle.
  $2,500-$6,000 (£1,550-£3,720)

Machine Guns

Model 1910
Maxim (SPM).
**$16,500-$25,000
(£10,230-£15,500)**
Peter Suciu

Model 1905 Maxim.
  $18,000-$35,000 (£11,160-£21,700)
Model 1910 Maxim (SPM).
  $18,000-$35,000 (£11,160-£21,700)
Model DP 28. **$17,500-$22,500 (£10,850-£13,950)**
Model DPM. **$17,500-$22,500 (£10,850-£13,950)**
Model DShK M38. **$42,500-$45,000 (£26,350-£27,900)**
Goryunov SG43. **$25,000-$35,000 (£15,500-£21,700)**

SPAIN

Handguns

Spanish Astra 300 9mm
automatic pistol. **$360 (£223)**
HA.com

Spanish Astra 600 semi-
automatic pistol with Nazi
proof marks. **$290-$900
(£180-£558)**
Rock Island Auction Co.

Astra 400 (Model 1921) pistol. **$100-$450 (£62-£279)**
Astra 400 pistol (Republican copy).
  $200-$500 (£124-£310)
Astra 300 pistol. **$150-$550 (£93-£341)**
Astra 300 pistol, Nazi-proofed. **$190-$500 (£118-£310)**
Astra 600 pistol. **$250-$750 (£155-£465)**
Astra 600 pistol Nazi-proofed. **$290-$900 (£180-£558)**
Astra 900 pistol. **$500-$1,800 (£310-£1,116)**
Astra 900 pistol, German used (sn 32788-33774).
  $750-$2,700 (£465-£1,674)
Astra 901 machine pistol.
  $15,000-$25,000 (£9,300-£15,500)
Astra 902 machine pistol.
  $15,000-$25,000 (£9,300-£15,500)
Astra 903 machine pistol.
  $15,000-$25,000 (£9,300-£15,500)
Astra 904 machine pistol (Model F).
  $15,000-$25,000 (£9,300-£15,500)
Royal MM31 machine pistol (1st model).
  $20,000-$30,000 (£12,400-£18,600)
Royal MM31 machine pistol (2nd model).
  $15,000-$25,000 (£9,300-£15,500)

Super Azul machine pistol.
$15,000-$25,000 (£9,300-£15,500)
Royal MM34 machine pistol.
$15,000-$25,000 (£9,300-£15,500)
Llama Model IX pistol. **$200-$600 (£124-£372)**
Star Model 1914 pistol. **$200-$600 (£124-£372)**
Star Model CO pistol. **$200-$500 (£124-£310)**
Star Model A pistol. **$150-$400 (£93-£248)**
Star Model A Super pistol. **$175-$450 (£109-£279)**
Star Model M (MD) machine pistol.
$6,500-$9,500 (£4,030-£5,890)
Star Model B pistol. **$175-$400 (£109-£248)**

Submachine Guns

Star Z-45. **$14,000-$17,500 (£8,680-£10,850)**

Rifles

Spanish Mauser M1933 standard model short rifle. **$250-$900 (£155-£558)**
Rock Island Auction Co.

Mauser M1916 short rifle. **$175-$400 (£109-£248)**
Mauser M1916 carbine. **$150-$550 (£93-£341)**
Mauser M1933 standard model short rifle.
$250-$900 (£155-£558)
Mauser M1943 short rifle. **$125-$400 (£78-£248)**

UNITED STATES

Handguns

Colt U.S. Army Model 1917 double-action revolver. **$300-$1,250 (£186-£775)**
HA.com

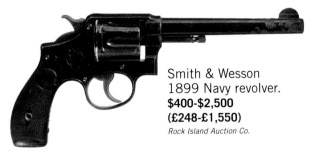

Smith & Wesson 1899 Navy revolver. **$400-$2,500 (£248-£1,550)**
Rock Island Auction Co.

Smith & Wesson Model 1917 revolver. **$400-$1,200 (£248-£744)**
PoulinAntiques.com

Remington UMC Model 1911 pistol. **$1,700-$6,000 (£1,054-£3,720)**
PoulinAntiques.com

U.S. Ithaca Model 1911A1 pistol. **$800-$2,000 (£496-£1,240)**

U.S. 1944 Remington Rand Model 1911A1 semi-automatic pistol. **$1,000 (£620)**
HA.com

U.S. 1943 Union Switch Model 1911A1 semi-automatic pistol. **$2,500 (£1,550)**
HA.com

Colt Model 1911A1
British Lend-Lease pistol.
$2,340 (£1,451)
PoulinAntiques.com

U.S. General Motors
Guide Lamp FP-45
Liberator single-shot
clandestine pistol.
$3,737 (£2,317)
Rock Island Auction Co.

Colt U.S. Army Model 1917 revolver.
   $300-$1,250 (£186-£775)
Colt Official Police revolver (U.S. Army-marked).
   $300-$750 (£186-£465)
Colt Commando revolver (U.S. Army-marked).
   $250-$850 (£155-£527)
Cold Detective Special revolver (U.S. Army-marked).
   $250-$850 (£155-£527)
Colt Model 1911 pistol, serial number below 101.
   $10,000-$50,000 (£6,200-£31,000)
Colt Model 1911 pistol, serial number 100-500.
   $5,000-$25,000 (£3,100-£15,500)
Colt Model 1911 pistol, serial number 501-1000.
   $5,000-$25,000 (£3,100-£15,500)
Colt Model 1911 pistol, four-digit number, with fire
   blue parts. **$2,500-$18,000 (£1,550-£11,160)**
Colt Model 1911 pistol, four-digit number without
   fire blue parts. **$2,000-$6,500 (£1,240-£4,030)**
Colt Model 1911 pistol, four-digit number, Navy,
   with fire blue parts. **$3,500-$17,500 (£2,170-£10,850)**
Colt Model 1911 pistol, four-digit number, Navy,
   without fire blue parts.
   $1,800-$8,500 (£1,116-£5,270)
Colt Model 1911 pistol, serial number 3501-3800,
   USMC. **$3,500-$18,000 (£2,170-£11,160)**
Colt Model 1911 pistol, serial number 36401-
   37650, USMC. **$1,800-$8,000 (£1,116-£4,960)**
Colt Model 1911 pistol, five-digit number, Navy.
   $1,700-$8,500 (£1,054-£5,270)
Colt Model 1911 pistol, five-digit number, Army.
   $2,000-$5,000 (£1,240-£3,100)

Remington UMC Model 1911 pistol.
   $1,700-$6,000 (£1,054-£3,720)
Colt Model 1911 pistol, six-digit number, Army.
   $750-$3,500 (£465-£2,170)
North American Arms Model 1911.
   $10,000-$35,000 (£6,200-£21,700)
Cold Service Model Ace .22 caliber pistol.
   $1,500-$6,500 (£930-£4,030)
Colt Model 1911A1 pistol, transition model, 1924.
   $1,600-$6,000 (£992-£3,720)
Colt Model 1911A1 pistol, transition model, 1937.
   $2,000-$8,000 (£1,240-£4,960)
Colt Model 1911A1 pistol, 1938 production.
   $1,500-$9,500 (£930-£5,890)
Colt Model 1911A1 pistol, 1939 production.
   $1,200-$6,500 (£744-£4,030)
Colt Model 1911A1 pistol, 1940 production.
   $1,200-$4,800 (£744-£2,976)
Colt Model 1911A1 pistol, 1941 production.
   $1,500-$5,000 (£930-£3,100)
Colt Model 1911A1 pistol, 1942 production.
   $850-$2,600 (£527-£1,612)
Colt Model 1911A1 pistol, 1942 Navy.
   $1,400-$4,000 (£868-£2,480)
Colt Model 1911A1 pistol, 1943 production.
   $750-$2,500 (£465-£1,550)
Colt Model 1911A1 pistol, 1943 production with
   commercial slide. **$1,000-$2,500 (£620-£1,550)**
Colt Model 1911A1 pistol, 1943 production,
   Canadian-marked. **$850-$2,500 (£527-£1,550)**
Colt Model 1911A1 pistol, 1944 production.
   $800-$2,500 (£496-£1,550)
Colt Model 1911A1 pistol, 1945 production,
   GHD-marked. **$800-$2,500 (£496-£1,550)**
Colt Model 1911A1 pistol, 1945 production,
   JSB-marked. **$1,250-$3,500 (£775-£2,170)**
Colt Model 1911A1 pistol, 1945 production, no
   mark. **$650-$2,750 (£403-£1,705)**
Ithaca Model 1911A1 pistol.
   $700-$1,900 (£434-£1,178)
Remington Rand M1911A1 pistol, 1942-43
   production. **$850-$2,200 (£527-£1,364)**
Remington Rand M1911A1 pistol, 1943
   production. **$650-$1,800 (£403-£1,116)**
Remington Rand M1911A1 pistol, 1943-45
   production. **$650-$1,800 (£403-£1,116)**
Singer Model 1911A1 pistol, educational order,
   1941. **$14,000-$45,000 (£8,680-£27,900)**
Union Switch M1911A1 pistol, 1943 production.
   $1,000-$4,000 (£620-£2,480)
Colt Military Woodsman Match pistol.
   $450-$2,800 (£279-£1,736)
Smith & Wesson Model 1899 Navy revolver.
   $400-$2,500 (£248-£1,550)
Smith & Wesson Model 1917 revolver.
   $400-$1,200 (£248-£744)
Smith & Wesson Victory Model revolver.
   $250-$650 (£155-£403)
Smith & Wesson Model 11. **$250-$600 (£155-£372)**
High Standard Model B-U.S pistol.
   $300-$850 (£186-£527)

High Standard Model USA/Model HD.
  $250-$1,000 (£155-£620)
High Standard Model USA/Model HD-MS.
  $5,000-$6,000 (£3,100-£3,720)
Guide Lamp Liberator .45 caliber pistol.
  $300-$4,000 (£186-£2,480)

Flare Pistols

U.S. Navy Mk IV flare pistol. **$75-$150 (£47-£93)**
AdvanceGuardMilitaria.com

U.S. Navy Mk V flare pistol. **$150-$200 (£93-£124)**
AdvanceGuardMilitaria.com

U.S. International Flare Signal Co. pistol. **$200-$300 (£124-£186)**
AdvanceGuardMilitaria.com

U.S. M8 Army Air Force flare pistol. **$115-$225 (£71-£140)**
AdvanceGuardMilitaria.com

U.S. Sklar flare pistol. **$85-$165 (£53-£102)**
AdvanceGuardMilitaria.com

Remington Mk III flare pistol. **$125-$165 (£78-£102)**
Sedgley Mk IV Navy flare pistol. **$75-$150 (£47-£93)**
Sedgley Mk V Navy flare pistol. **$150-$200 (£93-£124)**
Harrington & Richardson MK VI flare pistol.
  $200-$350 (£124-£217)
International brass frame flare pistol.
  $200-$300 (£124-£186)
International Model 52. **$300-$350 (£186-£217)**
Sklar flare pistol. **$85-$165 (£53-£102)**
M8 Army Air Force flare pistol. **$115-$225 (£71-£140)**

Submachine Guns

Harrington & Richardson Reising 50/55 submachine gun. **$5,000-$9,500 (£3,100-£5,890)**
JamesDJulia.com

Colt U.S. Navy over-stamped Thompson Model 1928 submachine gun. **$26,450 (£16,399)**
JamesDJulia.com

U.S. Thompson Model 1928A1 submachine gun. **$18,500-$28,000 (£11,470-£17,360)**
Amoskeag Auction Co.

U.S. Thompson M1/M1A1 submachine gun.
$18,000-$25,000 (£11,160-£15,500)

JamesDJulia.com

General Motors/Guide Lamp
M3A1 submachine gun.
$20,700 (£12,834)

Rock Island Auction Co.

Reising 50/55. **$5,000-$9,500 (£3,100-£5,890)**
Thompson Model 1921AC/21A, 1921/28 Navy.
 $20,000-$35,000 (£12,400-£21,700)
Thompson Model 1928A1.
 $18,500-$28,000 (£11,470-£17,360)
Thompson M1/M1A1.
 $18,000-$25,000 (£11,160-£15,500)
United Defense M42.
 $12,500-$20,000 (£7,750-£12,400)
M3. **$15,000-$22,500 (£9,300-£13,950)**
M3A1. **$15,000-$22,500 (£9,300-£13,950)**

Rifles

Johnson Model 1941 rifle. **$1,000-$4,500
(£620-£2,790)**

PoulinAntiques.com

U.S. M1 Garand semi-automatic rifle, serial number
range 410000-3880000. **$700-$3,500 (£434-£2,170)**

PoulinAntiques.com

U.S. Inland M1 carbine. **$525-$1,900 (£326-£1,178)**
Rock Island Auction Co.

Winchester M1 rifle, serial number range 2305850-
2536493. **$900-$3,000 (£558-£1,860)**

PoulinAntiques.com

Harrington & Richardson M1 rifle.
$700-$2,000 (£434-£1,240)

PoulinAntiques.com

Winchester T3 carbine with
original pattern M-2 infrared
sniper scope and accessories.
$15,000-30,000, (£9,300-£18,600)
Rock Island Auction Co.

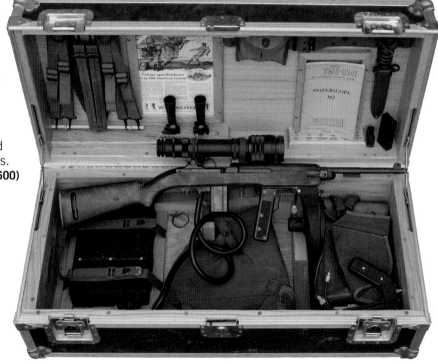

U.S. M1903 .30-06 caliber Springfield bolt-action rifle. **$660 (£409)**

HA.com

U.S. Model 1903A3 rifle. **$350-$1,000 (£217-£620)**

PoulinAntiques.com

U.S. Springfield M1 rifle, gas trap, serial number 81-52000. **$7,500-$30,000 (£4,650-£18,600)**

Rock Island Auction Co.

U.S. Model 1903A4 sniper rifle. **$3,500-$5,000 (£2,170-£3,100)**

Rock Island Auction Co.

Pedersen rifle. **$7,500-$17,500 (£4,650-£10,850)**
Pedersen carbine. **$10,000-$19,000 (£6,200-£11,780)**
Model 1903 rifle. **$250-$850 (£155-£527)**
Model 1903 rifle, modified. **$300-$850 (£186-£527)**
Model 1903A3 rifle. **$350-$1,000 (£217-£620)**
Model 1903A4 sniper rifle.
 $3,500-$5,000 (£2,170-£3,100)
Model 1917 rifle. **$250-$750 (£155-£465)**
IBM M1 carbine. **$525-$1,900 (£326-£1,178)**
Inland M1 carbine. **$525-$1,900 (£326-£1,178)**
Irwin Pedersen M1 carbine.
 $650-$4,000 (£403-£2,480)
National Postal Meter M1 carbine.
 $525-$2,000 (£326-£1,240)
Rockola M1 carbine. **$550-$2,200 (£341-£1,364)**
Saginaw (Grand Rapids) M1 carbine.
 $550-$2,000 (£341-£1,240)
Standard Products M1 carbine.
 $550-$1,900 (£341-£1,178)
Winchester M1 carbine. **$550-$2,500 (£341-£1,550)**
M1A1 paratrooper carbine.
 $1,500-$4,500 (£930-£2,790)
M2 carbine. **$7,000-$12,500 (£4,340-£7,750)**
T-3 carbine with M2 Sniper Scope.
 $10,000-$30,000 (£6,200-£18,600)
Springfield M1 rifle, gas trap, serial number
 81-52000. **$7,500-$30,000 (£4,650-£18,600)**
Springfield M1 rifle, gas port, serial number ca.
 500000-410000. **$750-$4,000 (£465-£2,480)**
Springfield M1 rifle, serial number
 410000-3880000. **$700-$3,500 (£434-£2,170)**
Winchester M1 rifle, serial number 10000-100500.
 $3,000-$10,000 (£1,860-£6,200)

"I was with the squad that was out front. We were the point. They always wanted a BAR (Browning automatic rifle, which I carried and used) out front."

— John Francis Shindelar, USMC

Winchester M1 rifle, serial number
 100501-165000. **$1,200-$5,500 (£744-£3,410)**
Winchester M1 rifle, serial number
 1200000-1380000. **$1,000-$3,250 (£620-£2,015)**
Winchester M1 rifle, serial number
 2305850-2536493. **$900-$3,000 (£558-£1,860)**
Winchester M1 rifle, serial number
 1601150-1640000. **$1,500-$3,500 (£930-£2,170)**
Harrington & Richardson M1 rifle.
 $700-$2,000 (£434-£1,240)
International Harvester M1 rifle.
 $500-$2,500 (£310-£1,550)
Lend-Lease M1 rifle. **$700-$2,500 (£434-£1,550)**
Johnson Model 1941 rifle.
 $1,000-$4,500 (£620-£2,790)
Harrington & Richardson Reising Model 60 rifle.
 $750-$2,000 (£465-£1,240)
Harrington & Richardson Model 65 .22 caliber rifle.
 $150-$500 (£93-£310)

Shotguns

Winchester Model 12 trench gun with bayonet.
$3,276 (£2,031)

PoulinAntiques.com

Winchester Model 97 trench shotgun. **$850-$4,500 (£527-£2,790)**
Rock Island Auction Co.

U.S. Army Remington Model 11 shotgun with Cutts compensator. **$1,000-$2,500 (£620-£1,550)**
Rock Island Auction Co.

Stevens Model 520-30 trench gun. **$500-$2,500 (£310-£1,550)**
Rock Island Auction Co.

Ithaca Model 37 trench gun.
  $1,000-$3,500 (£620-£2,170)
Remington Model 10 trench gun.
  $2,500-$12,500 (£1,550-£7,750)
Remington Model 11 military riot gun.
  $1,000-$2,500 (£620-£1,550)
Remington Model 31 military riot gun.
  $500-$1,800 (£310-£1,116)
Savage Model 720 riot gun.
  $850-$2,500 (£527-£1,550)
Stevens Model 520-30 trench gun.
  $500-$2,500 (£310-£1,550)
Stevens Model 620A trench gun.
  $1,000-$2,500 (£620-£1,550)
Winchester Model 97 take-down.
  $850-$4,500 (£527-£2,790)
Winchester Model 12 trench gun.
  $800-$5,000 (£496-£3,100)

Machine Guns

U.S. Westinghouse Browning Model 1917 machine gun with tripod, mount, water can and hose.
$28,750 (£17,825)
Rock Island Auction Co.

U.S. Model 1918 Browning automatic rifle. **$28,750 (£17,825)**
JamesDJulia.com

U.S. Browning M1917/M1917A1 water-cooled machine gun. **$15,000-$25,000 (£9,300-£15,500)**
JamesDJulia.com

U.S. Browning M1919A1/A2/A4/A6 air-cooled machine gun. **$20,000-$25,000 (£12,400-£15,500)**
JamesDJulia.com

U.S. M1918A1 Browning automatic rifle ("BAR"). **$20,000-$30,000 (£12,400-£18,600)**
PoulinAntiques.com

"I was the bazooka man for our squad— well, actually for more than one squad. I had the bazooka, and I had never fired the bazooka. I knew about the bazooka; I knew what it did and how it looked, but I had never fired one."

— Robert L. Jackson, 3rd U.S. Infantry Division

U.S. Browning M2/M2HB .50 machine gun. **$18,000-$40,000 (£11,160-£24,800)**
JamesDJulia.com

Fairchild Aerial Camera Corp. Army Air Corps machine gun camera for training air crew. **$420 (£260)**
HA.com

Browning M1917/M1917A1 water-cooled machine gun. **$15,000-$25,000 (£9,300-£15,500)**
Browning M1919A1/A2/A4/A6 air-cooled machine gun. **$20,000-$25,000 (£12,400-£15,500)**
Browning M2/M2HB .50 machine gun. **$30,000-$40,000 (£18,600-£24,800)**
Browning automatic rifle ("BAR") M1918/ M1918A1. **$20,000-$30,000 (£12,400-£18,600)**
Johnson M1941/M1944 automatic rifle. **$20,000-$25,000 (£12,400-£15,500)**

YUGOSLAVIA

Handguns

Model 1891 revolver. **$350-$2,000 (£217-£1,240)**
Model 1898 revolver. **$150-$750 (£93-£465)**
Model 1910 FN Browning pistol. **$150-$550 (£93-£341)**
Model 1922 FN Browning pistol. **$300-$600 (£186-£372)**

Rifles

M90(t) short rifle. **$130-$500 (£81-£310)**
M24 short rifle. **$175-$800 (£109-£496)**
M24 carbine. **$175-$850 (£109-£527)**
FN M30 short rifle. **$150-$600 (£93-£372)**
FN M24 carbine. **$175-$800 (£109-£496)**

Machine Guns

ZB30J. **$17,000-$25,000 (£10,540-£15,500)**

Chapter 6

Bayonets, Knives, Daggers & Swords

Blades of one variety or another hold the fascination of many World War II collectors. The idea of soldiers marching into battle with bayonets affixed or brandishing large fighting knives or samurai swords in bloody hand-to-hand combat is a hard notion to dislodge from the spirited collector's mind. Even though blade-related wounds of any variety (including sword- or saber-inflicted) were minimal during the war, the weapons that *could* have delivered such a wound are at the top of many collectors' "premium pieces" list. In fact, there are many collectors who focus only on blades and forgo any other paraphernalia related to the war.

Bayonets are a rather straightforward item to collect. Rarely reproduced, plentiful, and with an endless variety, bayonets present a collector with the opportunity to assemble a diverse and meaningful collection for a minimum amount of cash.

Knives, on the other hand, present a bit cloudier picture. The knife was often regarded as a personal sidearm. As a result, many knives were personalized by soldiers. These field alterations can either increase or decrease the value. Unfortunately, outside of collecting types of specific issue examples, knife collecting can become quite subjective, making it hard to determine consistent values.

In the collecting world, if one mentions "dagger," it is generally assumed that the reference is to a personal, ceremonial sidearm of the Third Reich. Other nations presented its soldiers with daggers, but German daggers captured the fancy of collectors from the very beginning of the hobby. German dagger and sword collecting is one of the most thoroughly researched area in the hobby. Plenty of books are available to new collectors to guide them into the hobby with a degree of certainty. Before buying or selling a German dagger, take the time to do some research—a slight difference in a marking can mean the difference between hundreds or even thousands of dollars.

Japanese swords (referred to generically as "samurai swords") present another minefield in the hobby. Thankfully, there are a number of books and websites dedicated to explaining the nuances of Japanese blade collecting. Again, the difference of a few markings or components can mean the difference between a $300 and a $3,000 blade.

Though often used interchangeably, the terms "sword" and "saber" denote two very different forms of weapon. A sword is a long, straight-bladed weapon with the primary function to denote rank or status. A saber, on the other hand, is a curved-blade weapon with the sole function to enable the user to strike a blow. Sabers were usually intended for mounted personnel.

BULGARIA

Bulgaria National Youth Leader's dagger.
$4,200-$5,500 (£2,604-£3,410)
Hermann-Historica.de

Bulgarian Labor Service Leader's dagger.
$5,000-$5,750 (£3,100-£3,565)
Hermann-Historica.de

Bulgarian Army officer's saber. **$175-$300 (£104-£186)**
Hermann-Historica.de

CHINA

Chinese Nationalist Air Force dagger. **$500-$675 (£310-£419)**
AdvanceGuardMilitaria.com

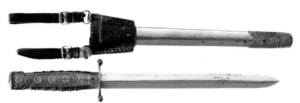

Chinese Nationalist Model 1924 officer's dagger.
$850-$1,100 (£527-£682)
Hermann-Historica.de

ENGLAND

Pocketknives

British Pattern of 1944 pocketknife.
$35-$55 (£22-£34)
AdvanceGuardMilitaria.com

Bayonets

British P.1907 bayonet. **$85-$115 (£53-£71)**
AdvanceGuardMilitaria.com

Combat Knives

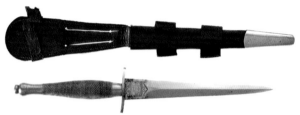

Fairbairn-Sykes fighting knife, circa 1940.
$1,200-$1,700 (£744-£1,054)
Hermann-Historica.de

FINLAND

Finnish Winter War Model 1928 bayonet.
$200-$265 (£124-£164)
AdvanceGuardMilitaria.com

GERMANY

German fighting/boot knife.
$265-$325 (£164-£202)
Chris William

Luftwaffe Fallschirmjager gravity
knife. **$595-$1,300 (£369-£806)**
AdvanceGuardMilitaria.com

German ersatz multi-blade folding
pocketknife. **$75-$115 (£47-£71)**
AdvanceGuardMilitaria.com

Values at a Glance

Commonly encountered blades:

- British P.1907 bayonet with scabbard
  $85-$115 (£53-£71)
- German K98 bayonet with scabbard
  $85-$145 (£53-£90)
- German Army officer's dagger
  $395-$900 (£245-£558)
- German SA dagger $500-$800 (£310-£496)
- German Hitler Youth dagger
  $350-$795 (£217-£493)
- German Army officer's Dove Head saber
  $185-$475 (£115-£295)
- Japanese Type 30 bayonet with scabbard
  $85-$145 (£53-£90)
- Japanese Type 95 Army NCO sword
  $350-$900 (£217-£558)
- U.S. M3 knife with M8 scabbard
  $165-$225 (£102-£140)
- U.S. M1 10" bayonet with scabbard
  $95-$175 (£59-£109)

German soldier's pocketknife. **$70-$95 (£43-£59)**

AdvanceGuardMilitaria.com

Bayonets

German 84/98 Mauser rifle bayonet, no scabbard. **$35-$55 (£22-£34)**

AdvanceGuardMilitaria.com

German dress bayonet with scabbard. **$100-$145 (£62-£90)**

AdvanceGuardMilitaria.com

84/98 Mauser bayonet with troddel and tropical belt. **$800 (£496)**

Hermann-Historica.de

German dress bayonet with scabbard. **$85 (£40)**

AdvanceGuardMilitaria.com

German police short dress bayonet and scabbard. **$125-$175 (£78-£109)**

AdvanceGuardMilitaria.com

German 84/98 Mauser rifle bayonet and scabbard and frog. **$95-$145 (£59-£90)**

AdvanceGuardMilitaria.com

German police dress bayonet, Coppel. **$275-$325 (£171-£202)**

AdvanceGuardMilitaria.com

German short dress bayonet with frog and knot. **$150 (£93)**

Hermann-Historica.de

German short K98 bayonet with single-etched blade, portepee and frog. **$525 (£326)**
Hermann-Historica.de

German short K98 single-etched dress bayonet with frog and noncommissioned officer's portepee. **$250-$350 (£155-£217)**
Hermann-Historica.de

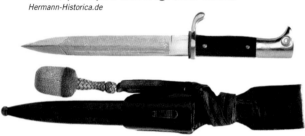

Luftwaffe dress K98 bayonet with single-etched blade and frog. **$560 (£347)**
Hermann-Historica.de

Short bayonet of the NSDAP Reich School in Feldafing. **$995 (£617)**
Hermann-Historica.de

Daggers

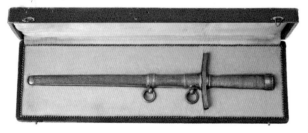

Honor dagger for high leaders of Hitler Youth. **$40,000-$55,000 (£24,800-£34,100)**
Hermann-Historica.de

Third Reich NSKK enlisted man's dagger. **$850-$2,150 (£527-£1,333)**
Hermann-Historica.de

Model 1938 dagger for subordinate leaders of the RLB, with leather hanger. **$1,000-$1,800 (£620-£1,116)**
Hermann-Historica.de

Third Reich Kriegsmarine officer's dagger. **$800-$1,200 (£496-£744)**
AdvanceGuardMilitaria.com

Hitler Youth member's dagger. **$350-$795 (£217-£493)**
HistoryHunter.com

Model 1936 SA service dagger for members of the NSKK-Motorboat Standarte with portepee and chain hanger. **$12,325 (£7,642)**
Hermann-Historica.de

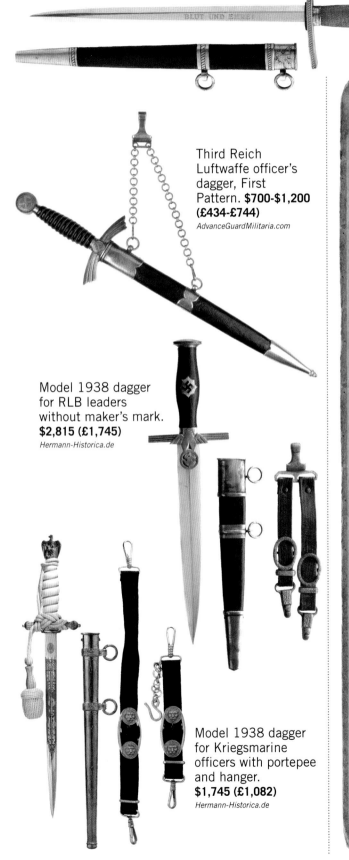

M1937 dagger for Hitler Youth leaders. **$2,800-$3,800 (£1,736-£2,356)**
HistoryHunter.com

Third Reich Luftwaffe officer's dagger, First Pattern. **$700-$1,200 (£434-£744)**
AdvanceGuardMilitaria.com

Model 1938 dagger for RLB leaders without maker's mark. **$2,815 (£1,745)**
Hermann-Historica.de

Model 1938 dagger for Kriegsmarine officers with portepee and hanger. **$1,745 (£1,082)**
Hermann-Historica.de

Collecting Hints

Pros:

- Swords, knives, bayonets, and daggers are impressive. More than other relics, a blade will capture the attention of young, old, male, and female. There is a lot of "wow" factor for the dollar when you own and display a sword, dagger, or knife.

- Swords, knives, bayonets, and daggers are relatively stable. As long as you don't handle the blades and you store the relics in a low humidity environment, deterioration will be minimal.

- Research has been intense in this area. Good references are available to assist a collector in determining origin, use, and scarcity.

- Due to the materials involved, bayonets, knives, daggers, and swords are plentiful.

Cons:

- Because iron is the primary material, these items are prone to rust if not stored in a dry environment.

- Japanese samurai swords and German daggers sell for very large sums. The high values have lured some into creating swords and daggers by assembling pieces or by manufacturing forgeries.

- This is an area of the hobby where repairs and replacement of missing parts seems to be an accepted norm. It can be difficult to ascertain if the grip on a sword or all of the parts of it were always there, or if they had been expertly replaced over the last 20 years. This sort of alteration does not seem to be regarded as inappropriate within the hobby, so it is up to the collector (and not the dealer) to know exactly what he is examining.

Availability: ✪ ✪ ✪ ✪
Price: ✪ ✪ ✪ ✪
Reproduction Alert: ✪ ✪ ✪

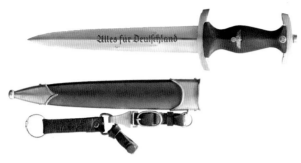

Model 1933 SA service dagger with three-piece leather hanger. **$850-$1,350 (£527-£837)**
Hermann-Historica.de

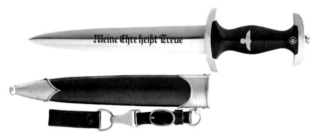

Model 1933 SS service dagger with leather hanger. **$3,500-$7,500 (£2,170-£4,650)**
Hermann-Historica.de

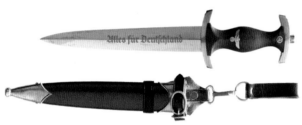

Model 1933 SA service dagger with etched dedication, "In treuer Kameradschaft. Josef Einöder – Sturmbannführer," and vertical leather hanger. **$3,350 (£2,077)**
Hermann-Historica.de

Model 1936 SS service dagger with chain hanger and portepee. **$7,000-$15,000 (£4,340-£9,300)**
Hermann-Historica.de

SA dagger with Röhm inscription removed from reverse of blade. **$750-$1,100 (£465-£682)**
AdvanceGuardMilitaria.com

Third Reich Army officer's dress dagger with hanger and portepee. **$395-$900 (£245-£558)**
AdvanceGuardMilitaria.com

Model 1934 Hewer for RAD enlisted men/junior leaders, with leather hangers. **$1,800-$2,500 (£1,116-£1,550)**
Hermann-Historica.de

Favorite Find: World War II Knuckle Knife

by Harold Ratzburg

My favorite militaria collectible is one that I have had for more than 60 years. How I came about it makes an interesting story, and remembering those ancient days brings a warm glow to my heart.

Way back in the days of the Korean Police Action, I was a young "flyboy" in the U.S. Air Force (also known as a "bus driver" to the U.S. Army "ground pounders" who we AF guys called "the Army guys").

By a happy sequence of circumstances, I was assigned to the U.S. Occupation Forces in post-war Germany instead of shipped to the shooting war zone of Korea. Other members of the Radar Repairman class from which I graduated (a school at Keesler Air Force Base, Mississippi) were sent to Korea and spent part of their enlistment blowing up air bases ahead of the Chinese forces.

With incredible good luck, I wound up as a supply clerk in a U. S. Air Force Intelligence Squadron in Ulm an der Donau, West Germany. We lived and had our offices in three large German villas. As a young collector working in supply, I had the keys and access to all parts of those villas. The villas had previously been occupied right after the war by the U.S. Army's Civil Intelligence Corps (CIC) and the Criminal Investigation Department (CID).

On one of my first forays "liberating" any military souvenirs I might find (before someone else found them), I climbed into the attic of one of the villa's garages. There, in the dust, I found a nice U.S. M3 fighting knife and an odd-looking knuckle knife. Who had left them there, I have no idea, but now they were mine!

The knuckle knife was a mystery to me. I had never seen anything like it. There were no markings on it. I knew what the World War I U.S. Mark I fighting knife looked like, and it made sense to me that a German soldier from World War I had brought one home as his trophy from the trenches and tried to copy it.

The blade was rather crudely made and looked more like a spear point than a fighting knife, but I knew how to fix that. I took it to a German knife craftsman in town and had him grind it down to my specifications for a pack of cigarette, which was the accepted currency in those post-war days.

For years I told other collectors the story of my

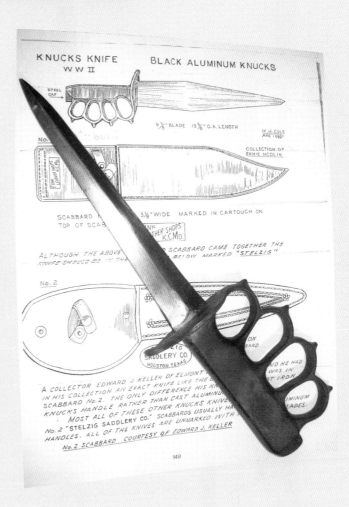

German copy of an American Mark I fighting knife.

About 30 years passed when I paged through a copy of M. H. Cole's book, US Military Knives Bayonets & Machetes, and there was my knife! It turns out it was really American-made by an unknown maker. According to Cole's information, all of the other known knucks in private collections were unmarked like mine, and all had a variety of blades. Some were made with a cast iron knuckle handle. Some of those found in private collections came in a leather scabbard made by Stelzig Saddlery Co. of Houston, Texas.

It probably affected the value of my knife when I had the blade ground down, but I do like it better the way it is.

Does that new knowledge make me feel different about my favorite knife? Nope, no way! The knife still lies on my desk, doing its job for over 60 years now—that is, being a paperweight and a handy letter opener.

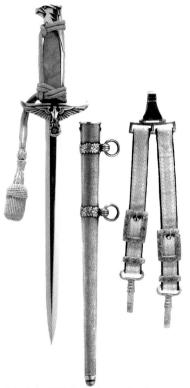

Model 1938 diplomat's dagger with hanger and portepee. **$7,000-$13,000 (£4,340-£8,060)**
Hermann-Historica.de

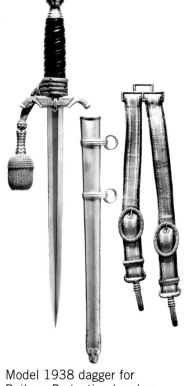

Model 1938 dagger for Railway Protection Leaders, with suspension and portepee. **$3,500-$5,500 (£2,170-£3,410)**
Hermann-Historica.de

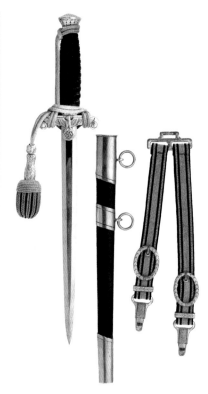

Model 1937 dagger for Land Customs Officers, with portepee and hanger. **$3,700-$8,000 (£2,294-£4,960)**
Hermann-Historica.de

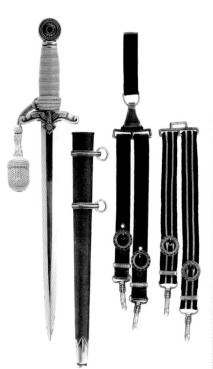

Model 1938 TeNo (Technical Emergency Corps) leader's dagger. **$10,000-$16,000 (£6,200-£9,920)**
Hermann-Historica.de

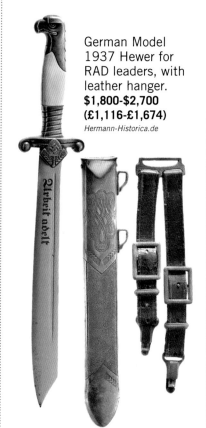

German Model 1937 Hewer for RAD leaders, with leather hanger. **$1,800-$2,700 (£1,116-£1,674)**
Hermann-Historica.de

Model 1939 diplomat's dagger in gold issue with hanger and portepee. **$10,000-$16,500 (£6,200-£10,230)**
Hermann-Historica.de

Vertical hanger for the Model 1933 SS service dagger. **$400-$535 (£248-£332)**

Hermann-Historica.de

Third Reich Red Cross enlisted Hewer. **$500-$1,200 (£310-£744)**

AdvanceGuardMilitaria.com

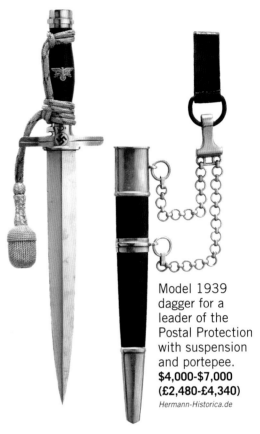

Model 1939 dagger for a leader of the Postal Protection with suspension and portepee. **$4,000-$7,000 (£2,480-£4,340)**

Hermann-Historica.de

Model 1934 DLV flyer's dagger with chain hanger and portepee. **$5,000-$8,000 (£3,100-£4,960)**

Hermann-Historica.de

Model 1937 NSFK service dagger (flyer's knife) with hanger. **$1,500-$2,500 (£930-£1,550)**

Hermann-Historica.de

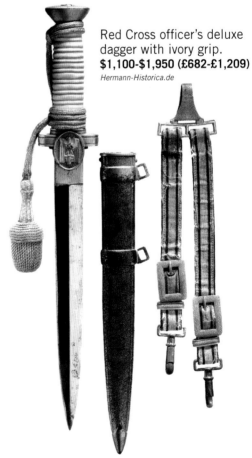

Red Cross officer's deluxe dagger with ivory grip. **$1,100-$1,950 (£682-£1,209)**

Hermann-Historica.de

Swords and Sabers

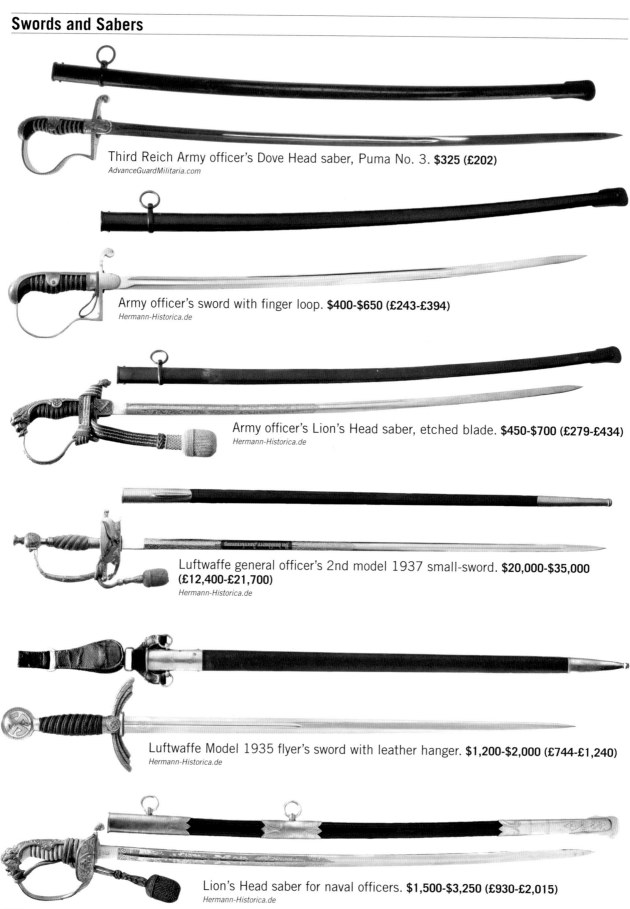

Third Reich Army officer's Dove Head saber, Puma No. 3. **$325 (£202)**
AdvanceGuardMilitaria.com

Army officer's sword with finger loop. **$400-$650 (£243-£394)**
Hermann-Historica.de

Army officer's Lion's Head saber, etched blade. **$450-$700 (£279-£434)**
Hermann-Historica.de

Luftwaffe general officer's 2nd model 1937 small-sword. **$20,000-$35,000 (£12,400-£21,700)**
Hermann-Historica.de

Luftwaffe Model 1935 flyer's sword with leather hanger. **$1,200-$2,000 (£744-£1,240)**
Hermann-Historica.de

Lion's Head saber for naval officers. **$1,500-$3,250 (£930-£2,015)**
Hermann-Historica.de

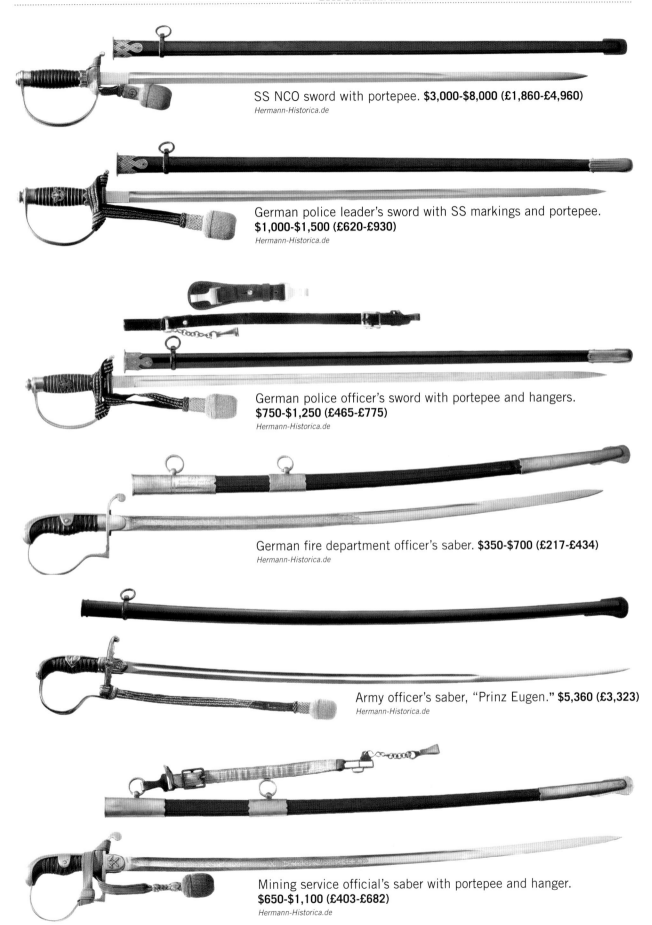

SS NCO sword with portepee. **$3,000-$8,000 (£1,860-£4,960)**
Hermann-Historica.de

German police leader's sword with SS markings and portepee.
$1,000-$1,500 (£620-£930)
Hermann-Historica.de

German police officer's sword with portepee and hangers.
$750-$1,250 (£465-£775)
Hermann-Historica.de

German fire department officer's saber. **$350-$700 (£217-£434)**
Hermann-Historica.de

Army officer's saber, "Prinz Eugen." **$5,360 (£3,323)**
Hermann-Historica.de

Mining service official's saber with portepee and hanger.
$650-$1,100 (£403-£682)
Hermann-Historica.de

Third Reich Army officer's
Panther Head saber.
$400-$800 (£248-£496)
AdvanceGuardMilitaria.com

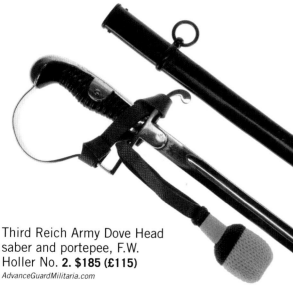

Third Reich Army Dove Head
saber and portepee, F.W.
Holler No. **2. $185 (£115)**
AdvanceGuardMilitaria.com

Third Reich Army
officer's Dove Head
sword, Alcoso.
$595 (£369)
AdvanceGuardMilitaria.com

ITALY

Italian Navy officer's sword.
$200-$350 (£124-£217)
HA.com

Italian M91 Carcano bayonet with frog.
$100-$155 (£62-£96)
AdvanceGuardMilitaria.com

Model 1937 MVSN
leader's dagger with
portepee and hanger.
**$1,400-$1,750
(£860-£1,085)**
Hermann-Historica.de

Model 1937 dagger
for leaders of the
Fascist Militia MVSN.
$1,000 (£620)
Hermann-Historica.de

Italian Fascist MVSN high leader's dagger with scarce white grip and chain hanger. **$1,792 (£1,111)**

HA.com

JAPAN

Bayonets

Japanese Type 30 training bayonet, Nagoya Arsenal. **$85-$135 (£53-£84)**

AdvanceGuardMilitaria.com

Japanese "Last Ditch Defense" pole bayonet, Jinsen Arsenal. **$200-$285 (£124-£177)**

AdvanceGuardMilitaria.com

Japanese Type 30 bayonet, Tokyo/Kokura. **$100-$145 (£62-£90)**

AdvanceGuardMilitaria.com

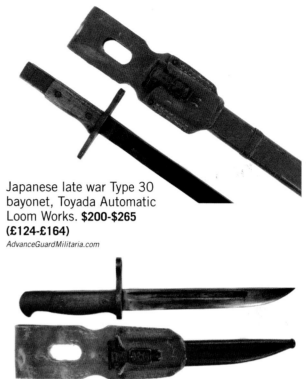

Japanese late war Type 30 bayonet, Toyada Automatic Loom Works. **$200-$265 (£124-£164)**

AdvanceGuardMilitaria.com

Japanese "Paratrooper bayonet" fighting knife. **$2,500-$3,250 (£1,550-£2,015)** AdvanceGuardMilitaria.**com**

Daggers, Swords/Sabers

Japanese police dirk. **$250-$400 (£155-£248)**

HA.com

Japanese Second Pattern naval officer's dagger. **$450-$875 (£279-£543)**

Hermann-Historica.de

Japanese dagger with cloth-wrapped grip. **$1,135 (£704)**

HA.com

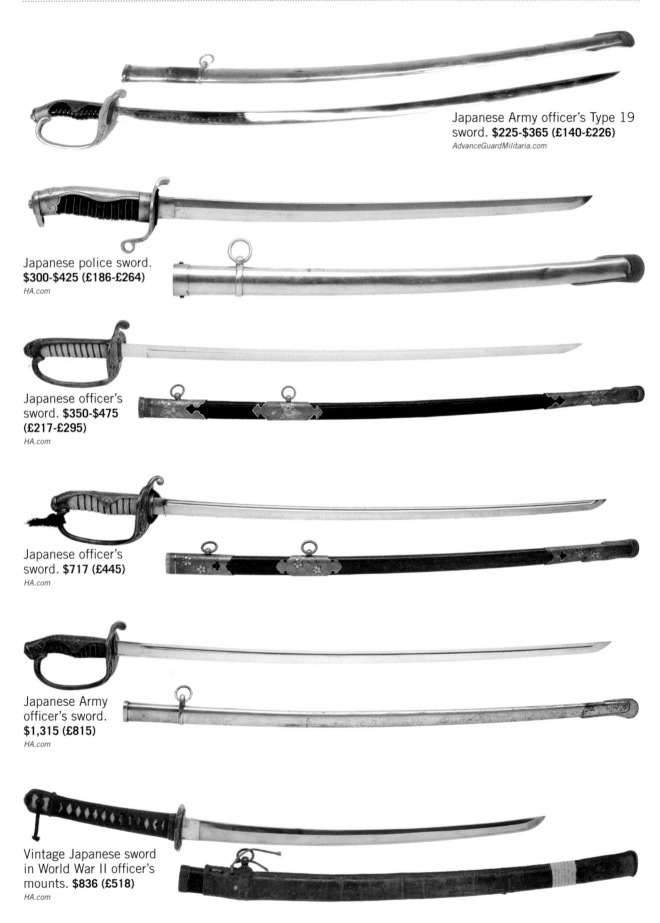

Japanese Army officer's Type 19 sword. **$225-$365 (£140-£226)**
AdvanceGuardMilitaria.com

Japanese police sword. **$300-$425 (£186-£264)**
HA.com

Japanese officer's sword. **$350-$475 (£217-£295)**
HA.com

Japanese officer's sword. **$717 (£445)**
HA.com

Japanese Army officer's sword. **$1,315 (£815)**
HA.com

Vintage Japanese sword in World War II officer's mounts. **$836 (£518)**
HA.com

Japanese officer's sword with signed tang. **$650-$1,500 (£403-£930)**
HA.com

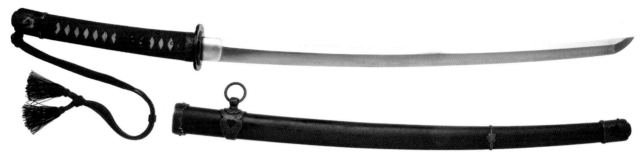

Japanese officer's sword with old blade, unsigned tang, World War II
officer's mounts and old iron tsuba with gold highlights. **$2,390 (£1482)**
HA.com

Japanese officer's sword with old blade with high wavy temper line
and signed tang, "Bishu Norimitsu Nagafune." **$538 (£334)**
HA.com

Japanese officer's sword with standard officer's handle mounts,
heavily flowered brass tsuba and green military wrap. **$658 (£408)**
HA.com

Showa Period Japanese sword with World War II mounts. **$840 (£839)**
HA.com

Japanese Naval Landing Force officer's sword. **$500-$850 (£310-£527)**
HA.com

Japanese Navy officer's sword. **$750-$1,350 (£465-£837)**
HA.com

Miscellaneous Parts and Accessories

Japanese Type 94 sword tassels, all ranks. **$150-$200 (£93-£124)**
AdvanceGuardMilitaria.com

Japanese Army leather sword knot, enlisted and warrant officers. **$150-$200 (£93-£124)**
AdvanceGuardMilitaria.com

Japanese naval sword knot. **$175-$225 (£109-£140)**
AdvanceGuardMilitaria.com

Japanese Type 97 naval sword tassels, all ranks. **$150-$200 (£93-£124)**
AdvanceGuardMilitaria.com

POLAND

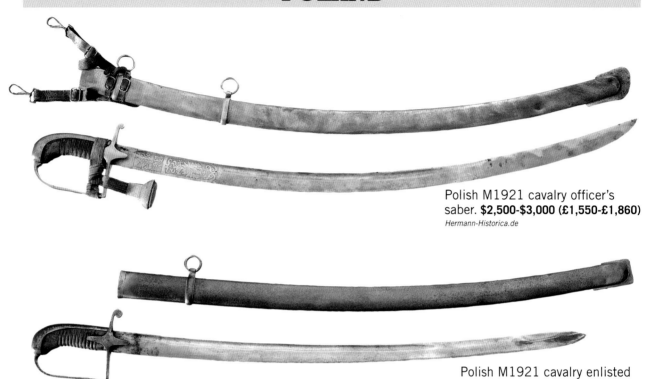

Polish M1921 cavalry officer's saber. **$2,500-$3,000 (£1,550-£1,860)**
Hermann-Historica.de

Polish M1921 cavalry enlisted saber. **$1,000-$1,500 (£620-£930)**
Hermann-Historica.de

SOVIET UNION

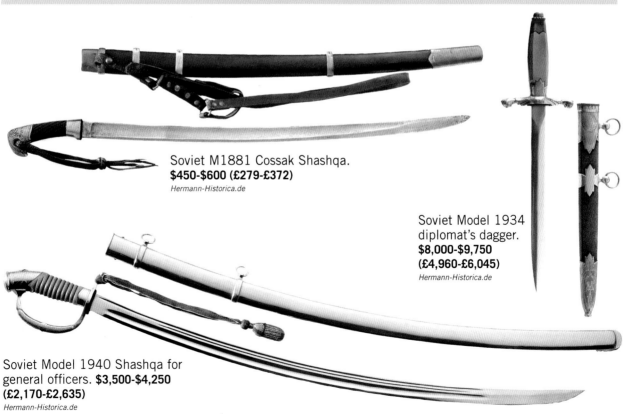

Soviet M1881 Cossak Shashqa.
$450-$600 (£279-£372)
Hermann-Historica.de

Soviet Model 1934 diplomat's dagger.
$8,000-$9,750 (£4,960-£6,045)
Hermann-Historica.de

Soviet Model 1940 Shashqa for general officers. **$3,500-$4,250 (£2,170-£2,635)**
Hermann-Historica.de

"The Italians were armed with carbines. The bayonet was attached to the carbine and you could bend it with your bare hands."

— Joyce W. Gerling, 34th U.S. Infantry Division

SWITZERLAND

Swiss Model 1943 dagger with officer's portepee. **$315-$465 (£195-£288)**
AdvanceGuardMilitaria.com

UNITED STATES

Pocketknives

United States Paratrooper M2 pocketknife. **$350-$450 (£217-£279)**
AdvanceGuardMilitaria.com

United States TL-29 pocketknife. **$35-$50 (£22-£31)**
AdvanceGuardMilitaria.com

Belt Knives

First Special Service Forces V-42 Stiletto scabbard. **$650-$750 (£403-£465)**
AdvanceGuardMilitaria.com

U.S. knuckle knife scabbard. **$200-$265 (£124-£164)**
AdvanceGuardMilitaria.com

U.S. PAL RH 36 fighting knife. **$55-$75 (£34-£47)**
AdvanceGuardMilitaria.com

USMC Ka-Bar fighting knife. **$250-$350 (£155-£217)**
HA.com

United States Fighting knife U.S. fighting knife made from an M1906 bayonet. **$65 (£40)**

U.S. commercial fighting knife by E.G. Waterman & Co. **$40-$65 (£25-£40)**
AdvanceGuardMilitaria.com

U.S. Navy PAL Mark 1 fighting knife. **$65-$125 (£40-£78)**
HA.com

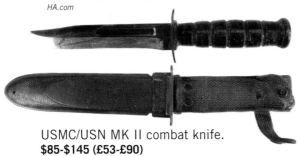

USMC/USN MK II combat knife. **$85-$145 (£53-£90)**
AdvanceGuardMilitaria.com

U.S. fighting utility knife, Robeson. **$50-$95 (£31-£59)**
AdvanceGuardMilitaria.com

U.S. field-modified fighting utility knife. **$95 (£59)**
AdvanceGuardMilitaria.com

U.S. theater-made case fighting knife. **$135 (£84)**
AdvanceGuardMilitaria.com

U.S. M3 trench knife with M8 scabbard. **$200-$265 (£124-£164)**
AdvanceGuardMilitaria.com

USMC hospital corpsman's knife. **$125-$200 (£78-£124)**
AdvanceGuardMilitaria.com

U.S. Pacific Theater Australian-made knuckle knife. **$475-$550 (£295-£341)**
AdvanceGuardMilitaria.com

United States V-44 fighting/survival knife. **$350-$450 (£217-£279)**
AdvanceGuardMilitaria.com

U.S. Taylor Huff D-guard knuckle fighting knife with original scabbard. **$2,500-$3,000 (£1,550-£1,860)**
AdvanceGuardMilitaria.com

U.S. World War II-modified 1918 Mark I trench knife and theater-made scabbard. **$550-$700 (£341-£434)**
AdvanceGuardMilitaria.com

Machetes

U.S. M1939 machete. **$100-$145 (£62-£90)**
AdvanceGuardMilitaria.com

U.S. case survival machete, non-folding. **$45-$75 (£28-£47)**
AdvanceGuardMilitaria.com

U.S. survival knife LC-14-B. **$140-$185 (£87-£115)**
Minnesota Military Museum

Bayonets

U.S. M1917 rifle bayonet. **$165-$225 (£102-£140)**
Author's Collection

U.S. M1 bayonet, American Fork & Hoe. **$95 (£59)**
AdvanceGuardMilitaria.com

U.S. M1905 bayonet, arsenal reconditioned. **$225-$285 (£140-£177)**
Author's Collection

U.S. USN MK I training bayonet. **$185-$235 (£115-£146)**
AdvanceGuardMilitaria.com

U.S. M1 10" bayonet, Oneida Ltd. **$135-$175 (£84-£109)**
AdvanceGuardMilitaria.com

U.S. M4 bayonet with leather handle and scabbard. **$65-$125 (£40-£78)**
AdvanceGuardMilitaria.com

Swords

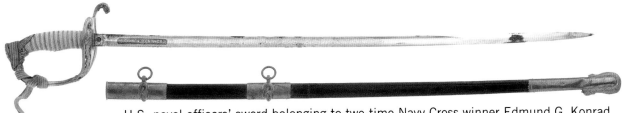

U.S. naval officers' sword belonging to two-time Navy Cross winner Edmund G. Konrad. **$480 (£298)**
HA.com

M1902 saber belonging to Gen. Douglas MacArthur. **$7,170 (£4,445)**
HA.com

U.S. Navy officer's sword attributed to Allan G. Wussow. **$210 (£130)**
HA.com

YUGOSLAVIA

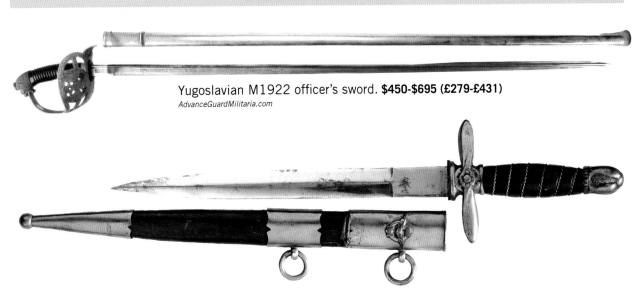

Yugoslavian M1922 officer's sword. **$450-$695 (£279-£431)**
AdvanceGuardMilitaria.com

Yugoslavian Model 1937 Air Force officer's dagger. **$700-$1,000 (£434-£620)**
Hermann-Historica.de

Chapter 7

Personal Items

Looking at a military dealer's list or perusing the Internet often leaves one with the impression that personal items carried or used during World War II abound and are available for minimal investment. That is only partially true.

This is a frustrating area in which to collect, and even more so, to describe. There are many items that were made or used during the time period of 1939-1945. That does not mean that a soldier used the item or carried it in his knapsack. Many of the items that can be loosely tossed into this category rely on imagination and very little on documentation. Selling personal items, or "smalls," is a profitable business. Simple utilitarian antiques can often be found for a few dollars at an antiques show or flea market. With some wishful thinking and some clever writing, an average mid-20th-century item can immediately become a soldier's item. Unfortunately, this wishful thinking is infectious, and soon, plenty of customers believe the romantic yarns spun by a dealer.

Toothpaste in vintage containers, sweetheart jewelry, personal toiletry items, or vintage canned goods—a lot of antiques are currently being imported that look period appropriate and are sold as World War II items. Again, it cannot be emphasized enough: buyer beware! If you are in the market for items that are typical of the period (or that simply look good), then you will have no shortage of available artifacts to purchase. On the other hand, if you stick with items that have a *known* provenance linking them to a soldier, or the time period of 1939-1945, be prepared to pay! Personal items that were actually carried or used by a soldier are harder to find and document—for the simple reason that they were *used*. The items were, by their very intent, expendable. Survival after 60 years was not the goal when these items were manufactured.

Patience and study is the best defense against acquiring World War II personal items that are wishfully ordained but woefully lacking in documentation. Limit yourself to known entities—items with a strong provenance or documented period use.

Closely examine the items in this chapter. You will notice that the items that have a known association with a World War II soldier sold for strong prices. The rest of the items are low-level collectibles. Resist the

Values at a Glance

Commonly encountered personal items and trench art:

- German Army soldbuch $65-$95 (£40-£59)
- German Wehrmacht folding fork and spoon $25-$35 (£16-£22)
- Germany Army identification disc $55-$95 (£34-£59)
- Japanese good luck flag $145-$225 (£90-£140)
- Japanese sake cup with military theme $15-$35 (£9-£22)
- U.S. supper K ration 1944 $145-$165 (£90-£102)
- U.S. soldier's "housewife" sewing kit $25-$30 (£16-£19)
- U.S. souvenir pillow $10-$45 (£6-£28)
- Trench art ashtray made from shell $15-$25 (£9-£16)
- Allied active service Bible $10-$20 (£6-£12)

Collecting Hints

Pros:

- Genuine articles identified to a soldier are a very immediate link to the soldier's life.
- An item with a strong, proven provenance is a good investment. The prices of these items keep going up.
- Collecting personal items allows World War II enthusiasts to inject a bit of their own personalities into the hobby by collecting items that appeal directly to them.

Cons:

- Few items with solid provenance have survived. Personal items that are identified as having belonged to a soldier are uncommon. Those that do exist are often part of a larger grouping of items associated with the soldier, further driving the price beyond a beginner's reach.
- This area is inundated with items represented as World War II when, in fact, there is no provenance to support the claims.
- World War II experts are not usually experts in decorative arts. Therefore, a lot of items that look era-appropriate are represented as typical of items from the World War II-era.
- Provenance for items is often "created" by a dealer looking to increase the value of a relatively common World War II-era item. Many items that never had any association can suddenly become part of a group, or in the worst case, sprout markings that identify them to a soldier.
- Personal items do not follow any set of regulation designs or patterns, so it is difficult to clearly identify an item as having been made or used before or during the war.

Availability: ✪ ✪ ✪ ✪ ✪
Price: ✪ ✪
Reproduction Alert: ✪ ✪ ✪

temptation to believe a soldier *could* have used it. Just saying it doesn't make it so. Visit museums and study books and period magazines to determine a sense of construction and use of items from the World War II era.

Personal items might seem—at first—the easiest arena in which to begin collecting. It is, in fact, the most difficult. Because civilian-produced and used items followed no "regulation" pattern or order, the variety is endless. For example, notice the number of toiletry kits listed here. It's easy to think a soldier would have needed this to shave and keep clean in the field, yet very few have solid provenance linking them to a soldier.

To successfully collect in this area, a person must first familiarize himself with the material culture of the mid-20th-century. A lot of time and effort can be spent studying decorative arts to hone the skill of recognizing period-appropriate civilian ware. It is much easier to recognize an M1923 riflemen's cartridge belt or an M1carbine than it is to determine whether a can of body powder or a toothbrush dates to World War II.

GERMANY

Entertainment

Third Reich Winterhilfswerk donation can, Vienna.
$155-$185 (£96-£115)

AdvanceGuardMilitaria.com

Souvenir book of Japanese Major Kobyashi's visit to Rovaniemi, Finland, in February 1943.
$50-$65 (£31-£40)

AdvanceGuardMilitaria.com

Third Reich Luftwaffe identification book for British, American, German, and Soviet aircraft. **$35-$45 (£22-£25)**

AdvanceGuardMilitaria.com

Luftwaffe book, *Fliegende Front.*
$165-$185 (£102-£115)

AdvanceGuardMilitaria.com

Third Reich soldier's stationery and reading material. **$35-$45 (£22-£28)**

AdvanceGuardMilitaria.com

Identification

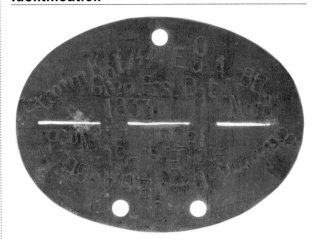

Third Reich SS soldier's identification tag.
$185-$235 (£115-£146)

AdvanceGuardMilitaria.com

Fifteen Third Reich casualty memorial cards.
$75-$100 (£47-£62)

AdvanceGuardMilitaria.com

Third Reich Army identification disc,
Infantry Ersatz Battalion. **$55-$75 (£34-£47)**

AdvanceGuardMilitaria.com

German soldier's leather coin purse.
$25-$35 (£16-£22)

AdvanceGuardMilitaria.com

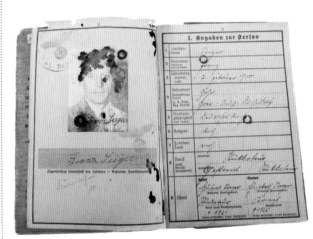

Third Reich Wehrpass, Luftwaffe. **$35-$65 (£22-£40)**

AdvanceGuardMilitaria.com

Third Reich grenadier's soldbuch. **$65-$95 (£40-£59)**

AdvanceGuardMilitaria.com

Third Reich Wehrpass, Army. **$35-$65 (£22-£40)**

AdvanceGuardMilitaria.com

Lighting

Third Reich
Bakelite carbide
lantern. **$75-$85
(£47-£52)**

AdvanceGuardMilitaria.com

Mess and Ration-Related

Third Reich folding fork
and spoon. **$25-$35
(£16-£22)**

AdvanceGuardMilitaria.com

Army soldier's field fork, knife, and spoon set.
$55-65 (£34-£40)

AdvanceGuardMilitaria.com

Third Reich RAD
mess hall plate.
$35-$45 (£22-£28)

AdvanceGuardMilitaria.com

Small Third Reich
Bakelite container.
$20-$30 (£12-£19)

AdvanceGuardMilitaria.com

Kriegsmarine fork.
$20-$25 (£12-£16)
AdvanceGuardMilitaria.com

Luftwaffe spoon.
$15-$20 (£9-£12)
Author's Collection

Favorite Find: Piece of Japanese Airplane Propeller with a Story

by Robert Jaques, aviation historian

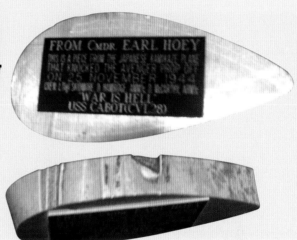

The favorite item in my military collection is a cut piece of propeller from a Japanese "KATE" kamikaze airplane that sheared off a turning propeller of a Navy TBM.

The TBM and its three-man crew were ready for take-off from the deck of the carrier USS Cabot (CVL-28) on Nov. 25, 1944, when the kamikaze attack occurred. The Cabot had four smokestacks on the starboard side. The kamikaze came down between the smokestacks, sheared off the turning propeller, crashed and exploded on the carrier deck.

Amazingly, all three crewmembers got out of the TBM without a scratch. During the clean-up process, an officer picked up a 12" section of the Japanese propeller and kept it.

After the war, the officer, Cdr. Earl Hoey, cut the propeller remnant into 1" thick pieces to give to the TBM three-man crew and friends.

At a USS Cabot reunion years ago, Cdr. Hoey auctioned off one of the pieces as a fund-raiser for the organization. My winning bid bought this propeller piece.

On my piece is a plaque that reads:

This is a piece from the Japanese plane that knocked the Avenger prop off on 25 November 1944.

Crew: LT (jg) Howard Skidmore, D. Hambidge, D. McCarthy

WAR IS HELL

USS CABOT (CVL 28)

SUICIDE PLANE GRAZES TORPEDO PLANE ON NOVEMBER 25, 1944. THE ZEKE CRASHED INTO THE PORT GUN TUB.

Third Reich bunker heater/small cooking stove. **$100-$125 (£62-£78)**
AdvanceGuardMilitaria.com

Japanese soldier's service records bag. **$20-$30 (£12-£19)**
AdvanceGuardMilitaria.com

Japanese Army identification tag. **$65-$85 (£40-£53)**
AdvanceGuardMilitaria.com

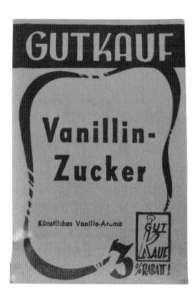

German sugar packet. **$5-$12 (£3-£7)**
Charles D. Pautler

German beer bottle, Herm Goering restaurant. **$45-$65 (£28-£40)**
AdvanceGuardMilitaria.com

JAPAN

Individual Items

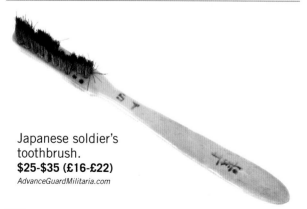

Japanese soldier's toothbrush. **$25-$35 (£16-£22)**
AdvanceGuardMilitaria.com

Japanese wounded soldier's hospital robe. **$145-$165 (£90-£102)**
AdvanceGuardMilitaria.com

Japanese cargo tags, GI souvenirs. **$25-$35 (£16-£22)**
AdvanceGuardMilitaria.com

Japanese soldier's cigarette case. **$30-$40 (£19-£25)**
AdvanceGuardMilitaria.com

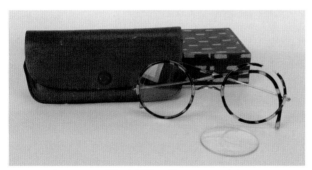

Japanese World War II-era eyeglasses and case. **$25-$45 (£16-£28)**
AdvanceGuardMilitaria.com

Japanese soldier's cigarettes. **$35-$50 (£22-£31)**
AdvanceGuardMilitaria.com

Good Luck Flags and Sennibari

Japanese Thousand Stitch Attacking Tiger Senninbari and personal flag. **$185-$360 (£115-£223)**
AdvanceGuardMilitaria.com

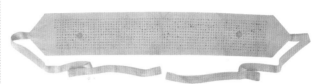

Japanese Thousand Stitch Senninbari. **$200-$235 (£124-£146)**
AdvanceGuardMilitaria.com

Japanese personal banner, 30cm x 78cm. **$25-$45 (£16-£28)**
AdvanceGuardMilitaria.com

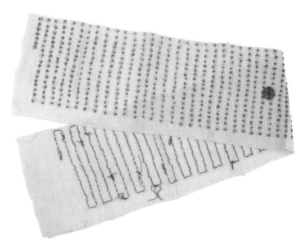

Japanese Thousand Stitch Senninbari, no casing. **$85-$115 (£53-£71)**
AdvanceGuardMilitaria.com

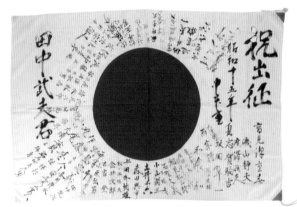

Japanese good luck flag, congratulations on enlistment, 72cm x 108cm. **$165-$185 (£102-£115)**
AdvanceGuardMilitaria.com

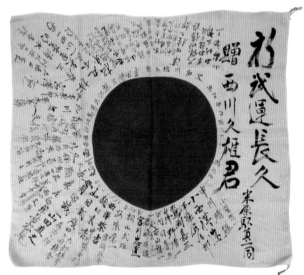

Japanese good luck flag, 72cm x 82cm. **$195-$215 (£121-£133)**
AdvanceGuardMilitaria.com

Sake Cups, Bottles, and Trays

Japanese sake cup with artillery motif. **$20-$25 (£12-£16)**
AdvanceGuardMilitaria.com

Japanese sake cup with battle flag motif. **$20-$30 (£12-£19)**
AdvanceGuardMilitaria.com

Japanese sake cup with army star. **$10-$15 (£6-£9)**
AdvanceGuardMilitaria.com

Japanese sake cup with crossed flags, 1st Regiment Tokyo Guards. **$40-$60 (£25-£37)**
AdvanceGuardMilitaria.com

Favorite Find: Prisoner of War Camp Model

By Bruce R. Tuttle

This prisoner-made presentation model of the camp and document lot came from Captain Fred B. Fimbres of the 232nd Infantry, commander of a camp for German POWs near Salzburg, Austria. The documents include a 42nd Division certificate of merit awarded to Captain Fimbres, cited to have "performed his duties as Commander of Camp Hallein Disarmed Enemy Forces Stockade in a consistently superior manner. With untiring energy and outstanding organizational ability, he reorganized the guards and prisoners of the camp, and after only one week, he had the security administration and the camp as a whole operating at the peak of efficiency."

The model came with several copies of letters from General Harry Collins (42nd Division) concerning his inspection of the DEF camp in March 1946, a March 1945 World News 42nd Division Signal Corps field newspaper, a report prepared by Captain Fimbres concerning his investigation of the escape of a German prisoner from a different camp, a memo to 42nd Division unit commanders concerning preparations for accepting the surrender of German Field Marshal Kesselring in May 1945, and a folding map showing the path taken by the 42nd Division during the war.

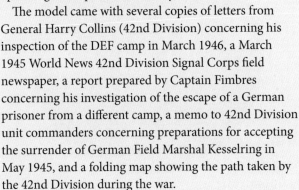

The highlight of the group, though, is the souvenir made for Captain Fimbres by the senior Austrian officer at Camp Hallein. Measuring 52cm long x 32cm wide x 7cm tall (20.5" x 12.5" x 2.75"), the walnut veneer box has a beautiful wood inlay of Hohensalzburg Castle atop Festungsberg hill in the center of the hinged lid. With the lid open, the base holds a detailed carved wood scale model of the camp, including all the barracks, commandant's house, hospital, soccer pitch, the adjacent railway, 42nd Division sign over the main entrance, guard towers, etc.

A metal plaque is attached to the interior lid: "To our patron / Mstr. Fred G. Fimbres / Former Capt. U.S. Army 232nd Inf. / that you never forget your camp / Camp Hallein, May 1946" with signature and "Austrian Camp Commander."

If Hallein sounds familiar, it should—this was the location of the salt mines worked by slave labor under the Germans, and where Hermann Goering cached the artwork he looted from Nazi-occupied Europe. It was also a hotbed of post-war "Werewolf" SS guerilla activity for many months after the fall of Berlin.

As we have learned in very recent history, the days and months following the fall of a brutal dictator can be as dangerous as the shooting war itself, and Captain Fimbres appears to be one of those talented officers successful in bringing order to the chaos, earning both the praise of his superiors as well as the gratitude and friendship of former foes. A unique and beautiful POW item!

Japanese Army lacquer sake cup. **$35-$45 (£22-£28)**
AdvanceGuardMilitaria.com

Japanese sake cup, Red Cross. **$20-$25 (£12-£16)**
AdvanceGuardMilitaria.com

Japanese inverted helmet sake cup.
$25-$35 (£16-£22)
AdvanceGuardMilitaria.com

Japanese Army lacquer sake cup, family crest.
$30-$40 (£19-£25)
AdvanceGuardMilitaria.com

Japanese sake cup with machine gun motif.
$35-$45 (£22-£28)
AdvanceGuardMilitaria.com

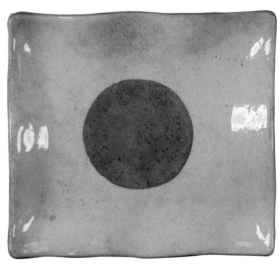

Japanese sake tray. **$20-$25 (£12-£16)**
AdvanceGuardMilitaria.com

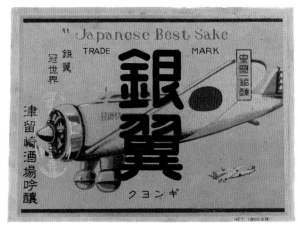

Japanese sake bottle label, dive bombers. **$25-$35 (£16-£22)**

AdvanceGuardMilitaria.com

Japanese sake bottle label, Army theme. **$15-$20 (£9-£12)**

AdvanceGuardMilitaria.com

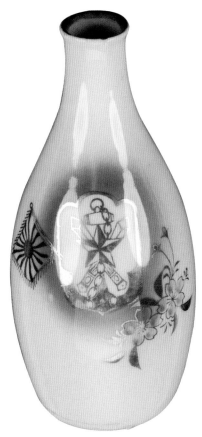

Japanese sake bottle, veteran commemoration. **$45-$55 (£28-£34)**

AdvanceGuardMilitaria.com

Japanese sake bottle, 19th Infantry. **$65-$85 (£40-£53)**

AdvanceGuardMilitaria.com

Japanese sake bottle, memory of war in China. **$60-$80 (£37-£50)**

AdvanceGuardMilitaria.com

UNITED KINGDOM AND UNITED STATES

Entertainment

United States bundles of America playing cards, two decks. **$15-$20 (£9-£12)**

AdvanceGuardMilitaria.com

Army issue phonograph. **$250-$350 (£155-£217)**

Charles D. Pautler

Army travel-sized checkers game. **$35-$50 (£22-£31)**

AdvanceGuardMilitaria.com

Parker Brothers checkers game in military service packaging. **$35-$40 (£22-£25)**

AdvanceGuardMilitaria.com

Rations/Foodstuffs

U.S. B-unit of the Army C-rations. **$100-$145 (£62-£90)**

Author's Collection

U.S. D-Bar. **$65-$125 (£40-£78)**
Author's Collection

U.S. supper K-ration, 1944. **$145-$165 (£90-£102)**
AdvanceGuardMilitaria.com

Religious Items

U.S. boxed breakfast K-ration in the 1941-style brown pasteboard carton. **$135-$150 (£84-£93)**
Author's Collection

Catholic soldier's field prayer kit. **$35-$50 (£22-£31)**
AdvanceGuardMilitaria.com

U.S. breakfast K-ration in the 1943-style box. **$135-$175 (£84-£109)**
Author's Collection

U.S. boxed dinner K-ration in the 1943-style blue and tan camouflaged carton. **$135-$185 (£84-£115)**
Author's Collection

British active service Bible, 1939. **$10-$20 (£6-£12)**
AdvanceGuardMilitaria.com

British RAF active service Bible, 1939. **$15-$25 (£9-£16)**
AdvanceGuardMilitaria.com

U.S. pocket Bible with metal cover.
$35-$50 (£22-£31)
AdvanceGuardMilitaria.com

Sewing Kits

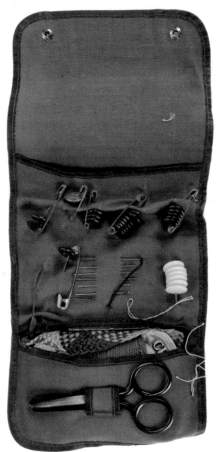

U.S. soldier's "housewife" sewing kit.
$10-$15 (£6-£9)
AdvanceGuardMilitaria.com

U.S. soldier's "housewife" sewing kit. **$25-$30 (£16-£19)**
Author's Collection

U.S. sewing kit, Coke. **$20-$30 (£12-£19)**
AdvanceGuardMilitaria.com

Sporting Goods

U.S. Navy/Marine Corps Special Services softball bat, ball, and two gloves.
$325-$400 (£202-£248)
AdvanceGuardMilitaria.com

USMC baseball glove. **$160-$185 (£99-£115)**
Charles D. Pautler

U.S. Army Special Services football. **$60-$85 (£37-£53)**

AdvanceGuardMilitaria.com

U.S. Army Special Services baseball/softball catcher's mask. **$150-$175 (£93-£109)**

AdvanceGuardMilitaria.com

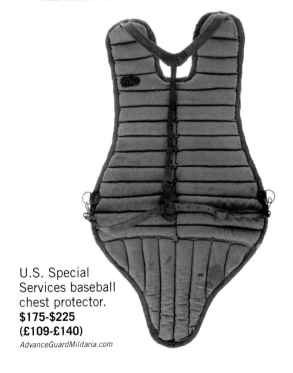

U.S. Special Services baseball chest protector. **$175-$225 (£109-£140)**

AdvanceGuardMilitaria.com

Tobacco/Smoking Accessories

Wings cigarettes. **$45-$65 (£28-£40)**

Charles D. Pautler

Wartime-pack of Camel cigarettes for domestic distribution. **$45-$65 (£28-£40)**

Charles D. Pautler

Philip Morris & Co. cigarettes with label indicating that they are not for sale and are to be used only for distribution to the Armed Forces. $65-$85 (£40-£53)

Charles D. Pautler

An unopened carton of wartime Camels is prized by collectors today just as it was by soldiers during World War II. **$300-$400 (£186-£248)**

Charles D. Pautler

Chesterfield cigarettes from a K-ration box. **$15-$25 (£9-£16)**

Charles D. Pautler

U.S. foxhole lighter. **$25-$35 (£16-£22)**

AdvanceGuardMilitaria.com

U.S. Dunhill service lighter. **$25-$35 (£16-£22)**

AdvanceGuardMilitaria.com

U.S. World War II-era chewing tobacco in patriotic packaging. **$20-$30 (£12-£19)**

AdvanceGuardMilitaria.com

U.S. Occupation-era CBI cigarette case. **$55-$65 (£34-£40)**

AdvanceGuardMilitaria.com

U.S. Occupation Zone cigarette case with Nurnberg War Crimes DI. **$285-$325 (£177-£202)**

AdvanceGuardMilitaria.com

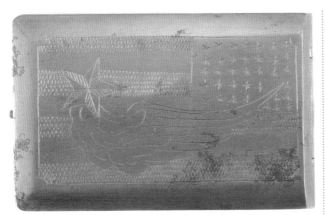

U.S. aviation theme trench art cigarette case.
$50-$65 (£31-£40)
AdvanceGuardMilitaria.com

U.S. Occupation-era constabulary cigarette case.
$75-$95 (£47-£59)
AdvanceGuardMilitaria.com

AAF 9th Air Force cigarette case. **$75-$95 (£47-£59)**
AdvanceGuardMilitaria.com

British Middelsex Regiment cigarette
case, Africa Service. **$65-$75 (£40-£47)**
AdvanceGuardMilitaria.com

Toiletries/Personal Hygiene

British Royal Navy tooth soap. **$20-$25 (£12-£16)**
AdvanceGuardMilitaria.com

U.S. soldier's Gillette
safety razor kit, two in
box. **$10-$15 (£6-£9)**
AdvanceGuardMilitaria.com

GI Pro-Kit (prophylactic). **$45-$55 (£28-£34)**
AdvanceGuardMilitaria.com

U.S. GI's personal items. **$45-$55 (£28-£34)**
AdvanceGuardMilitaria.com

U.S. Army/Marine personal items. **$25-$35 (£16-£22)**
AdvanceGuardMilitaria.com

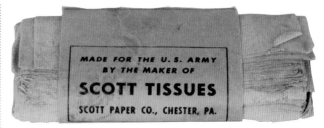

Issue toilet paper. **$10-$12 (£6-£7)**
Author's Collection

U.S. OD cotton handkerchiefs, lot of nine.
$10-$20 (£6-£12)
AdvanceGuardMilitaria.com

British soldier's issue foot powder. **$10-$12 (£6-£7)**
AdvanceGuardMilitaria.com

Army issue foot powder. **$10-$15 (£6-£9)**
AdvanceGuardMilitaria.com

Soldier's personal kit. **$20-$30 (£12-£19)**
Author's Collection

Watches

AAF Type A-11 watch, Waltham. **$145-$165 (£90-£102)**
AdvanceGuardMilitaria.com

U.S. Army wristwatch, Elgin. **$175-$195 (£109-£121)**
AdvanceGuardMilitaria.com

AAF navigator's stopwatch. **$45-$85 (£28-£53)**
AdvanceGuardMilitaria.com

Various Nations

Trench Art, Commercial Souvenirs

German tray with shot glasses. **$75-$95 (£47-£59)**
AdvanceGuardMilitaria.com

Third Reich ring with swastika. **$45-$65 (£28-£40)**
AdvanceGuardMilitaria.com

Third Reich bronze Hitler statue. **$95-$145 (£59-£90)**
AdvanceGuardMilitaria.com

Large presentation swastika, Hitler's 44th birthday. **$125-$165 (£78-£102)**
AdvanceGuardMilitaria.com

Japanese ceramic coin bank. **$55-$65 (£34-£40)**

AdvanceGuardMilitaria.com

Japanese ceramic figure, Japanese Army pilot. **$100-$125 (£62-£78)**

AdvanceGuardMilitaria.com

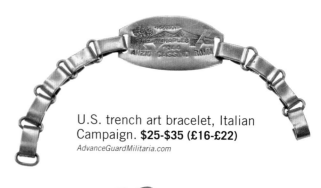

U.S. trench art bracelet, Italian Campaign. **$25-$35 (£16-£22)**

AdvanceGuardMilitaria.com

AAF pilot's identification bracelet. **$55-$65 (£34-£40)**

AdvanceGuardMilitaria.com

AAF bombardier wing badge bracelet. **$30-$40 (£19-£25)**

AdvanceGuardMilitaria.com

Hungarian trench art commemorating war in Russia. **$125-$135 (£78-£84)**

AdvanceGuardMilitaria.com

Italian Fascist Party desk ornament. **$125-$165 (£78-£102)**

AdvanceGuardMilitaria.com

AAF identification bracelet. **$25-$35 (£16-£22)**

AdvanceGuardMilitaria.com

U.S. trench art bracelet, "Jap Zero."
$40-$60 (£25-£37)
AdvanceGuardMilitaria.com

U.S. AAF bombardier's silver ring. **$65-$85 (£40-£53)**
AdvanceGuardMilitaria.com

U.S. AAF ring. **$55-$65 (£34-£40)**
AdvanceGuardMilitaria.com

1st Cavalry Division souvenir
pennant, 1943. **$50-$65 (£31-£40)**
AdvanceGuardMilitaria.com

U.S. AAF Tyndall Field souvenir
stuffed animal. **$35-$45 (£22-£28)**
AdvanceGuardMilitaria.com

AAF 14th Air Force silk scarf. **$65-$95 (£40-£59)**
AdvanceGuardMilitaria.com

Canadian RCAF souvenir scarf. **$15-$25 (£9-£16)**
AdvanceGuardMilitaria.com

USMC Marine-related souvenir textile lot.
$25-$35 (£16-£22)
AdvanceGuardMilitaria.com

British RAF souvenir pillow cover.
$20-$25 (£12-£16)
AdvanceGuardMilitaria.com

U.S. 97th Division 387th Infantry
souvenir textiles. **$10-$20 (£6-£12)**
AdvanceGuardMilitaria.com

U.S. 137th Field Artillery souvenir pillow.
$10-$20 (£6-£12)
AdvanceGuardMilitaria.com

AAF souvenir pillow cover, Langley Field.
$10-$15 (£6-£9)
AdvanceGuardMilitaria.com

AAF souvenir pillow cover, Air Transport.
$10-$15 (£6-£9)
AdvanceGuardMilitaria.com

AAF souvenir pillow cover, Wright Field.
$15-$20 (£9-£12)
AdvanceGuardMilitaria.com

U.S. 634th Tank Destroyer Battalion souvenir
pillow. **$35-$65 (£22-£40)**
AdvanceGuardMilitaria.com

CBI theater-made souvenir pillow cover,
Bullion. **$40-$55 (£25-£34)**
AdvanceGuardMilitaria.com

CBI Bullion wall hanging, 1944.
$25-$35 (£16-£22)
AdvanceGuardMilitaria.com

United States soldier's trench art on
Japanese canteen. **$55-$65 (£34-£40)**
AdvanceGuardMilitaria.com

Ashtray and lighter. **$15-$20 (£9-£12)**
AdvanceGuardMilitaria.com

USN VPB-135 ashtray stand. **$65-$85 (£40-£53)**
AdvanceGuardMilitaria.com

U.S. .50 caliber cigarette lighter. **$25-$35 (£16-£22)**
AdvanceGuardMilitaria.com

AAF Tactical Air Force ashtray. **$15-$25 (£9-£16)**
AdvanceGuardMilitaria.com

Coast artillery ashtray and lighter. **$15-$25 (£9-£16)**
AdvanceGuardMilitaria.com

Desktop cigarette lighter, 20mm. **$35-$45 (£22-£28)**
AdvanceGuardMilitaria.com

Trench art lighter, 20mm. **$25-30 (£16-£19)**
AdvanceGuardMilitaria.com

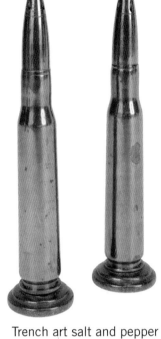

Trench art salt and pepper shakers. **$10-$15 (£6-£9)**
AdvanceGuardMilitaria.com

Eagle trench art shell. **$30-$40 (£19-£25)**
AdvanceGuardMilitaria.com

Fist full of bullets trench art. **$25-$30 (£16-£19)**
AdvanceGuardMilitaria.com

Trench art on Italian shell, Algiers. **$55-$65 (£34-£40)**
AdvanceGuardMilitaria.com

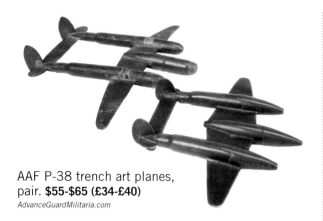

AAF P-38 trench art planes, pair. **$55-$65 (£34-£40)**
AdvanceGuardMilitaria.com

Trench art lamps, pair. **$35-$50 (£22-£31)**
AdvanceGuardMilitaria.com

AAF identified souvenir plaque. **$15-$20 (£9-£12)**
AdvanceGuardMilitaria.com

AAF Far East Air Forces paperweight.
$25-$35 (£16-£22)
AdvanceGuardMilitaria.com

U.S. trench art hand grenade dish.
$65-$85 (£40-£53)
AdvanceGuardMilitaria.com

Persian Gulf Command trench art tankard.
$55-$75 (£34-£47)
AdvanceGuardMilitaria.com

Philippines hand fan made from Occupation money. **$10-$15 (£6-£9)**
AdvanceGuardMilitaria.com

AAF CBI lunch box. **$45-$65 (£28-£40)**
AdvanceGuardMilitaria.com

AAF Wright Field souvenir bowl.
$20-$35 (£12-£22)
AdvanceGuardMilitaria.com

Trench art multi-shot vase. **$15-$20 (£9-£12)**
AdvanceGuardMilitaria.com

Trench art stiletto letter opener.
$30-$40 (£19-£25)
AdvanceGuardMilitaria.com

Trench art lamp, entered Army in 1941.
$25-$35 (£16-£22)
AdvanceGuardMilitaria.com

U.S. 83rd Division trench art shells, pair. **$35-$45 (£22-£28)**
AdvanceGuardMilitaria.com

U.S. Persian Command trench art plate.
$10-$20 (£6-£12)
AdvanceGuardMilitaria.com

Chapter 8

Groupings

The phone rings. The voice on the line says he is answering your ad for World War II mementoes. Would you be interested in his dad's uniform? After a few questions, you conclude the uniform has been stripped of all insignia, but you decide to look at it, just in case. When you visit the home, the Ike jacket is indeed stripped of any insignia except for an embroidered 15th Air Force insignia. "Not bad," you think. "With the identification of their dad and the patch, this is about an $85 (£53) uniform." Before making a fair offer, you ask the all-important question, "Do you have anything else from your dad's service years?"

The question leads to discussing just what the vet's children remember seeing. First, they pull out a tattered but respectable A-2 flight jacket, and you recognize the painted insignia of the 98th Bomb Group. Together with the Ike, this "group" just jumped in value to about $500 (£310).

After asking about any medals or awards, they produce a box containing a three-award medal ribbon bar with Air Medal mounted by three bronze subsequent award oak leaf clusters, Good Conduct, and European campaign ribbon with four stars; loose embroidered 15th Air Force shoulder sleeve insignia, the man's identification tag, an un-engraved Air Medal with three bronze subsequent award oak leaf clusters on the ribbon, a silver Air Crew wing badge, and a few original photographs taken from his B-24 in formation flight, one inscribed. The value has suddenly jumped to around $900 (£558)!

A final inquiry about paperwork produces a file that includes the 1945 98th Bombardment Group listing of the Group's 14 Battle Participation Awards, the March 28, 1944 98th Bombardment Group 200th Mission commemorative letter, and an informative brief history of operations to that date with special note of their heroic participation in the first raid on the Ploesti oil fields. Further examination produces a document listing AAF men to be sent to the United States for "rehabilitation, recuperation and recovery," with this particular vet's name listed among them. What started out as a simple stripped Ike jacket has suddenly become a $1,200+ (£744+) "grouping."

Get It All

Collecting groupings is a relatively new phenomenon in the hobby. Many early collectors were satisfied by simply collecting their specialty, be it helmets, collar discs, patches, or whatever niche they defined as their own. This led to the proliferation of stripping uniforms for the particular piece of interest. Furthermore, dealers had been convinced they could make more money by splitting up groups—selling the helmet to a headgear collector, collar discs and shoulder patches to insignia collectors, and discarding the bulky uniforms. The logic, at the time, was that the uniforms took up too much space for the amount of monetary return they offered.

For many years, World War II collecting remained nameless, especially in regard to relics of the Axis. "Identified" items just didn't seem to matter to most collectors.

This all changed as more former American Civil War collectors moved into the World War II arena. This group of collectors had learned very early that the value of a photograph, weapon, or uniform increased dramatically if the name of a soldier was attached to it.

The former Civil War collectors were attracted by the plentiful supply of World War II relics and the relative ease of finding identified pieces. It didn't take long for dealers to recognize this emerging market.

Today, the same dealers who, years ago, thought nothing of plucking a patch from a jacket's shoulder or a pair of wings from the breast are now gathering every scrap of paper, every personal hygiene item, and every piece of clothing a soldier was issued to offer groupings for sale.

Know Your Source

Whereas patch and insignia stripping has subsided in recent times, "assembling" groupings has proliferated. For some, it is an overwhelming temptation to put a group together. It increases values and moves items that aren't that desirable in the first place.

Collecting Hints

Pros:
- Groupings provide a real sense of the soldier to whom the items originally belonged.
- Groupings provide an opportunity to avoid becoming a "type" collector. They provide variety.
- Research potential is extremely high, leading the collector to interesting connections.
- Groupings usually make impressive displays that are engaging and interesting for both experienced scholars and casual observers.

Cons:
- Groupings can be difficult to store. Because so many different materials make up a grouping, it can be a challenge to find a storage environment that accommodates all pieces.
- Material can be split apart inadvertently, leading to the loss of historical continuity of a group. Owning a grouping requires vigilance and dedication to maintaining the integrity of the material.
- Groupings require a greater monetary investment than individual items.
- Because of the variety of material that can be combined to form a grouping, it can be tempting for sellers to marry items together. It is imperative that the collector knows and trusts his sources.

Availability: ✪ ✪
Price: ✪ ✪ ✪
Reproduction Alert: ✪ ✪ ✪

For example, consider this scenario: A U.S. Army Class A tunic with a 3rd Army patch is worth about $35 (£22). An unscrupulous dealer could add some armor collar discs ($10/£6), a pair of 1940 cavalry boots ($125/£78), mounted breeches ($15/£9), a visor cap ($45/£28), an unnamed Purple Heart ($65/£40), and a story about how this belonged to "one of Patton's tankers who was wounded at the Bulge." As such, this grouping, with a face value of $295 (£183), could be marketed for as much as $650 (£403). More important to the unscrupulous dealer, though, is that the grouping would permit him to get rid of items that would otherwise be very difficult to sell.

"The American soldier is, by nature, a collector of mementos from wherever he has been. I came home with or shipped guns, swords, daggers, knives, and helmets. Nazi paraphernalia, beer steins, and the skin of a red deer I shot, a book of Albrecht Duhrer's paintings, and a tapestry of a hunting scene. Also enough beautiful leather gloves for the entire family for Christmas."

— Robert G. Hansen, U.S. Army

The Key is Provenance

Many soldiers marked their belongings (U.S. soldiers used their surname initial followed by the last four digits of their serial number). If all pieces in a grouping are marked similarly, that provides strong evidence that everything belonged to the same soldier.

Other than buying directly from the veteran or his/her family, one has to be able to trust his source. Is your source the type to add (or even worse, strip away) a pair of wings, a patch, or a piece of field gear? Resist the temptation of a great grouping if you don't know your dealer's reputation, or worse yet, if you do know the reputation and it isn't impeccable.

A Different Kind of Collecting

Those who specialize in groupings tend not to develop the expertise of a "type collector." Whereas a helmet collector will know and recognize variations in helmet liners, a groupings collector is more interested in the story of the soldier who wore the helmet. The joy for the groupings collector is in the amount of information he can learn about the military career of the soldier whose items he owns.

A downside to a grouping, though, can be in how to display it. Groupings require a great deal of flexibility. A patch collector will never need to worry about display torsos or adequate closet space. A medal collector will never need to be concerned about leather dry rot. A headgear collector will never wonder how to preserve brittle documents. A bayonet collector will rarely be concerned about light levels. But all of these things are the concern of a groupings collector. In fact, the concerns a local historical museum faces in regards to preservation, handling and display are the same that a groupings collector faces.

Another facet of group collecting is assembling "typical" uniforms and equipment. Not necessarily belonging to any one specific soldier, these conglomerations represent what a soldier most likely would have worn or used at a particular point in time. This style of collecting has been fast gathering momentum as people want to purchase and show complete displays. These assembled groupings have value for the sense of history they impart, but should not command prices much different than the combined values of the individual pieces in the group.

Groupings, more so than specialized "type collections," impart the sense of the soldiers who made the sacrifice to serve their countries. Like the local historical museum, the groupings collector enjoys the sense of putting the personality back into the objects.

CANADA

Canadian Uniform and Equipment Group

Assembled group for officers or enlisted personnel: Mk III steel helmet with cotton chinstrap, battledress blouse with trousers, two shirts, short black leather boots, web gaiters, wool tie, trouser belt, map case, basic pouches, brace attachments, Enfield breech cover, web belt, haversack, haversack L straps, cross straps, entrenching tool with cover dated, bayonet frog, camouflage net, brown canvas Bren magazine carrier/ vest, ammunition bandoleer, revolver ammunition pouch, canteen and cover, rifle pull-through, two field dressings, brown enamel mug, Mk II service respirator with pouch, and aluminum mess tin. Also included is a reproduction Colt. 45 pistol and a spare parts case for a Bren. **$2,145 (£1,330)**
Hermann-Historic.de

FRANCE

Captain with 4th Regiment of Moroccan Spahis

Pre-1944 U.S. M1 steel helmet with fixed loops with French captain bars on front and unit insignia (yellow 4 on red lozenge) on both sides; same markings on liner, except for number 4; red-backed 4th RSM collar patches; pair of lieutenant's shoulder strap slip-ons; pair of captain's shoulder strap slip-ons; and pastel portrait of an officer signed "Lesur" and labeled "Guy" on back. **$1,340 (£831)**
Hermann-Historic.de

French Officer's Group, 1940

Wood and canvas foot locker with painted markings, "2e Corps d'Armée Etat-Major, Mr Menier Commandant," contains brown wool tunic with fall collar for major of 51st Infantry Regiment and two ribbon bars; pair of breeches; Sam Browne belt; two green shirts; and two wool knit puttees. **$200 (£124)**
Hermann-Historic.de

Free French Foreign Legion Group

British Mark II steel helmet in original finish with tricolor lozenges on sides (one over a probable Royal Artillery flash), marked "1938, 1C576 94 Co. Ltd" with name scratched into paint, damaged patent leather lining, French leather chinstrap attached with brass wire; kepi for enlisted personnel; and blue wool cholera belt. **$1,235 (£766)**

Hermann-Historic.de

French Colonel Léon Edmond Simonin (1888-1967)

Ecole spéciale militaire shako with tuft, full dress shako with cassowary plume, set of epaulets with thin red fringes; pair of white gloves; Pattern 1935-37 steel helmet for motorized troops with rubber crown pad; wooden cane engraved for 517th GBC (tank battalion group); leather map case; pair of full dress senior officer epaulettes with thick silver fringes and officer's ID card in leather wallet. The 18th BCP badge is pinned on a World War 1 Croix de Guerre fourragère. Six medals with ribbons, Officier de la Légion d'Honneur, Croix de Guerre 1914-18 and 1939 with palms, Croix du Combattant, and World War 1 and Interallied medals, with documents for mention in dispatches, and Légion d'Honneur certificate. Also included is 1931 pattern full dress cape; blackened wooden trunk; commercial pattern brown canvas leggings; leather saber hanger; leather compass case; leather leggings; two pairs of stirrups; leather box for detachable collars and cuffs; two large leather map cases; and two leather and web coat straps for officer's saddle. **$3,485 (£2,161)**

Hermann-Historic.de

French Artillery Lieutenant Uniform: 1939-40

Assembled group: Garrison cap without piping; four pocket tunic with open collar, artillery buttons, 11th Artillery Regiment collar tabs and lieutenant's stripes on cuffs; putty-colored officer's breeches; poplin uniform shirt with two pleated pockets, shoulder straps; commercial silk tie; brown leather Sam Browne belt with sword straps; map case with strap; eight 1940s Michelin road maps; pair of 1936 pattern 8x24 binoculars with case and strap; ANP-31 service gas mask with commercial carrier; and high-top hobnailed shoes and leggings. **$670 (£415)**

Hermann-Historic.de

Free French Navy (FNFL) Sailor's Uniform

Reconstruction with original seaman's cap with "Marine Nationale" tally; dark blue wool jumper and trousers; undated jumper with post-war blue collar, leather and canvas leggings; black leather ankle boots; leather suspension straps (nine adjustment holes); 1903/14 pattern leather belt; three 1916 pattern cartridge pouches; and 1888 pattern black leather bayonet frog. There is also a large, unbleached canvas sea bag. **$335 (£208)**

Hermann-Historic.de

Military Motorcyclist Uniform, 1940

Assembled group: 1938 pattern motorcyclist's canvas coat with wooden buttons; matching bib coveralls; leather and canvas gloves dated 1938; 1935 pattern shirt with round stamp, "Nord toile St-Etienne"; regulation tie; leather map case with snap hooks and seven 1940s Michelin road maps; undated poplin neck cloth; leather belt for enlisted personnel; 11-hole Y-straps; 1935 pattern ammunition pouches; mismatched pair of 1917 pattern high top hobnailed shoes; 1935 pattern tent section with camouflage loops and buttons; green canvas breech cover; canvas water bucket and wash basin; 1892 pattern haversack; 1877 pattern water bottle with strap and tin-plated cup; portable pick in its leather carrier; ANP-31 service gas mask with bag and accessories; 1939-dated field dressing; Monjardet candle lantern; housewife; two 1915 pattern gun oilers; button brush; and aluminum mess tin. **$750 (£465)**

Hermann-Historic.de

1940 Pilot's Complete Flight Suit

Complete set to outfit a French pilot from Battle of France (May 10-June 25, 1940), including brown leather-covered hard shell flight helmet with brown japanned metal snap fittings for goggle strap guides, straps and earphone cover attachments, lace adjustment in back, and chinstrap with two metal ring closure; interior has brown leather liner with "finger" crown adjustment; pair of goggles with blue and white elastic band with metal cam buckle adjustment; "Type L 400" insulated flight coverall marked with January 1940 date; flying boots of shearling with leather side out and dyed dark brown, zipper side access with functional zippers, leather soles, and black rubber heels, fleece interior has nomenclature tag "Type L 340," also dated "January 1940." **$1,850 (£1,147)**

www.AdvanceGuardMilitaria.com

Commando Uniform for 1er Bataillon de Fusiliers-Marins

Assembled group: Green commando beret with cap badge for 1er Bllon FM Commando; 1940 pattern battledress blouse with "France" and "No 4 Commando," shoulder titles, combined operations unit insignia, sergeant stripes, and specialty badge for heavy machine gunner on right sleeve; pair of 1940 pattern battledress trousers; 1937 pattern web belt, shoulder straps, two basic pouches and bayonet frog, water bottle, entrenching tool (rusted handle), revolver holster, and ammunition pouch; 1944 flotation belt; rifle ammunition bandoleer; camouflaged face veil; toggle rope; and web anklets with mismatched pair of hobnailed combat boots. **$4,020 (£2,492)**

Hermann-Historic.de

Favorite Find: Another Time, Another Place

By Larry J. Menestrina

It just seemed too good to believe. But there I was with Mr. Forest S., who invited me to his house in south-central Kansas to look at his World War II military souvenirs. It all started on a wintry afternoon in December 2004, during a conversation I had with an old veteran who visited a museum in my hometown of Wichita, Kansas, where I have an extensive display of German and Russian World War II uniforms and artifacts.

Forest came to the museum on a day when I happened to be wearing my father's Ike jacket and talking to visitors about the various German and Russian uniforms I had on display from my personal collection. Forest walked over to one of the German combat uniforms and said to me, "You know, I have something like this down in my basement, but I think it's a camouflage uniform the Germans wore."

This really perked up my ears. I was trying to control my excitement when I asked him to explain what his old German uniform looked like. He said it was a jacket and maybe pants—that's all he could remember because it had been a long time since he had seen all those things.

I showed him around the rest of the World War II exhibit. Before he left, I made sure I had his name and address. It had been a great pleasure speaking to him and listening to his war stories.

Christmas came and my family and I drove to Indiana to visit my parents, who themselves had unique experiences in World War II. My mother had been a German BDM girl and my father had been a U.S. Army soldier, European theater.

Before I left for Indiana, I sent Mr. S. a Christmas card with a reminder that I would like to visit him sometime after the holidays and see his World War II stuff. Later, I contacted Mr. S. again. He invited me to come over on the following Saturday afternoon. I could hardly wait—the excitement was getting stronger each day. I daydreamed of what he might have stored away in his basement and what he might want to do with it. Hopefully, he would consider selling it to me. Or he might tell me that he was going to give it all to his son. I've had that happen to me several times during my 40 years of collecting. A guy shows you what he's brought back and you think you're going to have a chance to buy

Larry Menestrina acquired his "Favorite Find"—a grouping of items brought home from World War II by a single veteran—because of a museum display that he prepared for a local museum.

it, but then it all falls through because he's going to give it to a family member who probably has little to no interest in it. So what can you do?

I arrived at Mr. S.'s house and we walked downstairs to the basement, which was dimly lit. For a few seconds I couldn't see where he had gone. I could hear clothing hangers clanging around. I heard him say, "Where did I put it?" He finally pulled a piece of clothing from one of the hangers and laid it on a pool table in the middle of the basement. He walked back to what I presumed was a clothing rack and pulled down another item from a hanger and placed it on the pool table. I slowly walked over to the pool table to see what he had retrieved.

GERMANY

By this time he had found the pull string for a light, and I saw a beautiful German camouflage winter jacket with tan and water colors (the Marsh 44 pattern). Next to the jacket was a matching pair of pants with the original camouflage braces still attached. I gently felt the jacket, touching the rare and well-preserved German winter uniform with awe. I hoped there would be more—what else was he going to dig out?

He walked back to the clothing rack and brought another piece of clothing to the pool table. This time it was an enlisted man's Luftwaffe flieger blouse. I very gently touched each uniform item, relishing the feel and smell of the old cloth. I asked him how he acquired these items and he said he found most of the stuff at a German supply depot near Worms, Germany.

The veteran walked over to another side of the basement and showed me an old plywood box. He told me that a German prisoner of war had made it for him. One by one, he slowly pulled out his war souvenirs: U-boat binoculars still in the case, Luftwaffe pilot wrist compass, German silver Wound Badge, Kriegsmarine Navy dagger, and German Army helmet.

After we looked at his war souvenirs, he went back to the clothing rack and took down another uniform item and gently laid it on the table. After the war, he had a German tailor modify his Army overcoat so that it was cut down to just below the waist. The old Army coat still had an ETO Advanced Base insignia, sergeant stripes, and five Overseas Service bars sewn onto the sleeves.

Mr. S.'s first thought was to give all these items to me, knowing that I would take care of them and put them on display at the museum. In my heart I knew I couldn't accept them without paying him something. So I offered him what I could afford to pay. He accepted my offer.

I am forever grateful to Mr. Forest S. for giving me the opportunity to acquire original veteran war items. As promised, I applied my tender loving care to each item and for several years displayed the German camouflage uniform in the museum's World War II exhibit, forever keeping alive its memory.

Mr. S. wanted people to remember his time as a soldier from another time and another place. I intend to do exactly that.

Generalmajor Max Hoffmann's Uniform Tunic and Archives

Max Hoffmann (1883-1957) was Oberstleutnant in 1931 in charge of troop training grounds at Münsingen. In 1933, he commanded Biberach defense district and in 1935 that of Sigmaringen; 1940 brought a similar command at Stuttgart. In 1942, he was in charge of prisoners of war in Wehrkreis II. He was discharged in 1944. Field blouse of field gray gabardine with dark green collars and granular gold buttons with sewn-on shoulder boards with plain underlay, red collar tabs with gold Larisch embroidery, gold cello-embroidered eagle (resewn) with contrasting brown feathers, War Merit Cross buttonhole ribbon, small field orders clasp, Iron Cross 1st Class of 1914, Wound Badge in black 1918, and War Merit Cross 1st Class with Swords of 1939. Archives includes Appointment of 1902 to Leutnant in Grand Duke of Mecklenburg Jäger Battalion Nr. 14, and to Oberleutnant dated 1911; possession document for Iron Cross 2nd Class of 1914; award for officer's equestrian show jumping 1926; appointment to Oberst (Colonel) dated 18 January 1937 with signatures in ink by Adolf Hitler and Blomberg; appointment with award folder to Generalmajor (Brigadier) with ink signature of von Brauchitsch; documents for Long Service awards 4th through 1st Classes; the War Merit Cross of 1939 with Swords 1st and 2nd Class; and Feldpost items. **$11,390 (£7,062)**
Hermann-Historic.de

Signal Unit Officer's Grouping

Rare cap for officers of Nachrichtentruppe (Information Section) with yellow piping and dark green cap band; six pairs of shoulder boards in various ranks, three pairs of collar tabs and two embroidered breast eagles for officers; saber for officers with leather hanger; officer's identification tag: "1.N.E.A.6."; two pistol holsters; belt buckle; cuff title; HJ/DJ insignia; student's cap; framed 1939 copper sheet document with dedication "Dem Sieger im Keulenweitwurf - Ernst Moritz Arndt Schule." **$1,250 (£775)**

Hermann-Historic.de

Generalleutnant Friedrich Zickwolff's (1889-1944) Field Tunic and Breeches

Old-pattern field tunic in field gray tricot cloth with dark green collar, red piping on button facing, golden buttons, sewn-in shoulder boards and red collar patches with golden Larisch embroidery (slightly darkened), breast eagle missing, affixed Iron Cross 1st Class of 1914, Wound Badge 1918 in black and six-piece field orders clasp, green silk lining with Berlin tailor's tag; breeches of stone gray cloth with broad red stripes, leg closure with laces and small buttons, signs of usage on stripes at height of boots. Generalleutnant Zickwolff was appointed Generalleutnant in 1941 and on June 2, 1942, he was awarded Knight's Cross as Kommandeur of 113th Infantry Division. Until seriously wounded in August 1943, he commanded the 343rd Infantry Division. On Sept. 17, 1944 he died as a result of his wounds. **$6,030 (£3,739)**

Hermann-Historic.de

NSKK Medical Doctor's Service Uniform

Brown gabardine tunic with silver buttons and gold-brown silk liner with black velvet collar tabs with silver corded edges and gold-colored metal applications, silver collar cord, woven silver sleeve eagle and lozenge, standard arm band; black gabardine riding breeches. **$2,145 (£1,330)**

Hermann-Historic.de

Political Section Leader's Uniform

Visor cap of brown gabardine with brown velvet lace stripes, blue piping, gilt metal insignia; coat of brown gabardine with gold Party buttons, brown collar tabs in rank of section leader, blue piping and applied national eagle with oak leaf, left sleeve with armband for local chapter leader; brown service shirt with tie and NSDAP member's badge; riding breeches of brown gabardine; belt with RZM stamping; pistol holster stamped "RZM 2/35" with pin-attached national eagle; and brown leather boots in officer's quality. **$5,895 (£3,655)**

Hermann-Historic.de

Luftwaffe Pilot's Summer Uniform

Summer flight helmet with larynx microphone, aviator goggles with tieback; summer combination with "Ri-Ri" zip closures and "Prym" buttons, arm compass, brown leather belt with aluminum buckle and pistol holster; lined leather boots with lateral zip closures and heating connections. **$1,200 (£744)**

Hermann-Historic.de

Afrikakorps Uniform Ensemble of Unteroffizier Africa

Assembled group: M40 reed green field cap with insignia with sand-colored background cloth; reed green tropical field tunic of cotton material with depot stamp, all accessories, national emblem, shoulder boards with green piping, collar patches and NCO braid; long reed green trousers with depot stamp; iron belt buckle and web belt; and short leather tie-up shoes with web linen trim and reed green tongue. Equipment includes web magazine pouch and four magazines; canteen with cup; bread bag with cigarette lighter; Y-straps and rucksack; modern copy of MP 38/40 shoulder guard and carry strap; uniform on movable mannequin. **$10,720 (£6,646)**

Hermann-Historic.de

Medals and Uniform of Luftwaffe Pilot August Högl

Comprehensive collection of observer and later pilot August Högl, winner of German Cross in gold, member of Battle Wing 200, Fighter Group West and East, Fighter Wing 105, Battle Wing 30 and 3rd Long Range Reconnaissance Squadron 122: four-pocket tunic with rank of first lieutenant for flying personnel of blue-gray wool fabric with silk lining, silver colored buttons, shoulder boards, collar patches and ribbon for Iron Cross 2nd Class sewn to tunic; awards in group include Combined Pilot's and Observer's badge, second model in zinc, German Cross in gold in 1957 version, and Front Flight Clasp for reconnaissance units, gold version; two hangers for Luftwaffe dagger; triangle calculator by Dennert & Pape from February 1943 and no. "FL 23825-1"; "aer-adjuvator" by Junkers Dessau for crews with glider training; heavy Luftwaffe gray leather greatcoat from 1930s; wooden model of four-engine FW 200 with dedication of Luftgau Signal Regiment 7 from Augsburg-Pfersee; maps for flying formations; three handwritten service and training books, and special edition of front newspaper from 1940 for British aircraft. **$2,415 (£1,497)**
Hermann-Historic.de

Uniform and Awards of Lieutenant Karl Dammann, Sturmgeschützabteilung (Assault Gun Unit) 190

Special field jacket for armored crew members, issue piece, field gray felt cloth, gray lining with faded issue stamp, seven buttons, woven crew eagle, field gray collar boards with red piping and applied skulls, shoulder boards with red backing and applied "190"; visor cap for artillery or assault gun officers of field gray cloth; officer's field tunic of field gray cloth, green silk lining, dark green collar with silver embroidered collar boards with red stripes, shoulder boards with red backing and applied "190," silver embroidered officer's eagle; riding breeches of field gray cloth with lacing; award certificates include IC 1, IC 2, Assault Badge (rare print with eagle emblem), Wound Badge in black, Eastern Front medal and certificate book for the Reich Sport badge, service record with list of all battles and awards, two folders with propaganda company reports on Dammann's missions; three records of interviews given by Dammann to war correspondent in which Dammann describes how he "destroyed 16 Soviet tanks" with two assault guns during defense on the Crimea. **$9,115 (£5,651)**
Hermann-Historic.de

GREAT BRITAIN

Uniform and Equipment for British Soldier, Burma Campaign

Assembled group: Felt bush hat; helmet with net; Aertex bush jacket with belt (1944); Aertex shirt; pair of cotton field trousers; mosquito net/helmet cover; web gaiters; belt with cross straps, haversack L straps, large pack, bayonet frog, field first-aid dressing, long stretcher bearer's straps, canteen with cover, web machete sheath and small axe. **$750 (£465)**
Hermann-Historic.de

Uniform for Officer of Royal Navy, 1944

Unmarked duffle coat; blue battledress blouse, dated 1944 Officer's blue working dress blouse; pair of trousers; wool turtleneck sweater; mismatched pair of combat boots; web gaiters; web belt with suspension straps, suspender attachments and revolver ammunition pouch; "RN" armband; Mk I leather binoculars case and pair of captain's shoulder boards. **$735 (£456)**

Hermann-Historic.de

Uniform and Equipment for British Paratrooper

Assembled group: Denison smock (1942) Lightning zipper, Newey snaps; battledress trousers; 1945 oversmock; issue necktie; gaiters; web belt with cross straps and haversack L straps, basic pouches, and canteen with cover; issue camouflage net; entrenching tool and cover; 1944 rifle sling; canvas bandoleer; service respirator and bag; 1942 mess tin; Bren magazine pouches; and personal items including two issue shaving brushes and razors; 1943 Canadian field dressing; toilet roll and small bag for casual effects. **$1,600 (£992)**

Hermann-Historic.de

Uniform and Equipment for Royal Marine Commando

Assembled group: Denim battledress blouse with matching trousers; flannel shirt; camouflaged face veil/net; cap comforter; gaiters (1941); web belt with basic pouches and cross straps; rifle breech rope (1944); canteen and cover; toggle rope; 1944 life belt; and rare round web carriers for Vicker's K-Gun with straps (1944). **$780 (£484)**

Hermann-Historic.de

RAF No. 625 Squadron Pilot Officer's DFC Medal Group

Items belonging to Pilot Officer Noel R. Truman, Flight Engineer with Lancaster-equipped No. 625 Squadron. Medals: Cased Distinguished Flying Cross dated 1944 on lower arm and five-place medal bar: Reproduction DFC, 1939-45 Star, Aircrew Europe Star with France and Germany clasp, Defence Medal, and British War Medal. Separate pair of ribbon bars accompanies medals. Also included is embroidered Engineer wing with black backing; Bomber Command blazer patch; two snapshots of Lancaster crews; two Navigator and Air Gunner's Flying Log Books chronicling Truman's flight history; three copies of *Pilot's Notes* (one general, one for York CI, and third for Lancasters); fabric-backed map of IPC pipeline and RAF routes; three engineer log pages (only one filled out for flight in York CI); and large file of photocopied records pertinent to Truman's military service. The recommendation for his DFC included testaments from his Wing Commander who stated, "His skill in the handling of the engines and in all the duties assigned to a Flight Engineer have proved of the greatest assistance to his Captain...On the night of March 15, 1944, when

attacking Stuttgart, the aircraft was intercepted by an ME 410 which was damaged and probably destroyed by the guns of the aircraft, and the skill and co-operation of Pilot Officer Truman helped materially in making the work of his Captain as easy as possible; and so probably destroying the enemy aircraft." Accompanying the group are two World War I medals presented to Truman's father, Pvt. Cecil Truman, Royal Marines, who was taken prisoner during Battle of Canal du Nord in 1918: Victory Medal impressed, "PLY 1500-S-PTE. C. TRUMAN. RMLI" and 1914-20 War Medal impressed the same. **$3,350 (£2,077)**

www.AdvanceGuardMilitaria.com

RAF NCO Aerial Gunner's Tunic and Medals, KIA

Blue wool simplified airman's jacket with BeVo-style blue eagle shoulder flashes; Sergeant's chevrons and flat silk embroidered Aerial Gunner's wing on dark blue backing; original O.H.M.S. mailing box addressed to E.J. Payne containing three medals for Sergeant T.E. Payne (1939-45 Star, Air Crew Europe, and 1939-45 War). Sergeant Trevor Herrington Payne, 617 Squadron, was serving as front gunner on board Lancaster Mk. III JA898 when it left Coningsby on a bombing operation on Dortmund-Ems Canal near Ladbergen on Sept. 15-16, 1943. Thick fog prevented accurate bombing. Lancaster III JA898 was shot down by light flak while in target area and crashed between Recke and Obersteinbeck. Sergeant Payne, along with the rest of the crew, perished in the crash. Payne was one of the crewmembers who trained for the dam-busting missions. **$685 (£425)**

www.AdvanceGuardMilitaria.com

Uniform and Equipment for RAF Crew Member

Assembled group: Battledress blouse with matching trousers and suspenders; "Mae West" life preserver; leather-lined flying gloves; scarf of parachute material; and non regulation shirt and tie. **$565 (£350)**

Hermann-Historic.de

British Army Tank Unit Uniform, 1944-45

Assembled group: Tank crew overalls with DOT zippers, Newey snaps, and detachable hood; camouflaged face veil; brown wool knit gloves; 1942-dated webbing belt with RAC holster and reproduction Enfield revolver with lanyard; radio headset, WK 44 YA5000; and hand-held microphone, No 3 ZA 5371. **$670 (£415)**

Hermann-Historic.de

Uniform Group for British Soldier, 8th Army Soldier

Assembled group: South African sand-colored steel helmet; Aertex bush shirt dated 1943; tropical shorts (GMN 1943); gaiters dated 1943; undated khaki socks; and black leather military boots. Equipment includes: undated web belt, pair of basic pouches, cross straps, and haversack L straps, canteen and cover, entrenching tool and cover, large pack, and service respirator dated 1940 in pouch with fog paste and ointment tubes in metal box. **$1,150 (£713)**

Hermann-Historic.de

HOLLAND

Enlisted Man's Uniform and Equipment

Assembled group, uniform and accoutrements of Dutch fighting man: Green-gray wool tunic with standing collar, nonfunctional shoulder straps, inset breast pockets with pointed flaps, bronze rampant lion buttons and round cuffs; issue breeches of matching wool with inset watch, side and hip pockets, rear half belt with buckle and fitted calves and pair of English-made Fox Wellington Somerset wrap puttees; pair of Dutch pattern English-made black leather ankle boots dated "1944"; Model 1928 "Nieuw Model" helmet with bronze oval rampant lion crest; M31 side cap of green-gray wool with false upturned visor and folding neck cape; brown leather M15 belt with black-painted iron buckle, pair of brown leather M95 cartridge pouches, pair of brown leather Y-straps with pair of leather loops with buckles that allow suspenders to be worn without pouches. M95 Infantry bayonet has "T" pattern blade retaining 80% blued finish with "HEMBRUG" maker's stamp, hilt has wood grips with black leather scabbard and frog. Other equipment: tinned iron mess kit in age dark finish, dated "1-39," with field gray canvas and brown leather belt pouch issue; black leather and tan canvas shovel carrier with Belgian-made shovel; field gray canvas bread bag with shoulder sling; aluminum canteen; and field gray canvas single bag soft knapsack with leather shoulder slings; Type "G" gas mask with field gray canvas carry bag with sling with leather tabs. Personal items: zinc identity tag stamped with soldier's name and data, white neck cord, black soldier's ID book dated "1938" and individual dressing in natural linen wrapper with paper instruction labels. **$1,565 (£970)**

www.AdvanceGuardMilitaria.com

Infantry Officer's Uniform and Equipment

Early war uniform of captain as worn during Blitzkrieg period of 1940; tunic of bluish green-gray wool twill with standing collar piped in infantry dark blue with silvered rank stars, shoulder straps, blue piped cuffs and pleated patch breast and bellows skirt pockets, all with button flaps, bronze rampant lion buttons, collar lined with removable white celluloid standing shirt collar, three addition collars and set of cuffs with lion buttons; breeches of matching wool with dark blue seam piping and lace calves; shako-like rigid kepi covered in green-gray wool with fabric-covered celluloid visor, double row of gold soutache braid around band, orange and gold bullion national cockade and rampant lion insignia on obverse and brown leather chinstrap. Footwear: pair of black leather commercial ankle boots lined in white canvas and pair of black leather leggings. Sam Brown belt with brass fittings, shoulder sling and sword frog; automatic pistol holster with full flap and lift the dot snap, extra magazine pocket and belt loop; field gray cord and brown leather pistol lanyard; leather two-pocket clip pouch; binocular case with belt loops, lacking binoculars; and unmarked British-style whistler with brown cloth cord lanyard; map case with shoulder sling and dispatch case with full flap with aluminum-tipped closure strap, divided interior pouch and multiple drafting tool holders. **$895 (£555)**

www.AdvanceGuardMilitaria.com

HUNGARY

ITALY

Infantry Uniform and Equipment

The Hungarians were one of Nazi Germany's staunchest allies, and their armies fought in Russia and elsewhere on the Eastern Front. Basic uniform and equipment as issued to infantry private: khaki wool uniform of pattern adopted around 1922 consists of tunic with pointed roll collar, shoulder straps, and pleated patch breast and skirt pockets with scalloped flaps, collar has green wool infantry insignia with pointed ends and bronze St. Stefan crown buttons used throughout; trousers of matching wool with inset front and rear pockets with buttoned flaps; issue khaki wool field cap with folding neck cape held by two bronze crown buttons and matching fold-up cloth visor, obverse with bronze cockade painted in center with national colors; German-made khaki fine knit wool wrap puttees have friction buckles, metal hooks, and a woven label marked "Mars Gamasche." Other clothing: khaki wool double-breasted greatcoat with roll collar, shoulder straps, round cuffs, inset skirt pockets with scalloped flaps and rear half belt, green wool collar tabs and St. Stefan crown buttons; issue olive drab cotton pullover shirt with stand and fall collar, reinforcing shoulder yoke and patch breast pockets with flaps; pair of white corded canton flannel underdrawers, maker- and issue-marked with drawstring waist and tape ankle ties. Aluminum identification papers locket embossed with title "HUNGARIA" and grid pattern and unopened individual first aid dressing with OD waterproof cover dated "1943" constitute the soldier's personal effects. Group also includes M1935/38 steel helmet similar in design to German M35 but with strap loop on rear skirt. Equipment: brown leather belt with iron roller buckle and pair of matching M1917 "Austrian"-style two-pocket cartridge pouches, M1935 bayonet, folding shovel with pointed steel blade and brown leather carrier, tan linen canvas bread bag with adjustable shoulder sling, aluminum canteen and khaki canvas rucksack. Other equipment: rectangular aluminum mess kit, camouflage triangular shelter quarter, khaki rubberized gas mask, folding shovel and bayonet. **$3,950 (£2,449)**

www.AdvanceGuardMilitaria.com

Nizza Cavalry Regiment Officer's Uniform

Model 1937 officer's green-gray gabardine four-pocket tunic with crimson wool collar and piping on shoulder boards and cuffs, silvered five-point stars on collar, brass flaming bomb buttons, six-place ribbon bar over left breast pocket; Valore Militare, two awards of the Military Merit Cross, the Spanish Campaign Cross, Spanish Campaign medal, and a third Spanish Civil War-related decoration; brass and enamel 3rd Celere Division badge displayed on pocket and captain's rank braid above cuffs; breeches of matching wool with wide black side seam stripe divided by crimson piping; green-gray wool Model 1935 "Bustina" side cap with turned-up divided visor and folding earflaps, brass flaming bomb insignia on wool is snapped to front of visor and three gold bullion ranks stars are sewn to left side; green-gray issue pattern rayon knit shirt with matching wool knit necktie; pair of black leather riding boots. **$1,180 (£732)**

www.AdvanceGuardMilitaria.com

Alpini Officer's Service Dress Uniform

Model 1940 uniform for Sottotenente (2nd Lieutenant) of mountain troops: gray-green wool twill four-pocket tunic with open lapel collar with brass star on green wool "double flames" collar insignia; gold braid loop rank insignia on both cuffs; regulation dark olive plastic buttons; scarce regulation gray flannel shirt with rolled collar and shoulder straps; brown leather Sam Browne belt with shoulder strap and brass fittings, brown holster for small caliber Beretta automatic pistol and blue silk officer's dress sash with matching tassels. **$695 (£431)**

www.AdvanceGuardMilitaria.com

Fatigue Uniform and Cap

Model 1940 work uniform of gray and white "salt and pepper" mixed denim fabric, single-breasted jacket with wood buttons, white machine-woven collar star insignia on black field, shoulder straps and patch skirt pockets with flaps; trousers of matching denim with composition buttons, rear waist adjustment tabs with tape ties and straight legs that gather into cuffs with ties at ankle; Model 1934 "Bustina" side cap of matching gray mixed denim with turned-up front visor and folding earflaps with snaps. M40 fatigue uniform often saw service as a tropical combat uniform during hot Mediterranean summers. **$245 (£152)**

www.AdvanceGuardMilitaria.com

NORWAY

Infantry Uniform and Equipment

Although Norway may not jump readily to mind when listing the allied powers of World War II, their heroic resistance to the Nazi invaders was legendary at the time and an important chapter in the history of the Blitzkrieg. This group was collected some years ago for museum exhibition and has the basic uniform and equipment worn by a Norwegian infantryman during the early war period. M1912 gray-green wool tunic with fly front, stand and fall collar piped in red, pleated patch breast and inset skirt pockets, all with scalloped flaps, and red piped cuffs; straight-leg trousers of matching wool with side pockets, rear adjustment half belt, black-painted metal buttons and red side seam piping; gray-green wool field cap with cloth-covered visor and earflaps (variation of "Finnmarkslue" differing from regulation pattern in that it does not have red piping edging on earflaps), cap has applied construction wool cockade in national colors on obverse; steel helmet is Swedish-designed M31 retaining 80% field gray painted finish; black leather ankle boots with iron heel plates marked "Stal."; brown leather belt with nickel frame buckle and matching pair of brown pigskin M1875 cartridge pouches; Model 1894 Krag Jorgensen bayonet with 21.5cm blade marked with royal cipher and Kongsberg arsenal proof; German-style aluminum canteen, three-piece aluminum mess kit/cooking set with folding handles, dark tan canvas rucksack with gray leather trim, and salt and pepper gray herringbone canvas shelter quarter with hook and eye attachments and metal-tipped wooden tent pole. **$2,425 (£1,504)**

www.AdvanceGuardMilitaria.com

POLAND

Enlisted Man's Uniform and Equipment

Assembled group, 1939 Blitzkrieg-era uniform and basic equipment group as issued to a Polish combat soldier: wz. 37 Czapka field cap of olive drab wool with stitch reinforced visor and Polish square-cornered crown, obverse with Polish eagle and Amazon shield insignia stenciled in white paint, sides with folding neck cape secured with metal buckle in front; wz. 36 summer service tunic of grayish olive linen with roll collar, shoulder straps, four patch pockets with button flaps and zinc-crowned eagle buttons; straight-leg trousers of natural linen with side pockets and zinc utility buttons; natural linen issue collarless pullover shirt with zinc buttons; leather three-pocket cartridge pouches, wz. 22 bayonet, Linneman patent shovel with pointed blade converted from Imperial Russian shovel with brown leather Austrian-style carrier, wz. 33 olive canvas bread bag with web sling and aluminum wz. 38 canteen; 23/31 tinned iron mess kit and tinned iron folding spoon/fork combination; wz. 35 olive drab canvas knapsack; five leather equipment straps, wz. 32 rubber gas mask with head straps, hose and filter with "38"-dated OD canvas bag with web sling and instructions printed under flap. **$2,845 (£1,764)**

www.AdvanceGuardMilitaria.com

"In Chicago my discharge logo was sewed onto my sleeve, I received my discharge papers, was paid in full, and I was suddenly a civilian again!"

— Allen A. Johnson, 409th Infantry Regiment

SOVIET UNION

Early War Infantry Uniform and Equipment

Even though the fall of the Iron Curtain some years ago opened up a flood of Soviet World War II artifacts onto the collecting market, most were from the post-1943 period (and many much later). Items from the opening phases of the conflict, the Winter War, invasion of Poland and Operation Barbarossa, remain scarce. This group, assembled for museum display, includes most of what the Soviet conscript would have worn or carried during the opening salvos of the Great Patriotic War. Enlisted issue pullover M35 Gymnastiorka of olive drab denim with rolled collar showing black piped red infantry branch insignia, fly front placket, patch pockets with flaps, and coffin shaped elbow patches; breeches of OD cotton twill with quilted waistband, inset side and hip pockets, rear adjustment half belt, black composition buttons and ankle straps; black leather marching boots with pebble finish to legs and leather soles and heels with heel irons; Model 1936 steel helmet with short vent cover comb on top of crown retains 85% dark olive painted finish; olive cotton Pilotka side cap, lacking red star insignia, lined in gray with maker's mark; OD web and leather belt with iron roller buckle, pair of M93 Czarist pattern cartridge pouches, World War I Russian entrenching tool dated "1915" in khaki canvas cover, flap closed with Soviet button, apple green-painted aluminum canteen with OD cotton cover and belt loop, "1941" dated first aid dressing and "1938" dated MOD-08 gas mask with OD-painted metal filter and dark olive drab canvas haversack with adjustable web sling; German-inspired semi-ridged M36 knapsack of OD canvas with green oilcloth flap trimmed in brown leather, M36 aluminum mess kit and shelter half /poncho of OD canvas with early-style aluminum grommets and buttons in place of later toggles. **$2,475 (£1,535)**

www.AdvanceGuardMilitaria.com

UNITED STATES

Marine Corps Officer's Field Uniform

Assembled group: Camouflaged helmet cover/mosquito net; Army herringbone twill (HBT) hat; M41 USMC green dungaree HBT jacket with trousers; pistol belt; M41 suspension straps; pair of M3 binoculars and leather case; BAR belt with original USMC marking; 1944 leggings; M-2 jungle first aid kit; first aid packet and pouch; M41 second type haversack with first type knapsack; black enameled canteen with aluminum cup and Marine Corps cross flap cover; and pick mattock and cover. **$1,075 (£667)**
Hermann-Historic.de

Army Paratrooper Uniform

Assembled group: Wool knit cap; M42 jump jacket with 101st Airborne Division shoulder patch and arm flag marked "H-317-H"; jump trousers; scarf of camouflage parachute material; jump boots; M1936 pistol belt; M1936 musette bag; leg holster for folding stock M1A1 carbine (OD7 color, dated 1944); carbine magazine pouch; first aid packet with pouch; 1943-dated M1 ammunition bag with British-made strap; green canvas demolition bag; cavalry canteen extension strap; M1943 folding shovel with adjustable cover; 1944 canteen with British made 1944 cover; M1938 wire cutters; TL-122C flashlight and M227 signal lamp. **$2,280 (£1,414)**
Hermann-Historic.de

Navy "Tin Can" Sailor's Uniform and Souvenirs: USS Grayson DD-435

Fireman First Class Ken Worthington of Mishawaka, Indiana served aboard the hard-fighting Gleaves-class Destroyer USS Grayson. Dress blue jumper and trousers with honorable discharge insignia on jumper; blue work jumper; black silk scarf; blue wool flat hat with "U.S. NAVY" tally; "working whites" with trousers; blue denim bag; 1943 Bluejacket's manual; several Navy theme souvenir pillow covers; white porcelain ship's teacup with blue glaze trim and anchor insignia; American Campaign, Asiatic-Pacific Campaign, and World War II Victory medals; several "V-Mail" letters home; "Neptunus Rex" certificate dated August 1944 earned aboard AP-134 General R.L. Howe; and photocopies of other records; hardbound original 1943 edition of *Condition Red: Destroyer Action in the South Pacific* written by Cap. Frederick J. Bell, telling the tales of Grayson's exploits in early campaigns of the war. **$165 (£102)**

www.AdvanceGuardMilitaria.com

Airborne Troop Carrier Pilot's Grouping: D-Day Pilot and Author

Uniform, photos, and historical notes of Captain Donald Van Reken, a pilot who served with the 32nd Troop Carrier Squadron from the Normandy Invasion to the end of the War in Europe. Van Reken was copilot of a C-47 on D-Day that dropped a stick of Airborne Engineers, along with parapacks affixed to the underside of the fuselage that held 600 pounds of TNT, which the crew was not exactly pleased to discover. Van Reken's group includes his "pinks and greens," dark olive drab wool twill tunic with AAF shoulder insignia, Captain's rank, "U.S." and AAF winged prop lapel devices, "AMCRAFT" pinback silver Pilot's Wing badge, Distinguished Unit Citation, ribbon bar with Air Medal with two oak leaf clusters and ETO campaign with four campaign stars, and cuff with three overseas service bars; "pinks" trousers with matching fabric waist belt, officer's piped overseas cap with Captain's rank insignia; unengraved slot brooch Air Medal in presentation case; old copy of his official Army flight log; several snapshots; 9th and 12th Air Force shoulder insignias; identification tag; large map of France; map case grid insert; silk ETO "escape" map and B-4 flight bag; copies of squadron newsletter that he edited in the late 1980s and early 1990s; folder and binder packed with correspondence, photos, and research for squadron unit history. **$1,365 (£846)**

www.AdvanceGuardMilitaria.com

AAF 5th Air Force Pilot Captain's Uniforms: Silver Star Recipient

Group of four uniforms. First: Dark OD elastique wool four-pocket tunic with U.S. and Aviation devices on collar and lapels; bullion embroidered, cut-edge 5th Air Force patch and four bullion overseas bars on left sleeve; Captain's silver embroidered bars on shoulders; silver embroidered Pilot's Wing badge above sewn, six-place medal ribbon bar (Silver Star, Distinguished Flying Cross with one cluster, Air Medal with three clusters, Purple Heart, American Campaign, and Asiatic Theater with three stars); Distinguished Unit Citation (DUC) with three clusters pinned on right chest. Second: Khaki wool summer issue tunic with U.S. and Aviation devices on collar and lapels; embroidered felt AAF patch and four overseas bars on left sleeve; Captain's bars on shoulders; "Orber"-marked sterling Pilot's Wing badge above same ribbon bar combination; DUC with no clusters. Third: Heavy white cotton and U.S. and Aviation devices; Captain's bars; scarce Fox-marked Pilot's Wing badge over same medal bar combination; DUC has three clusters. Fourth: Privately tailored dark OD wool Ike-style jacket with U.S. and Aviation devices; embroidered felt AAF patch; Captain's bars, sterling-marked, hollow-back Pilot's Wing badge over sewn medal ribbon bars; DUC with three clusters. **$625 (£388)**

www.AdvanceGuardMilitaria.com

AAF Troop Carrier Pilot's Uniform

Flight Officer Wilfred H. Shaw grouping: Tunic, Ike jacket, shirt, visor cap and flight log. Dark olive green elastique wool tunic has double-clutch back "U.S." and Aviation collar and lapel devices, cut-edge Army Air Forces patch on left sleeve, Flight Officer bars on shoulders, and clutch-back sterling ASCO pilot's wings on left chest. Ike jacket has "U.S" and Aviation collar and lapel devices, Flight Officer rank insignia, embroidered felt Army Air Forces patch and two bullion tape overseas bars on left sleeve, embroidered felt Airborne Troop Carrier patch on right sleeve (both patches likely English-made) and pair of Fox-hallmarked pilot's wings on chest. Shirt is made from fine quality dark olive green wool. Visor cap exhibits wear and has typical "crusher-style" shape with soft visor. Shaw's stateside flight log included in which he recorded more than 229 hours piloting Fairchild trainers and Beechcraft AT-10s; portrait of Shaw in flight gear with an inscription to his mother on back. **$495 (£307)**
www.AdvanceGuardMilitaria.com

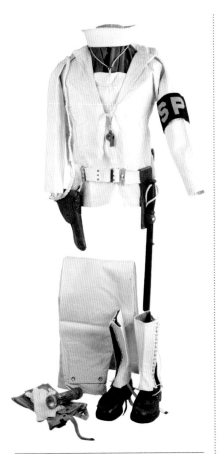

U.S. Navy Seaman Uniform

Assembled group: White hat; jumper and trousers; cotton gloves; Shore Patrol armband; metal first aid package in gray canvas cover; gray plastic flashlight marked USN; M1936 white parade belt; russet leather pistol holster with reproduction pistol and lanyard; green plastic whistle; white web belt equipment loop/hanger; white canvas pistol magazine pouch; Navy leggings; wooden club and white lanyard; 1944 Navy leggings; pair of whitened leggings; and pair of 1940 shoes. **$365 (£226)**
Hermann-Historic.de

U.S. Army Tanker Uniform

Assembled group: Hard fiber crash helmet marked "Rawlings 7 1/8" with R-14 earphones; second pattern tanker's jacket; matching second pattern, bib-front lined trousers; M-1936 pistol belt with M-1912 web pistol magazine pouch and M-1910 canteen; leggings; and leather and rubber shoepacs. **$670 (£415)**
Hermann-Historic.de

Uniform and Equipment for U.S. Soldier

Assembled group: Olive drab field jacket (collar repaired); pair of OD serge trousers; 1941 leggings; M-1923 rifle belt; 1942 suspension straps; canteen with cup; M-1926 lifebelt; field first-aid dressing in cardboard box in British-made pouch dated 1944; green vinyl waterproof cover for rifle; and M1943 folding shovel with 1944 cover. **$804 (£498)**
Hermann-Historic.de

Uniform and Equipment for USAAF Crew Member

Assembled group: B-10 cotton flying jacket with fur collar, Crown zipper, 20th Air Force patch on left shoulder, and initials on leather name tag; pair of M-1937 khaki cotton trousers; M-1938 matching shirt; khaki tie; A-10 summer flying helmet (no headphones); pair of M-1944 tinted Polaroid goggles; A-13A oxygen mask; blue rubberized Mae West life preserver; and white parachute silk scarf. **$538 (£334)**

Hermann-Historic.de

2nd Engineer Special Brigade Soldier's Uniform and Souvenirs

Grouping from Pvt. Ralph C. Brandau of Company F, 592nd Engineer Amphibian Regiment, 2nd Engineer Special Brigade: Ike jacket with "U.S." and Engineer discs, blue Amphibious Forces shoulder insignia and Engineer Amphibious Command patch on left pocket, Honorable Discharge insignia, Presidential Unit Citation ribbon with second award oak leaf, one long service stripe and five overseas service bars; medal ribbon bar includes Good Conduct, Asiatic-Pacific Campaign with one Invasion arrowhead device and four campaign stars, Liberation of Philippines with two stars, and World War II Victory. Issue trousers and shirt with blue Amphibious Forces shoulder insignia; 30cm x 21cm x 19cm box for Japanese technical equipment containing photographs; sewing kit and personal items kit; extra Amphibious Forces shoulder insignias; 592nd Regiment in-theater newspapers including Aug. 8, 1945 issue that discusses use of atomic bomb, other in-theater papers, soldier poetry, orders indicating he was to serve as (temporary acting) Technician 5th Grade, two printed "battle honors" papers listing accomplishments of 2nd Engineer Special Brigade and one of 592nd Regiment in particular; large tinted photo of Brandau wearing Ike jacket; post-war Hi-Standard "Model H-D Military" .22 long rifle caliber automatic pistol and brown leather holster. **$865 (£536)**

www.AdvanceGuardMilitaria.com

99th Division Infantryman's Uniform: Bronze Star Recipient

Uniform and medals of S/Sgt. John Weaver: Enlisted issue Ike jacket with "U.S." and Infantry discs, pinback 99th Division DIs, Staff Sergeant rank chevrons, honorable discharge insignia, one service stripe and four overseas service bars, 99th Division shoulder insignia, Belgian Croix de Guerre 1940 fourragere, Presidential Unit Citation, Combat Infantryman badge, and medal ribbon bar including Bronze Star, American Defense, Good Conduct, American Campaign, and European-African-Middle Eastern Campaign with one invasion arrowhead and three campaign stars; expert qualification badge with "Rifle" and "B.A.R."; two pairs of olive drab wool enlisted trousers; un-engraved Good Conduct and Bronze Star with initials "JRW" engraved on back, with original presentation box; honorable discharge pin; ID tags. **$350 (£217)**

www.AdvanceGuardMilitaria.com

Bibliography

World War II collectors are very fortunate. Thousands of volumes have been published on myriad collecting interests. The following is just a brief list of books that new collectors will find beneficial.

Ailsby, Christopher J. *A Collector's Guide to the Luftwaffe.* Hersham, Surrey, UK: Ian Allan Publishing, 2006.

Alberti, Bruno and Laurent Pradier. *USMC: Uniforms & Equipment 1941-45.* Paris: Histoire & Collections, 2007.

Angolia, LTC John R. *For Führer and Fatherland: Military Awards of the Third Reich, 2nd ed.* San Jose, CA: R. James Bender Publishing, 1985.

Angolia, LTC John R. *For Führer and Fatherland: Political & Civil Awards of the Third Reich.* San Jose, CA: R. James Bender Publishing, 1978.

Angolia, LTC John R. *Heroes in our Midst: WWII American Airborne, Early Years, Training, Jump Wings, Parachutes, Jump Helmets, Paramarines.* San Jose, CA: R. James Bender Publishing, 2013.

Armold, Chris. *Steel Pots: The History of America's Steel Combat Helmets.* San Jose, CA: R. James Bender Publishing, 1997.

Armold, Chris. *Painted Steel: Steel Pots, Volume II.* San Jose, CA: R. James Bender Publishing, 2000.

Beadle, Alan, *German Combat Awards, 1935-45.* Bridport, Dorset, UK: Alan Beadle Ltd., 2004.

Beaver, Michal D. with Kelly Hicks, *SS Helmets: The History and Decoration of the Helmets of the Black Corps.* Atglen, PA: Schiffer Military History, 2006.

Beaver, Michael D. with Mark A. Bando. *Insignia and Artifacts of the Waffen SS.* Mark A. Bando, 2012.

Beaver Michael D. with William Shea. *The Collector's Guide to the Distinctive Cloth Headgear of the Allgemeine and Waffen-SS.* Atglen, PA: Schiffer Military History, 2009.

Békési, László. *Stalin's War: Soviet Uniforms & Militaria, 1941-45 in Colour Photographs.* Ramsbury, Marlborough, Wiltshire, UK: The Crowood Press, Ltd., 2006.

Bellec, Olivier. *1940: Le Soldat Français* (two volumes). Paris: Histoire & Collections, 2010.

Berrafato, Enzo and Laurent. *Kriegsmarine: History, Uniforms, Headgear, Insignia, Equipment 1935-1945.* Atglen, PA: Schiffer Military History, 2012.

Besnard, Pierre. *U.S. Army Insignia 1941-1945, Vol. I.* Paris: Histoire & Collections, 2013.

Bouchery, Jean. *Allies in Battledress: From Normandy to the North Sea, 1944-45.* Paris: Histoire & Collections, 2012.

Bouchery, Jean. *From D-Day to VE-Day: The Canadian Soldier.* Paris: Histoire & Collections, 2003.

Bouchery, Jean and Philippe Charbonnier. *D-Day Paratroopers: The British, The Canadians, The French.* Paris: Histoire & Collections, 2004.

Brayley, Martin J. *Bayonets: An Illustrated History.* Iola, WI: KP Books, 2004.

Brayley, Martin J. *American Web Equipment, 1910-1967.* Ramsbury, Marlborough, Wiltshire, UK: The Crowood Press, Ltd., 2006.

Brayley, Martin J. *British Web Equipment of the Two World Wars.* Ramsbury, Marlborough, Wiltshire, UK: The Crowood Press, Ltd., 2005.

Brayley, Martin J. & Richard Ingram. *Khaki Drill & Jungle Green: British Tropical Uniforms, 1939-45 in Colour Photographs.* Ramsbury, Marlborough, Wiltshire, UK: The Crowood Press, Ltd., 2000.

Brayley, Martin J. & Richard Ingram. *The World War II Tommy: British Army Uniforms European Theatre 1939-45 in Colour Photographs.* Ramsbury, Marlborough, Wiltshire, UK: The Crowood Press, Ltd., 1998.

Brown, Christopher P. *U.S. Military Patches of World War II.* Paducah, KY: Turner Publishing Co., 2002.

Canfield, Bruce N. *U.S. Infantry Weapons of World War II.* Lincoln, RI: Andrew Mowbray Publishers, 1994.

Cano, Gustavo and Santiago Guillén. *Deutsche Luftwaffe: Uniforms and Equipment of the German Air Force (1939-1945).* Madrid, Spain: Andrea Press, 2013.

Clark, Jeff. *Uniforms of the NSDAP: Uniforms, Headgear, Insignia of the Nazi Party.* Atglen, PA: Schiffer Military History, 2007.

Clawson, Robert W. *Russian Helmets: From Kaska to Stalshlyem, 1916-2001.* San Jose, CA: R. James Bender Publishing, 2002.

Curley, Timothy J. and Neil G. Stewart. *Waffenrck: Parade Uniforms of the German Army.* San Jose, CA: R. James Bender Publishing, 2006.

Davis, Aaron, *Standard Catalog of Luger: Identification & Pricing for All Models, Every Variation.* Iola, WI: Gun Digest Books, 2006.

Davis, Brian L. *Badges & Insignia of the Third Reich, 1933-1945.* Poole, Dorset, England: Blandford Books, Ltd., 1983.

Davis, Brian L. *German Army Uniforms and Insignia, 1933-1945.* London: Arms and Armour Press, 1971.

Dawson, Jim. *Swords of Imperial Japan, 1868-1945.* Newnan, GA: Stenger-Scott Publishing Co., 1996.

DeSchodt, Christophe and Laurent Rouger. *D-Day Paratroopers: The Americans.* Paris: Histoire & Collections, 2004.

de LaGarde, Jean. *German Soldiers of World War Two.* Paris: Histoire & Collections, 2005.

de Quesada, Alejandro M. *Uniforms of the German Soldier: An Illustrated History from World War II to the Present Day.* London: Greenhill Books, 2006.

Dorosh, Michael A. *Dressed to Kill.* Ottawa, Ontario, Canada: Service Publications, 2001.

Dorsey, R. Stephen. *U.S. Martial Web Belts and Bandoliers: 1903-1981.* Eugene, OR: Collector's Library, 1993.

Emerson, William K. *Encyclopedia of United States Army Insignia and Uniforms.* Norman, OK: University of Oklahoma Press, 1996.

Enjames, Henri-Paul: *Government Issue: U.S. Army European Theater of Operations Collector Guide.* Paris: Histoire & Collections, 2003.

Enjames, Henri-Paul: *Government Issue: U.S. Army European Theater of Operations Collector Guide, Volume II.* Paris: Histoire & Collections, 2008.

Fisch, Robert. *Field Equipment of the Infantry, 1914-1945.* Sykesville, MD: Greenberg Publishing Co., Inc., 1989.

Foster, Col. Frank C. *Complete Guide to United States Army Medals, Badges and Insignia, World War II to Present.* Fountain Inn, SC: Medals of America Press, 2004.

Glenn, Harlan. *United States Marine Corps: Uniforms, Insignia and Personal Items of World War II.* Atglen, PA: Schiffer Publishing, 2005.

Glenn, Harlan. *"782 Gear" United States Marine Corps Field Gear and Equipment of World War II.* Atglen, PA: Schiffer Publishing, 2009.

Gordon, David B. *Equipment of the WWII Tommy.* Missoula, MT: Pictorial Histories Publishing Co., Inc., 2004.

Goebel, Katy Endruschat. *Women for Victory: American Servicewomen in World War II, Vol. I,* Atglen, PA: Schiffer Publishing, 2011.

Hertfurth, Dietrich. *Sowjetische Auszeichnungen, 1918-1991, 3rd ed.* Berlin: Dietrich Hertfurth, 1999.

Hewitt, Mike. *Uniforms and Equipment of the Imperial Japanese Army in World War II.* Atglen, PA: Schiffer Military History, 2002.

Hicks, Kelly. *SS-Steel: Parade and Combat Helmets of Germany's Third Reich Elite.* San Jose, CA: R. James Bender Publishing, 2004.

Hogg, Ian V. & John S. Weeks. *Military Small Arms of the 20th Century, 7th ed.* Iola, WI: Krause Publications, 2000.

Huart Laurent and Jean-Philippe Borg. *Feldbluse: The German Soldier's Field Tunic, 1933-45.* Paris: Histoire & Collections, 2007.

Hughes, Gordon, Barry Jenkins, & Robert A. Buerlein. *Knives of War: An International Guide to Military Knives from World War I to the Present.* Boulder, CO: Paladin Press, 2006.

Kibler, Thomas. *Combat Helmets of the Third Reich: A Study in Photographs.* Pottsboro, TX: Reddick Enterprises, 2003.

Kibler, Thomas and Robert Igbal. *Combat Helmets of the Third Reich, Vol. II.* Pottsboro, TX: Reddick Enterprises, 2005.

Kiesling, Paul. *Bayonets of the World: The Complete Edition.* Osterbeek, Holland: S.I. Publicaties BV, 2009.

Kruk, Alfred A. *Patronentaschen, Patronengürtel und Banduliere 1850-1950.* Münster, Germany: Alfred A. Kruk, 2000.

Labar, Raymond C. *Bayonets of Japan: A Comprehensive Reference on Japanese Bayonets.* Cleveland, TN: Raymar, Inc., 2008.

Lewis, Kenneth. *Doughboy to GI: U.S. Army Clothing and Equipment, 1900-1945.* Winton, Bournemouth, UK: Norman D. Landing Books, 2002.

Lucy, Roger V. *Tin Lids: Canadian Combat Helmets, 2nd ed.* Ottawa, Ontario, Canada: Service Publications, 2000.

Johnson, Thomas M. *Collecting the Edged Weapons of the Third Reich, Volume I.* Columbia, SC: LTC Thomas M. Johnson, 1977.

Lumsden, Robin. *Medals and Decorations of Hitler's Germany.* Shrewsbury: Airlife Publishing, Ltd., 2001.

Maguire, Jon A. *Gear Up! Flight Clothing & Equipment of USAAF Airmen in World War II.* Atglen, PA: Schiffer Military History, 1995.

Mason, Chris. *Paramarine: Uniforms and Equipment of Marine Corps Parachute Units in World War II.* Atglen, PA: Schiffer Military History, 2004.

Mirouze, Laurent. *World War II Infantry in Color Photographs.* London: Windrow & Greene Ltd., 1990.

Nakata, Tadao and Thomas B. Nelson. *Imperial Japanese Army and Navy Uniforms & Equipment, Revised Ed.,* Alexandria, VA: Ironside International Publishers, Inc., 1997.

Nash, Peter, *German Belt Buckles, 1845-1945.* Atglen, PA: Schiffer Military History, 2003.

Nelson, Derek and Dave Parson. *A-2 & G-1 Flight Jackets: Hell-Bent for Leather.* St. Paul, MN: MBI Publishing, 2002.

Niemann, Detlev. *Orders, Decorations, Award Documents, Miniatures and Cases of Issue: Price Guide Germany, 1871-1945.* Hamburg, Germany: Niemann Verlag, 2008.

Niewiarowicz, Ken. *Germany's Combat Helmets 1933-45: A Modern Study.* San Jose, CA: R. James Bender Publishing, 2009.

Prodger, Mick J. *Vintage Flying Helmets: Aviation Headgear before the Jet Age.* Atglen, PA: Schiffer Military History, 1995.

Rentz, Bill. *Geronimo! U.S. Airborne Uniforms, Insignia & Equipment in World War II.* Atglen, PA: Schiffer Military History, 1999.

Rio, Philippe. *The Soviet Soldier of World War Two.* Paris, France: Histoire & Collections, 2011.

Sáiz, Agustín. *Deutsche Soldaten: Uniforms, Equipment & Personal Items of the German Soldier 1939-45.* Drexel Hill, PA: Casemate Publishing, 2008.

Sáiz, Agustín. *Heitai: Japanese Infantryman, 1931-1945.* Madrid, Spain: Andrea Press, 2011.

Schwan, C. Frederick and Joseph E. Boling, *World War II Remembered: History in Your Hands: A Numismatic Study.* Port Clinton, OH: BNR Press, 1995.

Peterson, Phillip. *Standard Catalog of Military Firearms: The Collector's Price and Reference Guide, 7th ed.* Iola, WI: Gun Digest Books, 2013.

Silvey, M.W., Gary D. Boyd and Frank Trzaska. *U.S. Military Knives, Bayonets and Machetes Price Guide, 4th ed.* Knoxville, TN: Knife World Publications, 2000.

Smith, Jill Halcomb. *Dressed for Duty: America's Women in Uniform, 1898-1973* (two volumes). San Jose, CA: R. James Bender Publishing, 2001.

Stanton, Shelby. *U.S. Army Uniforms of World War II.* Harrisburg, PA: Stackpole Books, 1991.

Stein, Barry Jason. *U.S. Army Patches, Flashes and Ovals: An Illustrated Encyclopedia of Cloth Unit Insignia.* Insignia Ventures, 2007.

Strandberg, LTC John E. and Roger James Bender. *The Call of Duty: Military Awards and Decorations of the United States of America, 2nd ed.* San Jose, CA: R. James Bender Publishing, 2004.

Storey, Ed. *'37 Web: Equipping the Canadian Soldier.* Ottawa, Ontario, Canada: Service Publications, 2003.

Suermont, Jan. *Infantry Weapons of World War II.* Iola, WI: Krause Publications, 2004.

Sweeting, C.G. *Combat Flying Clothing: Army Air Forces Clothing During World War II.* Washington, DC: Smithsonian Institution Press, 1984.

Touratier, Guilhem and Laurent Charbonneau. *German Visor Caps of the Second World War.* Atglen, PA: Schiffer Military History, 2013.

Tulkoff, Alec S. *Grunt Gear: USMC Combat Infantry Equipment of World War II.* San Jose, CA: R. James Bender Publishing, 2003.

Vernon, Sydney B. *Vernon's Collectors' Guide to Orders, Medals & Decorations, 4th ed.* Temecula, CA: Sydney B. Vernon, 2004.

Warner, Jeff. *U.S. Navy Uniforms in World War II Series* (six volumes). Atglen, PA: Schiffer Military History, 2006.

Webster, David and Chris Nelson. *Uniforms of the Soviet Union 1918-1945.* Atglen, PA: Schiffer Military History, 1998.

Windrow, Richard and Tim Hawkins. *The World War II GI: U.S. Army Uniform, 1941-45 in Color Photographs.* Ramsbury, Marlborough, Wiltshire, UK: The Crowood Press, Ltd., 1993.

Glossary of Abbreviations

AAC: U.S. Army Air Corps
AAF: U.S. Army Air Force
AFB: U.S. Air Force base
ANC: U.S. Army Nurse Corps
ATS: British Auxiliary Territorial Service
AVG: American Volunteer Group
BAR: Browning Automatic Rifle
BeVo: Badfabrik Ewald Vorsteher, the major manufacturer of German cloth insignia. Today, collectors use the term to describe smooth, tightly woven cloth insignia.
CAC: U.S. Coastal Artillery Corps
CBI: China-Burma-India theater of operations
CPO: U.S. Chief Petty Officer
CWAC: Canadian Women's Army Corps
DAF: Deutsche Arbeitsfront, the German Labor Front
DAK: Deutsches Afrikakorps, the German Africa Corps
DI: distinctive insignia, usually U.S.
DLV: Deutsche Luftsport-Verband, German Air Sports Formation
DRGM: Deutsches Reichsgebrauchsmuster, German nationally used pattern
EGA: "Eagle, Globe and Anchor," the insignia of the United States Marine Corps
EM: enlisted man
ETO: European Theater of Operations
Ges. Gesch.: Gesetzlich Geschutzt, "legally protected"
Gestapo: GeheimeStaatspolizei, German Secret State Police
GHQ: General Headquarters, U.S. Army
GI: government issue
GPO: Government Printing Office
HBT: herringbone twill
HMAS: His Majesty's Australian Ship
HMCS: His Majesty's Canadian Ship
HMNZS: His Majesty's New Zealand Ship
HMS: His Majesty's Ship
HMSO: His Majesty's Stationery Office
HQ: headquarters
Id'ed: identified
IJA: Imperial Japanese Army
IJN: Imperial Japanese Navy
JAG: U.S. Judge Advocate General
KIA: killed in action
LDO: Leistungsgemeinschaft der Deutschen Ordenhersteller, German Administration of German Manufacturers
MIA: missing in action
MK: mark
MTO: Mediterranean Theater of Operations
NAS: U.S. Naval Air Station
NCO: noncommissioned officer
NSBO: Nationalsozialistische Betriebsorganisation, German National Socialist Factory Organization
NSDAP: Nationalsozialistische Deutsche Arbeiterpartei, the German Nazi party
NSFK: Nationalsozialistisches Fliegerkorps, German National Socialist Flying Corps
NSKK: Nationalsozialistisches Kraftfahrkorps, German National Socialist Motor Corps
OD: olive drab
OCD: Office of Civilian Defense
OCS: Officer Candidate School
OSS: Office of Strategic Services, U.S. organization to support underground operations
OT: Organization Todt
OWI: Office of War Information
POW: prisoner of war
PFR: Partito Fascista Repubblicano, Fascist Republican Party, the political arm of the RSI (q.v.)
PTO: Pacific Theater of Operations
PX: Post exchange
QMB: U.S. Quartermaster Board

QMC: U.S. Quartermaster Corps
RAD: Reichsarbeitsdienst, German National labor Service
RAF: British Royal Air Force
RAAF: Royal Australian Air Force
RAN: Royal Australian Navy
RCAF: Royal Canadian Air Force
RCN: Royal Canadian Navy
RCT: U.S. Regimental Combat Team
RB-Nr.: Reichsbetriebsnummer, German National Factory Code Number
RLB: Reichsluftschutzbund, German National Air Raid Protection Force
RM: Royal Marine(s)
RMA: Royal Marine Artillery
RN: Royal Navy
ROTC: U.S. Reserve Officer Training Corps
RSI: Repubblica Sociale Italiana, Italian Social Republic, the government established in North Italy by Mussolini after Italy capitulated in 1943.
RZM: Reichszeugmeisterie, German National Material Control Board
SA: Sturmabteilung, Nazi party "assault detachment," the "Brown Shirts"
SOS: U.S. Service of Supply
SS: Schutzstaffel, Nazi "protection squad"
SHAEF: Supreme Headquarters, Allied Expeditionary Force, Eisenhower's headquarters for D-Day
Showa: reign title used by Japanese Emperor Hirohito, 1926-1989
SOE: Special Operations Executive, British organization to support underground operations
SNLF: Japanese Special Naval Landing Force ("marines")
SPARS: U.S. Coast Guard Women's Reserve
TENO: Technische Nothilfe, German Technical Emergency Service
UDT: Underwater Demolition Team
USA: United States Army
USAAC: United States Army Air Corps
USAAF: United States Army Air Force
USAFFE: United States Army Forces in the Far East
USAFISPA: United States Army Forces in the South Pacific Area
USCG: United States Coast Guard
USCGR: United States Coast Guard Reserve
USFIP: United States Forces in the Philippines
USMC: United States Marine Corps
USMCR: United States Marine Corps Reserve
USMCWR: United States Marine Corps Women's Reserve
USN: United States Navy
USNR: United State Navy Reserves
USO: United States Service Organization
USQMC: United States Quartermaster Corps
USS: United States Ship
VB: U.S. Bomber plane or squadron
VC: U.S. Composite plane or squadron
VF: U.S. Fighter plane or squadron
VMF: U.S. Marine Fighter Squadron
VMJ: U.S. Marine Utility Squadron
VMSB: U.S. Marine Scout-Bomber Squadron
VP: U.S. Navy Patrol Squadron
VS: U.S. Navy Scouting Squadron
VT: U.S. Torpedo plane or squadron
VOS: U.S. Observation-Scout plane or squadron
WBA: Wehrmachtbekleidungsamt, German Armed Forces Clothing Office
WAAC: U.S. Women's Army Auxiliary Corps, created on May 14, 1942. Evolved into the Women's Army Corps (WAC) in July 1943.
WAC: U.S. Women's Army Corps, created in July 1943.
WAFS: U.S. Women's Auxiliary Ferrying Squadron
WASP: U.S. Women's Airforce Service Pilot
WAVES: U.S. Women Accepted for Volunteer Emergency Service
WIA: wounded in action
WD: U.S. War Department
WR: U.S. Women Reservist, USMC

Sources

Auction Houses

Amoskeag Auction Co., Inc.
250 Commercial St. #3011
Manchester, NH 03101
www.amoskeagauction.com

Boselys Military Auction
The White House, Marlow
Buckinghamshire SL7 1AH
England
www.bosleys.co.uk

Heritage Auctions
3500 Maple Ave., 17th Floor
Dallas, TX 75219-3941
HA.com

Hermann Historica OHG
Linprunstr. 16
D-80335 Munich
Germany
www.hermann-historica.de

History Hunter
Craig Gottlieb
722 Genevieve St., Suite H
Solana Beach, CA 92075
historyhunter.com

James D. Julia, Inc.
P.O. Box 830
Fairfield, ME 04937
www.JamesDJulia.com

Mohawk Arms, Inc.
P.O. Box 157
Bouckville, NY 13310
www.militaryrelics.com

Poulin Antiques and Auction Co.
199 Skowhegan Rd.
Fairfield, ME 04937
www.poulinantiques.com

Rock Island Auction Co.
4507 49th Ave.
Moline, IL 61265
www.rockislandauction.com

Wallis & Wallis
West Street Auction Galleries
Lewes, Sussex BN7 2NJ
England
www.wallisandwallis.com.uk

Dealers

Advance Guard Militaria
270 State Hwy HH
Burfordville, MO 63739
www.advanceguardmilitaria.com

Atlantic Crossroads, Inc.
P.O. Box 144
Tenafly, NJ 07670
www.collectrussia.com

Bay State Military Antiques
P.O. Box 296
Lunenburg, MA 01462
www.baystatemilitaria.com

Brock's
5742-A Bostwick Hwy
Bishop, GA 30621
www.brocksguns.com

Cowan's Auctions
6270 Este Ave.
Cincinnati, OH 45232
www.cowans.com

Falls Creek Collectables
P.O. Box 6304
Great Falls, MT 59406
www.fallscreekcollectibles.com

Helmut Weitze Fine Military Antiques
Neuer Wall 18, 2nd Floor
20354 Hamburg
Germany
www.weitze.net

Griffin Militaria
P.O. Box 226
Shoemakersville, PA 19555
www.GriffinMilitaria.com

Johnson Reference Books & Militaria
#403 Chatham Square
Fredericksburg, VA 22405
www.ww2daggers.com

Hayes Otoupalik
P.O. Box 8423
Missoula, MT 59807
www.hayesotoupalik.com

The Ruptured Duck
51 Morgan Rd.
Hubbardston, MA 01452-1602
www.therupturedduck.com

Stewart's Military Antques
P.O. Box 1492
Mesa, AZ 85211
www.stewartsmilitaryantiques.com

Vintage Productions
7266 Edinger Ave.
Huntington Beach, CA 92647
www.vintageproductions.com

Wartime Collectables
P.O. Box 165
Camden, SC 29020
www.wartimecollectables.com

Wittman Antique Militaria
P.O. Box 350
Moorestown, NY 08057
www.wwiidaggers.com

World Wide Military Exchange
2000 Bloomington Rd., Suite 200
Glendale Heights, IL 60139
www.wwmeinc.com

Index

DIVERSE
HISTORIC
AUTHENTIC

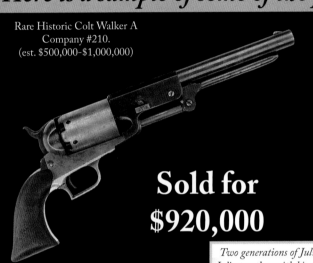

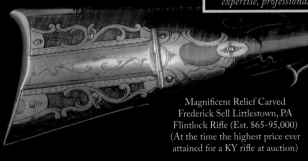
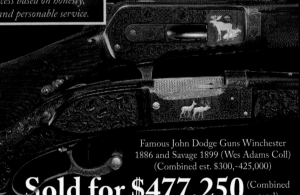

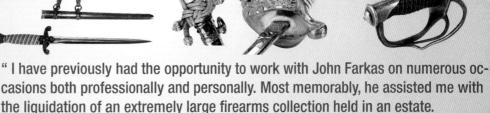

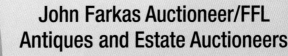
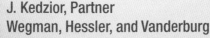

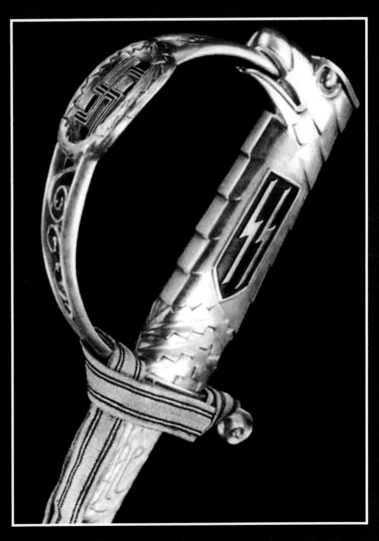

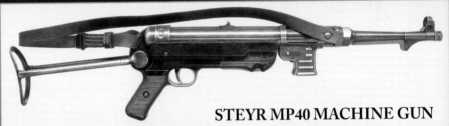

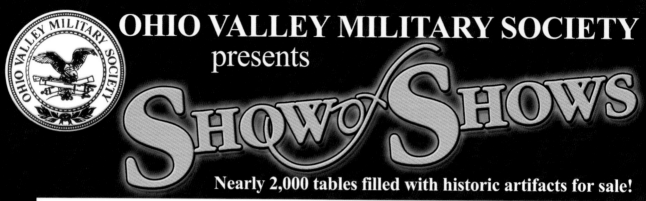

Jason Burmeister
MILITARIA

**Orders & Decorations, Documents, Embroidered Flags & Pennants,
Uniforms, Insignia, Headgear, Helmets & Edged Weapons**